Uncertain Rain

Sundry spells of Michael Field

What song the Syrens sang, or what name Achilles assumed when he hid himself among women

'By the way,' writes F.D.S. 'here's a mite of gossip. "Michael Field" is the pseudonym of <u>two</u> English women.'   *The Critic* (NY) 15 November 1890

<u>QUESTIONS</u> 1652. What is the real name of Michael Field, the writer of some original and interesting verse?   S.H.   Burlington, VERMONT
                                          The Critic (NY)   19 March 1892

Michael Field is always one. This writer— & he when a pronoun must come in.   Katharine Bradley writing to John Gray ca 1912 (YSK uf)

Uncertain Rain

Sundry spells of Michael Field

Chosen, annotated, but *not* edited
by Ivor C Treby

First published in 2002 by De Blackland Press
World copyright © Ivor C Treby 2002

A CIP catalogue record for this book
is available from the British Library.

ISBN 0-907404-08-1

Typeset by De Blackland Press
Printed on White Woodfree Bookwove and bound in Great Britain by
St Edmundsbury Press, Bury St Edmunds, Suffolk   250 copies only

Acknowledgements

This book is a third (and final) section of the planned selection of Michael Field poems under the collective title IN LEASH TO THE STRANGER; the first two sections (already issued) are A SHORTER SHĪRAZĀD and MUSIC AND SILENCE. The three sections combined now contain 404 annotated poems, the greatest number of Michael Field pieces ever published under a single title. What is more, 141— over one third of these poems— have never been seen in print until now.

As usual, I am grateful to the current copyright holders, Leonie Sturge-Moore and Charmian O'Neil, for authorising this first publication of a further fifty six Michael Field poems, amongst others, as well as the quotation of excerpts from the voluminous Michael Field papers and the relevant correspondence of Thomas Sturge Moore and his family. I must thank them too, as the copyright holders for Charles de Sousy Ricketts, for permission to use his sketch *The moon-horned Io* at page 35, and as an integral decoration throughout the cover.

I am also indebted to the Keeper of Western Manuscripts at the Bodleian Library, University of Oxford, and to the Curator of Modern Literary Manuscripts at the British Library, for permission to quote from the papers in their charge, and for allowing me access to the texts of the unpublished poems.

My ambition to draw on all surviving autographs, as well as the letters that Michael Field exchanged with John ('Dorian') Gray and Vincent McNabb, would have been unachievable without the co-operation, kindness, and patience of Bede Bailey (Blackfriars Archive); as also of Francis Collins (custodian of the Fortey Cache manuscripts). To them both, as ever, my deep gratitude. It is a pleasure to thank too Martha Vicinus, who at the very last minute drew my attention to two references new to me, JVM and FSZ. These are detailed on page 236.

I extend heartfelt apologies to any copyright holders whose rights have unwittingly been infringed (in particular to the heirs and assignees of the unknown photographer whose work appears on the back cover). Every effort has been made to trace all such, but without success.

Ivor C Treby   London, October 2002

Front cover: Detail of *The moon-horned Io*, a pen drawing by Charles de Sousy Ricketts, one of his decorations for Oscar Wilde's *The Sphinx*, London 1894 (T.C.5.b.3): by kind permission of The British Library.

And did you talk with Thoth, and did you hear the moon-horned Io weep? / And know the painted Kings who sleep beneath the wedge-shaped pyramid?

Back cover: Two rather grand ladies and an overweening dog; or just possibly Michael Field and Whym Chow on progress? If the latter, this is the only known pictorial record of the doggy Trinity. Neither date nor location is known. From an indistinct photograph stuck at ZJR 226a into the *Michael Field Journal* for 1903 (Add.MS. 46792), and here reproduced also by kind permission of The British Library.

References

The following abbreviations have been used in the notes:
H - prose in hand of Edith Cooper   M - prose in hand of Katharine Bradley
cf - compare with   du- dating uncertain   n - text note   pe- preface   rt - related to
s - stanza   sa - see also   uf - unfoliated   v - verse   v.i. - see below

Other citations are 3-letter codes (such as WDH, SMF, JAC, OCJ, QOC, YSA, ZJT).
These include published works of Michael Field, as well as significant other texts:

BLN -	Bellerophôn	C. Kegan Paul & Co.	London 1881
DDD -	Dedicated	George Bell & Sons	London 1914
LAG -	Long Ago	George Bell & Sons	London 1889
MCT -	Mystic Trees	Eveleigh Nash	London 1913
PAD -	Poems of Adoration	Sands & Co.	London 1912
SAS -	Sight and Song	Elkin Mathews	London 1892
SMF -	A Selection, Poems of Michael Field	Poetry Bookshop	London 1923
TNM -	The New Minnesinger	Longmans, Green	London 1875
TWF -	The Wattlefold	Basil Blackwell	Oxford 1930
UTB,C -	Underneath the Bough (two editions)	George Bell & Sons	London 1893
UTD -	Underneath the Bough	Mosher	Portland ME 1898
WAD -	Works and Days	John Murray	London 1933
WCF -	Whym Chow Flame of Love	Eragny Press	London 1914
WDH -	Wild Honey from various thyme	Fisher Unwin	London 1908
XFR -	Fair Rosamund	George Bell & Sons	London 1884
XFT -	The Father's Tragedy	George Bell & Sons	London 1885
XRB -	Ras Byzance	Poetry Bookshop	London 1918
XWA -	The World at Auction	Ballantyne Press	London 1898

FAL - Victorian Women Poets by Angela Leighton   Harvester Wheatsheaf 1992
FED - We are Michael Field by Emma Donoghue   Absolute Press 1998
FLF - Surpassing the Love of Men by Lillian Faderman   Morrow New York 1981
FMS - Michael Field by Mary Sturgeon   Harrap & Co London 1922
FWR - Men and Memories by William Rothenstein 1900-22   Faber London 1932
JCM - Carmina #8, The Poetry of Michael Field by Edwin Essex   1931
JTX - Textual Practice V4 #2 197, Poets and lovers by Christine White   1990
JYX - Yale Journal of Criticism 165-86 Sappho Doubled: MF by Yopie Prins   1995
MAS - Music and Silence The gamut of Michael Field De Blackland Press 2000
SZD - A Shorter Shīrazād 101 poems of Michael Field De Blackland Press 1999
VCR - Letters to "Michael Field" from C.S. Ricketts (1903-13)   Tragara Press 1981
VSW - Sappho: A Memoir and Translation by H.T. Wharton   Stott London 1885

★ SEE ALSO pp 236-7. Few of the above books are readily available in libraries.
Codes beginning with a J relate to newspapers and magazines, Q codes identify
Michael Field prose pieces. Codes beginning with an O or a Z indicate manuscripts
only accessible in the collections of the Bodleian Library at Oxford, or of the British
Library in London; Y codes signify manuscripts in other collections. For all these latter
a reader's ticket is unavoidable; shelf marks are fully listed in the key reference work:

MFC - The MICHAEL FIELD Catalogue a book of lists De Blackland Press 1998

This book also lists in chronological order by T number (such as T1137) some 1725
poems presently attributed to Michael Field.

Contents

Illustrations

The strange affair of Michael Field

I Poets

> *'I think the difference between me, & a true poet is this:— a true poet
> gives out his poetry, it is of him, as much as the fragrance is of the flower:—
> I suck a bit of sweetness here & there, & make honey of it, bee-fashion'*
> (Katharine Bradley, writing 28 February 1868, OYB 53b).

In May 1884 there was a household at Stoke Green, Bristol, which to all outward appearances was typically middleclass. It consisted of a married couple, James and Emma Cooper, their two daughters Edith and Amy, and Katharine Bradley, Emma's younger sister; to which one may probably add a couple of servants. Katharine and their widowed mother had originally lived with Emma and her husband in Kenilworth some 23 years previously, and it was here that the two girls were born, in 1862 and 1863; shortly after this Emma's health deteriorated, and her mother died. Katharine was then 21 and most of her time seems to have been spent looking after the two little girls; she was particularly devoted to the elder, Edith, who was just six years old. For a time this pattern had seemed set to change. Just after the death of her mother, Katharine became fleetingly entangled with, perhaps engaged to, a French sculptor turned stained glass artist; but he was to die suddenly, less than a month after they first met. The family moved several times, to Newton Leys in Derbyshire, then Solihull, then south to Bath, and eventually to Bristol.

Katharine had from a child shown a deep love of the classics and a natural talent for writing little poems, and her enthusiasms seem to have kindled a spark in Edith, who also began writing exotic plays when she was twelve. This fundamental division— Katharine for poetry and Edith for drama— set a pattern of interests which never substantially changed. In 1875 Katharine's first book of poetry THE NEW MINNESINGER was published by Longmans under the pseudonym 'Arran Leigh', and in 1881 she and her niece collaborated as 'Arran and Isla Leigh' on a second volume of drama and verse BELLEROPHÔN.

But May 1884 was pivotal, the month which saw the publication of their first major triumph, CALLIRRHOË / FAIR ROSAMUND, two separate plays bound together under yet another pseudonym, 'Michael Field'. This was a wise move, as a masculine name ensured their work would receive serious critical attention. And it succeeded beyond all reasonable expectation, attracting the enthusiastic praise of no less a poet than the ageing Robert Browning. The publication of H.T. Wharton's *Sappho* in 1885, containing the surviving fragments of that earlier poet's work, was to be the stimulus for LONG AGO (1889), "one of the most exquisite lyrical productions of the latter half of the nineteenth century"— so wrote John Miller Gray in *The Academy*. Browning had willingly overseen this work of his "two dear, Greek women" and his death that December was a great blow. From then on the die was cast; the rest of their lives they devoted to their high art, Katharine as 'Michael' and Edith as 'Field', although they always insisted that they functioned as a single artistic unit.

There was to be one final bizarre tweak to their artistic domino in August 1891, when Edith nearly died of scarlet fever on their visit to Dresden. Because of a dangerously high temperature, her hair was cut as short as a boy's, and the nurse subsequently referred to her as 'Heinrich'. In its anglicised form this nickname stuck, and Edith, although still 'Field', became commonly referred to as 'Henry' from that time on until her death in 1913.

Their Journal, WORKS AND DAYS, running almost without interruption from 1888 to 1914 (ZJB through ZKF) and abstracted in WAD, is an engrossing record of the daily life of Michael Field. The closet dramas (at least 40), and some 1725 poems, provide a parallel chronicle, almost as complete. But whereas Henry's life was a tumultuous drama, Michael's was a noble and beautiful poem. Back in 1877, the young Katharine wrote to Ruskin 'Do not ask me to give up dreaming or writing verses. I am afraid it wd. be quite impossible for me to do either' (OYR 34o). She never did.

II Lovers

> *"O Michael, you are not in the business!"*
> (Berenson, as reported by Henry, ZKC 81b)

Michael, in a well-known poem (T0538), described herself and her niece not only as poets, but also as lovers; I have already commented on this use of the word elsewhere (MAS 92). It is important to realise that the word 'lover', often indeed 'Lover', is used with a Shakespearian inclusiveness (as *Coriolanus V ii 14*) throughout their texts. One good example (see the note to *The*

Eternal Passer-by T0473) is its 1890 application to Edith's *mother*:

We were lovers together side by side   T0474, v1

An even more startling example is its application to Edith's *father*. On midsummer day 1906 Henry remembered 'Our great & terrible Lover— the dear Father' (ZJV 105b). One grimaces at a likely modern interpretation of that in some fevered misandric brain (especially the 'our'). In December 1897, after the traumatic Zermatt episode, Henry had written 'It is beautiful to think he ever approved our love, & has sealed it by his death' (ZJL 164b). Michael's affection for James is very clear in *Harmony* T0844.

Ruth Vanita, in her book on the unlikely bedfellows *SAPPHO AND THE VIRGIN MARY*, briskly pigeon-holes (on no stated grounds) Michael Field as an example of "the older woman who seduces the younger... Katherine Bradley, the aunt and lover of Edith Cooper" (FRV 30); she also maintains that they "sought out and maintained constant contact with homoerotically inclined men" (FRV 130). There is some ultimate truth in this (notably Ricketts and John 'Dorian' Gray), but so sweeping a generalisation must properly, if surprisingly, include (among many others whom they "sought out" and with whom they "maintained constant contact"), Ruskin, Browning, Berenson and McNabb. To state that they "sought out... homoerotically inclined men" *per se* is ludicrous— a discreet small ad in *The Academy* perhaps? It seems more to the point that they cultivated the company of *any person* who shared their (wide) "aesthetic" interests; on any count, such people would be few, and guaranteed to contain a high percentage of "homoerotically inclined men". Which brings to mind the anecdote of the man to whom an acquaintance complained about the "large numbers of queers, blacks and Jews in show-business": to which his interlocutor replied "If you took away the queers, blacks and Jews you wouldn't *have* any show business". And, one might add, most of the arts, and life's worthwhile things in general.

In (male) matters homoerotic, Michael Field displays a mixture of awareness and apparent innocence. On the one hand, Henry (writing from the *Weld Arms*, East Lulworth) refers to 'the strange hermit next door... No-one enters his house except (alas!) a boy belonging to the P.O. who often sleeps there and is loaded with presents. For long spaces of time the strange Monster sits with his hand in absorbed pose against his brow, his wigless baldness covered by a red hat. Then among the raspberries he appears in a

15

blond vivacious wig! We shall meet him again in <u>The Daily Mail</u>' (OCK 180-9o). On the other, Michael describes the "Painters" (SZD 52-3): '..it is inexpressibly droll to find 2 men living together exactly as Henry & I live. Ricketts adores Shannon as I adore Henry, & the fraternal two live in bliss working together at their woodcuts as we at our poems. They are both eminently beautiful, & of complexion quite ridiculously fair' (OCW 202or). Her choice of words *adores*, *fraternal* is particularly instructive. Henry even traced Michael's enthusiasm for Ricketts to her (Michael's) recognition of this mirrored *adoration*. 'The sympathy my Love feels with the Lover Ricketts made her responsive to him... How I enjoy the sight of it' (ZJG 48a). Once more one is conscious of the greater awareness of Henry; in July 1894 she writes: 'The brother-artists both adore Oscar— one hopes they don't imitate their idol in more than conversation' (ZJG 87a; sa *Motley* T0951).

They were also interested in '..Bessie Bell & Mary Grey.. two young women devotedly attached to one another' (OCW 70o); these Scots ladies had a triangular arrangement going with a male admirer in the second half of the seventeenth century. It all ended in tears when the youth inadvertently brought them a 'contagion' raging in Perth, and "the two gentle hermits.. unwittingly perished with their lover." In October 1889, Michael Field was at 'the wide silver Tay', and visited their tomb (ZJB 116b).

In a later contentious footnote Vanita remarks: "I agree with Leighton's emphasis on Michael Field's active assumption of the role of "lover," which I interpret as central to lesbian self-construction. I differ from her view that they lacked "socio-political commitment" (FAL 204), since I see them as activist members of Aestheticist circles that she reads as apolitical and masculinist (FAL 217-8) and I as anarchist, feminist, and proto-gay / lesbian" (FRV 264 n63). Leighton has my vote.

III Collaborators

> *'Ricketts confides to us that when we are each by ourselves we are <u>sane</u>— but when we are together we are <u>impossible</u> & <u>insane</u>,'*
> (H ZJN 103b)

Virginia Blain made a significant contribution to Michael Field scholarship with the rediscovery of the late Rothenstein letters (YVK), not least one written in 1907, in which Michael explained "that 'Michael' connoted the fiery archangel, while

'Field' came from pastures of the blessed" (JWH 245). The origin of "Michael" was never really in doubt, but the "Field" information is completely new. One does wonder, just a little, if Michael had re-invented the allusion; after all, 1907 was the year they became Catholics. Whilst "Michael Field" was to become their final publication name (sa MAS 47), it is interesting that for a time they used *only* the forename to denote their duality (as MAS 49 and ZCC 138o). This is also apparent in the following quotations. Michael wrote in the 1891 Journal 'Yesterday (July 21st) Amy & I went to Mrs. Chandler Moulton's. I saw Hardy, kind & austere. Near him was Theodore Watts. At the name of Michael he leapt into the air & glittered. Both these men found it <u>inscrutable</u>, <u>incomprehensible</u> that 2 people could write poetry together' (ZJD 56b). Henry took up the tale on the 28th: '...Sim introduced me to Theodore Watts— he shook hands with the whole Michael & we formed a trio on the sofa. When he heard we were aunt & niece, he exclaimed "It is more like a fairy-tale than ever." He told us at once he was deeply interested in our work..' (ZJD 60a). This particularly curious usage persisted as late as 1900 (MAS 19).

In June 1907 on a visit to Dublin they at last met Professor Dowden, who 'wanted to hear if one of us were the critic like Beaumont & the other the poet to be toned down like Fletcher; without prying, he set himself with eyes wrought to circumspection to find out the heart of our mysteries for himself' (H ZJW 144-5). Aunt and niece, usually rather reluctantly, explained their 'mysteries' on several occasions. Henry wrote to Browning on 30 May 1884: 'My Aunt & I work together after the fashion of Beaumont & Fletcher. She is my senior by but 15 Yrs. She has lived with me, taught me, encouraged me & joined me to her poetic life. <u>She</u> was the enthusiastic student of the <u>Bacchae</u>. Some of the scenes of our plays are like mosaic work— the mingled, various product of our two brains.... This happy union of two in work & aspiration is sheltered & expressed by "Michael Field". Please regard him as the author' (ZCL 9-10). Almost exactly two years later, writing to Havelock Ellis in a famous letter (which seems to have disappeared), Michael elaborated on this mosaic trope. 'As to our work, let no man think he can put asunder what God has joined. *The Father's Tragedy*, save Emmeline's song and here and there a stray line, is indeed Edith's work: for the others, the work is perfect mosaic: we cross and interlace like a company of dancing summer flies; if one begins a character, his companion seizes and possesses it; if one conceives a scene or situation, the

17

other corrects, completes, or murderously cuts away' (FMS 47). She also wrote to John Miller Gray (MFC 59) on Whit Sunday, 1889: "I weed Edith's garden she mine; then examining each other's withering heaps we exclaim— "Well, you might have spared that"— or, "that weak twining thing had yet a grace"— but the presiding horticulturist is ruthless, & it is borne away to the barrow' (ZCC 213-4).

Other significant aspects of their working methods have been elaborated on elsewhere (as at MAS 43,45,51,122,185). The poems often offer direct evidence. *Herself* T0217, bears directly on the collaboration; others, such as *Pen-prints* T0695, *Love growth* T0221, *Mood* T0901, *The New Song* T1214, show "the twain" working alone. Eventually the critics were aware that there was a team. Meredith asked 'wh: of us "does the <u>Males</u>"? (The highest compliment implied in any question asked of Michael)'; George Moore wanted to know '..who does the love-scenes— they are so good— "You get such words in them"' (H ZJE 85b;ZJL 62a). Henry noted in 1898 'the charge brought against us that one writes with a steel & one with a golden pen..' (ZJM 101b). Two years later she told Michael '"Your force is elemental— ... mine is of the spheres"' (ZJO 60b). But Michael had already observed in 1895:

> Mine is the eddying foam and the broken current,
> Thine the serene-flowing tide, the unshattered rhythm;　　　　T0724,v1-2

Much fascinating material has appeared in the last few years on collaborating authors in general and Michael Field in particular (see especially FBL, FWC and VWK). We will leave the topic with a final scene at Leicester in November 1909, where Michael chaired a meeting of the Catholic Women's League. The subject was "the Catholic strain in English Literature". When her own work was praised 'Michael with unnecessary generosity— openly declared that her name of Bradley was not known in literature— all the glory belonged to Michael Field, a name she shared with another, to whom the true honour was due— "my fellow" More wild applause— Fr. Placid grasps my hand below the platform & goes off murmuring "This beats the Incarnation. It takes two women to make one man!"' (H ZJZ 188a).

IV Roumanians

> 'I fall in love with Henry afresh; the Boy glows very delicately
> beautiful'　　　　　　　　　　　　　　　　　　　(M ZJR 101a)

18

In late September 1898 Ricketts was eager to tell Michael Field all about "The Roumanians... a people with Sapphic passion..". Henry wrote it all down. 'Again & again Ricketts reverts to his Roumanians— he delights in them, their faithfulness to the spectres of Pagan gods, their Brothers of the Sword (men who married men, with a train of bridesmaids— men, whose tied fingers were blessed by the Church) their Sisters of the Cross (women who married women, with a train of groomsmen, & were blessed by the Church foot tied to foot)— their powerful daring sentiment, their passionate utterance' (ZJM 95ab, sa ZJP 37a). One suspects that this is one of Ricketts's more inventive tarradiddles (or at least an inspired embroidery). An ethnographic footnote, at any rate, to interest Byatt's "Leonora Stern". How different, especially in Victorian times, from the home-life of our own dear Church!— and how much more enlightened.

"The Michaels" meanwhile pursued their own brand of gender-bending. In 1934 George Douglas, "a personal friend of the late Misses Bradley & Cooper" remembered "'Henry' was habitually 'full of fun', & if they played at being men, it was never for a moment in the uncouth or unsexed manner which one is inclined to associate with, for example, the Ladies of Llangollen or Christina of Sweden" (OZG 144-5). Presumably he never witnessed a cameo such as that recorded by Michael in July 1911: 'It seems indicated I should be cheered by a morning-pipe, so I begin.. to smoke to Henry, my feet on a low wicker chair' (ZKB 99b). But we know what he means; in public both women were the grandest of grand ladies. The imaginary stereotypes of Michael as the overbearing, trousered and pipe-smoking *butch* with Henry as the delicate *femme* are just that— imaginary. Apart from the single noted reference to a pipe, both in their respective physiques and dispositions, nothing could be further from the truth (see MAS 18).

It was possibly only the accident of his death that prevented Katharine marrying 'her supreme love' Alfred Gérente; but to state that she "seduced" Edith, presumably on the rebound, is that more grotesque. Katharine, the 'priest of the family', had too tender a conscience to contemplate such an enormity. If she was delighted but too scrupulous to encourage Francis Brooks, her young second cousin (SZD 27), she would hardly be likely to start a sexual relationship with her immediate, even younger, niece— and under her own sister's roof. A contrary case *might* however be made out. Did the winsome Edith "seduce" her susceptible aunt?

Michael, for all the external show, was essentially feminine; there was a strong male component in Henry's psyche (see the note to *Caenis Caeneus*, T0937   MAS 129). In her 'Confession' of January 1892, she faced unpalatable truths. Of her mother she writes 'She did not understand my need of freedom. She bound & overawed me where I wanted to be free & personal.. I suffered torments'. Whereas of Michael she could say: 'What a divine blessing it is to me to have my Love, who checks no self-expression, who brings beauty to my eyes, & gladness to my life, who loves me & whom I love with strenuous force, that is half-hidden by our caresses & humorous names, & utter familiarity! Alas, it *(ICT: Henry)* loves M̲an much less...' (ZJE 13b). It may be that Henry envied the freedom and apparent self-assurance of her aunt, saw a chance to achieve emancipation from what she considered suffocatingly rigid parental restraints— and took it. This makes her sound calculating, and to some extent I think she was; I think she would have had little compunction in ditching her aunt if Berenson had offered marriage. Michael was probably aware of this, but wisely gave her forest-room. Very early on Michael had recognised one of her own failings, a 'terrible intenseness that is almost a bane to me, ...there is a doglike clinging tenacity about me... I do not say it is well to have it' (OYB 80). In the long run the niece was to rely utterly on her aunt, and, in her own way, to return her love.

But that Henry was nothing so run-of-the-mill as a lesbian (or proto-lesbian for that matter) is indicated by an extraordinary Journal reference to Berenson in August 1912. She describes him as 'My life-friend, for whom I delayed the Perpetual Vow of Chastity for a whole year, because I had dreamt that in the future the wonder might happen that we could live together in friendship under a show of marriage' (ZKC 99a). Whether Michael was indeed to be relegated to a granny flat is not made clear, but when one considers the Palmer Worm was at that time eleven years married, one must also 'wonder' what plans Henry had in mind for his wife Mary. The phrase *under a show of marriage* is however the most revealing. Of George Douglas she had earlier written 'He is my ideal of what a husband shd. be, on the sensible French lines of no passion— but affection & respect' (OCK 122r). Henry seems to have been one of those unfortunates *incapable* of the transactions of physical love; as she grew older the glaciation increased, to her own very real distress. The climax of this is dramatically realised in *Milia Multa* (T1669, MAS 203).

V Masculinists

O Major / I've been a rager
On manly beauty throughout every clime
Ah me— what shall I see? / Bewitched I sure must be,
To think my joy will be fulfilled this time!   T0711

So Henry, on prospects of introduction to a male visitor at Dumfries in September 1895. (Her confessor Fitzgibbon would display an equal interest in a military escort in 1910.)

There is no doubt at all that both Michael and Henry were as susceptible to masculine beauty, and masculine charm, as most women (and not a few men) are. 'Hennie is falling in love with the Vet— and with his lovely eye-lashes' (M OCH 37o). Michael herself on Robert Bridges: '..he is besides a most handsome fellow, & Michael is trying through his publisher, to get a portrait' (ZCD 72r); and in 1887 of a more famous poet: '..when my hand was ungloved for tea, he caught it vehemently saying "And you do the lyrics." Truly Love, I wd. fain put back the clock of time 30 years & be loved by Robert Browning in his glorious manhood' (ZCL 244r). Henry recorded in 1897 'We talk even of my first love— Dr. Main, dead in disgrace— he who was Hippolyte to me at 17 when one's passion is still Dian's' (ZJL 33a). Her last lover, equally unattainable, was to be the Heavenly Bridegroom (T1669,72). Ursula Bridge proposes another love episode, with Arthur Symons (MFC 64) in June 1890; she believed that Henry "the more serious emotionally, was also the more sensual" (OZJ 218,34). For Henry's own views see also the note to T1167.

Bridge describes Michael as "a flirt and like many flirts not a sensual woman." There were two men— apart from Bridge's suggestion of a possible "flirtation" with Ernest Bell (MFC 55,OZR 205-6)— with whom Michael herself imagined an emotional involvement, Gérente (MAS 28), and Ricketts. Unfortunately both were non-starters. Her feelings for Ricketts are expressed in two beautiful, low-key poems of Summer 1903: *Missed Pleasures* T1127, and *A Symbol* T1129. They are perhaps most memorably encapsulated in her 1901 sonnet *Violets* T0948, in which she clearly acknowledges his prior commitment to his own Fellow:

That thou can'st never give my bosom ease;   T0948,v2

In 1906 she admits: 'The Painter can keep me young, but it is Hennie alone who can make me happy' (ZJV 111a). She should have accepted Francis Brooks (SZD 27,112). One cannot ignore Henry's superlative T0678 (SZD 56), but otherwise skips hastily by the infatuations of both women with Berenson. In 1901 they were dazzled by a comet-like transit of Kipling:

Pass, Pass, O Rudyard, with your handsome legs!   T1018,v2

Many such instances (as SZD 52, MAS 108) could be quoted.

Both women were willing to learn from men in general, and Ricketts in particular, courting his advice and criticism of virtually everything they wrote. In 1905 Michael told him 'You have delivered us into the glorious liberty of the male writer' (ZJT 137b). Six years later, trying to decide whether she wanted to become a Dominican Tertiary, but concerned that this might involve subjection to female authorities, she anxiously consulted McNabb. 'He assures Michael she wd. be under no dominion of women. He laughs very much at Michael's partiality to men' (H ZKA 185a). Henry seems to have preferred an obvious masculine presence in marriage. Writing of the Houghtons in August 1903 she says 'The husband & wife have outgrown the barriers of sex & become so much alike they are as brother & sister. I have seen this kind of marriage— unattractive because it is a confusion— the distinctness of sex-quality impaired' (ZJR 128a).

VI Feminists

Women should be liberated because, if they are not, they bore men so.
(Berenson, as reported by Michael, ZKF 69o)

If one now looks at the issue of "socio-political commitment", and considers first the case for Michael, we have Mary Sturgeon's assertion that "Katharine was a prime mover of the Anti-Vivisection Society in Clifton, and was its secretary till 1887" (FMS 21). Oxford still has the draft of her address to "ladies" advocating abolition of "State-registered vice", at den Haag in September 1883 (OPS 52-66). An entry in one of Katharine's early notebooks is especially revealing: '..when I look inward to my own life, I feel I was made for something nobler than to be an old spinster aunt & assist Lis in the care & education of her children. Such people may seem to be of use; but they are really superfluous' (OYB 49b). In a letter to Ruskin she writes 'I, Katharine Bradley, must exist, free in service, devoted, not fettered in love' (OYR 34r). There is also the clear affirmation in her letter to Isabelle Wedmore (page 57). So Katharine was a New Woman;

but she was not a man-supplanter. A *careful*, unprejudiced reading of *The New Minnesinger* (T0150), and her sonnet on the death of Frances Power Cobbe (T1164, MAS 158) make this plain— as also her mischievous *Adam & Eve* T0699 (MAS 103). In the same early notebook is the remark 'I should like to have been a page to some great man myself. Of all Shakespeare's women, I wd. choose the lot of Viola' (OYB 58b). She had only a lover's quarrel with man; the hurt came from the struggle to establish a right to be heard. A great-hearted woman, a fighter, and always an enthusiast; even as late as the Richmond days we find her campaigning against the despoiling of Cambridge Park. And she could make withering comments on women in general (MAS 153) and hardcore lesbians— whether or no she viewed them as such— in particular (MAS 103).

However, any attempt to pin the politically-correct rosette on her niece is doomed to ultimate failure. For Henry, history was more compelling than herstory. In the Journal for 1892 she 'confessed' to loving 'fads & causes not at all' (ZJE 13b). Fifteen years later, in September 1907, watching bathers in the 'women's tank', and taking a double swipe at both the female body and female suffrage, she comments 'such lack of the express & admirable if I had believed in the vote for the sex I should have drowned my belief & the vote forever' (ZJW 208b sa note to T0550, SZD 50). In another September, at a convent in Rottingdean in 1910, she inveighs against the nuns' modest collection of pictures: 'So it always is with women— the confession of chance in their selection of anything beautiful, the secret dropped they know nothing of Quality' (ZKA 164a). In December 1905 she had been even more dismissive: 'Where we breathe & have our being women are absolutely inferior creatures to men, as animals to human creatures' (ZJT 147b). Here surely she speaks as if she were essentially a man. And in August 1906, at the Blossoms Hotel in Chester, 'How I hate women-waiters— chill creatures vouching nothing! Oh for the velvet of meat & wine in a good waiter, the alacrity to a lady's smile & the sureness that her grateful purse will "tip"' (ZJV 146a). Here she is at her most feminine.

VII Femmes Damnées

> *'How could I confess my secret sins.. the anguish of the 3rd, 4th & 5th verses of Femmes Damnées..'* (H ZJW 69a)

23

Thus Henry in a tormented entry in the Journal for 09 April 1907, referring to the Baudelaire poem from *Les Fleurs du Mal*, a collection originally announced in 1845 under the title *Les Lesbiennes*. [Emma Donoghue invalidates her own conclusions by an unfortunate confusion of this poem with another by Baudelaire of identical name, FED 126.] Michael Field attempted a translation of this piece, probably in 1901, and his version of the relevant stanzas runs:

> *Others like sisters wander, slow and grave,*
> *Through craggy haunts of ghostly emanations,*
> *Where once Saint Anthony was wont to brave*
> *The purple-breasted pride of his temptations.*
>
> *Some by the light of resin-scented torches*
> *In the dumb hush of caverns seek their shrine,*
> *Invoking Bacchus, killer of remorses,*
> *To liven their delirium with wine.*
>
> *Others who deal with scapulars and hoods*
> *Hiding the whiplash under their long train,*
> *Mingle, on lonely nights in sombre woods,*
> *The foam of pleasure with the tears of pain.* (T1021, s3-5)

Henry's primary anguish seems not with the *temptations* of lesbianism— 'the delirious hy(p)notism of Dresden', but with her *purple-breasted pride*, and memories of the *whiplash*— 'the terrible wrong of my childhood & *its results*' (italics ICT; see the note to T1108, MAS 148). Possibly also a "guilt" at her Maenadic (maybe even masochistic?) enthusiasms, and the dubious obsession with Bacchus (T0727; sa T0415, SZD 38-9).

The 'results' might substantiate this writer's tentative theory of physical withdrawal; and peripherally explain Henry's seeking out for solace some garment of the absent Beloved (rather like Linus and his blanket). There *is* record of rare examples of Henry 'getting to grips' with her Fellow, as an amusing Journal entry in September 1894 by Michael: 'Then I come into the drawing-room & .. to Henry's side while he is listening to divine Chopin, fall asleep— I almost awake to hear— "I cannot keep my hands from this bushy head" & feel fingers plunging into my hair. In such wise spoke Bothwell to the Queen' (ZJG 129a); sa page 31.

When at last Henry steeled herself to the confessional, we have the (in)famous Journal entry of 07 December 1907 'Since I entered the Holy Catholic Church, I have never fallen into fleshly sin' (ZJX 53). Here I repeat my opinion voiced on an earlier (1988) occasion. "It is not overclear exactly what she means by this— she can hardly be claiming a blanket blamelessness— a sexual connotation seems inescapable. Yet here one will ride any one imagined hobby-horse at particular peril; especially for a modern reader her words are a deep well into which the sophisticate may peer and see only their own faces. Even IF substantive, it is at least possible the allusion amounts to no more than one of those wholesome solitary pastimes for which we need not look our best. It is scarcely our business" (MFC 42).

In August 1891, when Edith was ill with scarlet fever in Dresden, she was subject to advances from the woman (Schwester Christiane) who was set to nurse her. The nature of these advances is unmistakeable 'Schwester, while my Love is in the Garden, embraces me bodily... — her hand curls round my heart to feel the life beat & strays. "Die schöne Brust— O das schönes Bauch"— I don't know the German of the last exclamation! *(ICT: belly)* She makes me shiver, but I play with her passion like a child..' (ZJD 112a). There are two important points here. First, these advances were clearly most unwelcome. 'My Experiences with nurse are painful— she is under the possession of terrible, fleshly love, she does not conceive as such, & as such I will not receive it. Ah, why will Anteros make one cynical by always peering over the beauty of every love. . . why must his fatality haunt us?' (ZJD 110a). On visiting a hospital with a patient in November 1908, she would still remember Dresden and 'the lure of sin' (ZJY 185b). Secondly, Christiane's hunger was treated with an understanding and kindness which did the invalid much credit. Even if she had not been aware of such love before, she clearly knew what it was about from this point on. Of a train journey in August 1902 she writes 'We travel with two women— hermits in a pair, Nitche *(ICT: possibly Nietzsche?)* would call them— "Fellows" we call them. The lover is an intense-featured woman, whose love or ideals wd devour the very flesh off her— the beloved a silly little thing of about two & twenty with whitish blue eyes, & frolicsome smile. They look at each other from the centre of their eyes— & I know they are lovers' (ZJQ 140a).

There may have been other 'proto-lesbians' in the Michael Field circle, perhaps including Michael's friend of long-standing, Amy Bell (see T0591). This may explain an ambiguous remark by Henry in April 1900: 'She is blunt as most women on that side' (ZJO 54a). There was a particularly interesting Journal entry in

25

Michael's hand in August 1895. 'Amy Bell & a young girl with us. Is it because I am getting old, that the young girl, the normal, fresh, healthy, & sound as an apple kind, affects me as the most wonderful, & yet uninteresting phenomenon on earth. Why give it food? Why foster it as a species? It eats & drinks, & hangs on one with a weight heavy as custom' (ZJH 126b). But one can take another passage, written by Henry in January 1893, which points in the diametrically opposite direction. 'On Sunday she (Michael) saw <u>him</u>— Amy's <u>him</u>— a grave, simple young man' (ZJF 3b).

VIII Lesbians

Queen Dawn shall find us on one bed   T0318,v15

As for Michael Field himself, the only evidence for rumpy-pumpy, tenuous and ambiguous as that evidence is, is the shared bed (but see the note to T1194, MAS 161), and a scarce handful of Journal entries by Henry. One such occurs at the end of her account of Easter Sunday 1896, when James apparently did not want Michael to join the family inner circle for the annual devotion. 'We have to sing the Easter hymn in the salon to please Father— Michael cannot join— & when I would rejoin her in the Study I am locked out. She must have suffered abominably— I simply shivered with disquiet— a hopeless anxiety. . . .But Michael joined me in bed, talked only of <u>The Cup</u>, & took me to her breast & to young joyousness' (ZJK 52b). Perhaps— it all depends on one's mind-frame— more significant is an entry for New Year's Day 1893, 'My cruel Love leaves me for early service, an unsatisfied heathen in our little bed' (ZJF 3b). Donoghue quotes five other such scattered Journal remarks. Each of these, as she freely allows is "open to interpretation". But, as she rightly adds, "*together* (italics ICT) they clearly evoke a world of sexual joy" (FED 30). Such cumulative indications cannot be overlooked, or easily argued away .... perhaps!

Virginia Blain makes much of the 1885 letters, with their 'marital' salutations: "They provide a very rare instance of direct evidence of a Victorian lesbian relationship" (JWH 241,9). They provide of course nothing of the kind. They provide *circumstantial* evidence that Michael Field indulged a *verbal fantasy* of 'husbands and wives'. Blain herself admits this in so many words a few pages further on. "Although they *played* husband-wife *games* modelled on heterosexual marriage (italics ICT), it was only one of a range of intimacies available to them" (JWH 252). *Direct*

26

evidence is only obtainable with a flash camera through a bedroom window, and even this might be "subject to interpretation". A significant point, usually overlooked in all the voyeuristic excitement, is that Michael speaks of the 'marriage', from its inception, in an *explicitly literary* rather than (JWH 255 n24) an "explicitly genital" context. In *The Sign of the Bramble-bough*, Michael salutes (ICT italics):

My Poet-bride, sweet Song-mate, ...   T0191,v1

We should look more carefully at the notorious 1886 assessment of the Browning marriage (ZCL 229r, quoted at MAS 122) and the equally famous quotation from the Solemnization of Matrimony in the letter to Havelock Ellis already cited (page 17).

In any case, on the other side is more compelling evidence that if Michael Field was an 'item', it was (to modern eyes) a remarkably chaste one. There are remarks by both women that rebut any inference of physical congeries. Michael, in the undoubtedly erotic and sensuous *Cherry Song* of 1902, yet says:

Our love hath never made presumptuous sally   T1069,v5

In *Barren Love* (1900) we have the verse:

So coy. No fruit of it will ever be   T0908,v5

Henry wrote in 1903: 'Oh, what perfect joy there is in the way Michael & I love! .. So rarely love has this passionate discretion. We are free & more to each other with each year' (ZJR 222b).

The strongest contrary evidence comes from the period of the Catholic conversion in 1907. Henry, fearful that any priest, specifically Fitzgibbon, should 'tamper with our bond' (ZJW 76b), writes in the Journal 'There is nothing this young seminarist might not misconceive— even our Sacred Relation to each other. . . No, no! We must tear ourselves away from him...' (ZJW 72a). Michael had previously told Fitzgibbon that she had a 'maternal care' for her niece (ZJW 63b). It is *inconceivable* that either woman, in the awful sureness of the new faith and total commitment to it, would mince the truth either to the priest, or (especially) to herself.

Even Ruth Vanita eventually concedes "to read erotic imagery in their love-poems as self-aware is not to read lesbian consciousness into a nonerotic romantic friendship" (FRV 130). She

27

had rather given the game away with the statement "Michael Field's expansions of Sappho's fragments into lyrics in Long Ago (1889) turns out, *disappointingly* (italics ICT), to focus on Sappho's love for Phaon" (FRV 133). Lillian Faderman, for the present author, interprets most satisfactorily the "lesbianism" of the LONG AGO lyrics (MAS 61). Armstrong and Blain appear to realise that "The ambivalent relation between text and life disclosed in the work of.. 'Michael Field'.. suggests how problematic lesbian readings can be" (FAV xii). Yet Blain has no hesitation in labelling Michael Field as "most obviously lesbian", remarking further 'Theirs, of course, was a case of double perversion, since they were not only lesbian lovers, but being aunt and niece, they were incestuous lovers as well" (FAV 138-9). But as has been shown, the evidence is neither all black nor all white, but a nubilous, bewildering grey. Even *should* the smoke imply some fire, then as Emma Donoghue wisely and temperately observes, "Perhaps for the Michael Fields.. if sex was just one element in a balanced, spiritually enriching love, it did not make you a pervert" (FED 31).

Sturgeon has been gently mocked for "protecting" the reputation of the ladies, as if there was something "obscurely repellent" (FMS 29) in the domestic arrangements of Michael Field. Yet a homoerotic relationship, if such there was, is as natural and valid as a heteroerotic one. Were the ladies to roll nude on the living-room carpet at Reigate with a merino, a black one at that, to the enthusiastic if somewhat sticky applause of the assembled servants, parents and wider family (with the neighbours lining up for returns), it should not alter our admiration for their literary work, or of themselves as human beings. In fact, as long as the merino was consenting and the entertainment had PG rating, we might award them extra Brownie points for flair. Whatever they did to achieve their jollies was their business, and good luck to them; it does not damn them as poets or people, and is *not the point*. They put up their work, not their lives, for public scrutiny. If we *must* peer though the letter-box, the verdict is still: *not proven*.

The sexual charge of words was probably enough. Whether they called themselves Husband and Wife, Master and Boy, or Horsie and Persian Puss, the overall impression is that their private dreamworld was so charmed— with chivalry and troubadours, shells and pearls, lilies and tall white candles, tragic destiny and noble death before dishonour— they could still sleep in the same bed without the necessity of a drawn sword between them. They certainly need a knight errant in this century.

IX Eroticists

> *Women are to me*
> *Trumpets of flesh: I am their prophet, seer;*
> Phêmê, BELLEROPHÔN

Virginia Blain also quotes a 1993 article by one Paula Bennett: "Bennett suggests that all small but precious objects including buds, seeds, small flowers, berries and gems deserve (ICT: *deserve??*) to be read as potential clitoral symbols" (FAV 137). And, sure enough, Ruth Vanita enlightens us that "Clitoral imagery (buds, gems, seeds) is all pervasive in Field's writings" (FRV 265 n93). More! in Michael's beautiful *Cowslip-gathering* T0213, "the 'moist quiet' of the 'tender, marshy nook' studded with cowslips may be read as vulval" (FRV 120). "May be read" indeed; as McEnroe was wont to say, "You *can't* be *serious!*"

To find clitoral symbols in Michael Field's flowers and jewels and vulval analogues in her fountains and grottoes is to demonstrate (at best) the mind of an obsessed gynaecologist, and to open a public toilet in the drawing room of 'the most beautiful house in England' (one visitor's description of Paragon). And as basically silly. One might as well advance the famous handbag of *The Importance of Being Earnest* as a uterine symbol, in support of the 'womb envy' theory of aestheticism.

There is no room for ataraxy, let alone epiphany, in such po-faced clinical analyses, such cunning semantic stunts. It is a self-evident truth that *all* life, not just human, or female, is driven by the forces of replication: there is even the depressing probability that the apprehension of beauty, and all things ineffable, is only another mediation of generative stirrings. But with Michael's peerless love poems to Henry we enter a world where one can still feel human. The road to the Venusian ghetto is lined only with the shattered pillars and overthrown columns of the despised temples of Mars and Uranus. No one-eyed trouser-snake, it seems, shall tempt in, nor contaminate, that Eden. Such feminist sermons in stones and rhetoric in the running brook (with nary a fish on a bicycle) will agitate only regurgitators of the tired *cliché* and the latest passing fashion in the idle and essentially barren groves of literary academe. We can all play pseudo-scientific word games. Why is the bee such a constant motif in Michael's poetry; it has a sting: is it a penis? When, as often, it enters a flower, is this a "metaphorical field" for copulation? Is ANY 6-leg beastie a phallic symbol? Is there an occult significance in Michael's gift (*A Miracle* T0620) of a jewelled insect to Henry? Is there a Freudian implication in the fact that it is, of all insects, a fly? With its associations both of corruption and trousering? Is a rose *really* another four-letter word? Or is it the Virgin Mary? [An idea stolen, as in so much of guilt-drenched christianity, from the healthy hokum of paganism— in this case, Artemis]. Or may we agree with Dorothy Parker?

As urged once before (MFC 11) none of it has anything to do with the splendid tropes and metres of Michael Field. In such a context it is relevant to remember William Rothenstein's appraisal of the two women: 'With so much beauty to occupy them, they had no time for, and no patience with, the meaner objects which too many men and women pursue' (WAD x).

X Romanticists

> It is not *Athens* I desire— O Child,
> Thyself, thy small rose-body in my arms,
> Thy mutterings, & Thy fondness over me,
> Thy breath in waking, & Thy breath asleep.
>
> Procne, T0983 v19-22

Michael told George Barrett in March 1910 "— I am afraid it is an open secret that I am slightly attached to Henry"— "An open secret! It is as evident as the sun" the priest replied (ZKA 50b). Over two lifetimes she poured out lyrics in which the 'slight attachment' was made manifest; these included *She is my lady, O she is my love!* T0296, *Second Thoughts* T0662, *Old Ivories* T0884, *Vale!* T0888, and *Her Profile* T1215. To Michael, Henry was the significant other who was, at different times and in different aspects simultaneously 'lover', companion, younger sister, loving daughter. She was someone with whom to share her interests and emotional needs; in her niece's successes she saw a fulfilment of her own aspirations. Her initial "dominance" was the benevolent *in loco parentis* of the good teacher. As Henry fledged her wings Michael was content to withdraw, to sit on the side-lines and marvel (MAS 166). She did not want marriage because she did not want the problems of a family: '..mine is not the sort of nature for that; I am not fond of children as many women are. I do not like them constantly about me' (OYB 49b). What she *did* want was the stimulus of conversation, of active minds; any other needs became marginalised, peripheral. If a guest brought flowers, Henry was concerned with the flowers; Michael was more interested in the guest (H ZKC 43b, sa note to *Gifts* T0910).

For Henry, Michael was primarily a substitute mother or older sister, 'guardian & vigorous above me' (H ZKA 229a), with whom she felt safe— who would not grasp like Schwester Christiane, or pester her with 'fleshly love'. It is no wonder she never wrote her any 'love' poems, she did not think of her in the way she thought of Berenson. In fact she wrote her hardly *any* poems (*To A. Leigh* T0160 and *Temptation* T0978 are the only apparent examples). But in the sexually neutral ambience of the Whym Chow elegies, she could reveal her real love. Michael was more refuge than 'lover', a nest in which her agile brain might conjure nobler, more exotic lives— and bask in uncritical approval; from which she could make sorties into the exciting worlds of art, literature and human society— and then in safety return.

Henry's distress, on those few occasions when Michael was away, surfaces several times in the Journal. In November 1900 Michael escaped to a matinée, leaving Henry desolate. 'The house is lonely— even Whym Chow lives a memorial life on the stairs, & refuses my company, fixing eyes & ears in the direction of the front door. Michael wept to leave me by the misty river & in the silent rooms - - Michael must not do so again: it makes me more solitary, because apprehensive, & subject to attack from ghostly dread that mounts up out of the Past' (ZJO 158a). Again, one August day at Savernake in 1903, Michael 'stays away so long I think she will never return; & weep as the rain teaches how to weep— ...I did feel woe— woe, without her... (ZJR 99-100). In February 1897, she encouraged Michael to visit Amy Bell in Hastings '...she must have change. ..Amy *(ICT: her sister)* sleeps with me . . . I can get no sleep till I wrap up in my Love's yellow dressing gown that personates herself— a warm thing, of loving habit' (ZJL 15). In June 1894 'Then my Love leaves me to go with Rose Baker to <u>Phèdre</u>. I open her cupboard & see all her frocks— each a child of her very body, they are all so like her, & I kiss them as they hang before me. I go to sleep missing my Love...' (ZJG 77a). And a final example, dated March 1893 'I dreamt my Love was dead in the night & clasped her living form with the despair of expressing relief— My own Love, my Joy-bringer & With-enjoyer' (ZJF 34a). She knew Michael would not make of her those invasive physical demands with which she could not cope.

All the rest was fun, a "marriage" made not in Boston, but Bristol. It was part of a Kiplingesque "great Game", a "dressing up", both literally and metaphorically so important to Michael Field. The pantomime of their lives was performed on an invisible stage to an indifferent audience; the *show* of the relationship (but not its serious basis) a jest, no offence in't at all. If "friendship" meagrely describes it, it was Romantic rather than romantic.

XI Femmes sauvées

'My loved & I are so close & fresh to each other— we must cry a little. What we are to each other!— we mean to each other Earthly life; & into the next we are bound to run on together in our different natures along one channel of a love that cannot sever or dispart' (ZKB 95b)

Thus Henry in June 1911; it is in her prose, not her poetry, that one begins to appreciate the fact that Michael's devotion, after all, was not unreciprocated. The conversion to Catholicism in 1907 was the irrational solution to her realisation that death would fairly soon sever the 'Sacred Relation', that she would lose Michael as surely as they had lost Whym Chow. She was not to know then that it would be she who would die first, in a particularly loathsome manner. In February she spoke of 'my love for my Michael— my yearning to keep the glorious Union unbroken' (ZKB 38b). On an Easter Monday some 14 years before, she had defined that love, in a declaration that finally, perhaps, explains what she meant by the word "lover". 'When I love I love down to the Creator there is in the beloved & therefore our union cannot be temporary— in fact, is not. I only understand such love; I am in relation to no other. This binds me to Michael, to the Mother, to Robert Browning, to Bernhard..'(ZJL 45a). It was this pious hope that sustained her to the end. 'When we're together eternally our spirits will be interpenetrated with our love & our art under the beneson (sic) of the Vision of God' (ZKD 90b).

In Michael's 1912 poem *Lovers* T1679 (see MAS 204) they had become 'Lovers in Christ '; but in the earlier *The Art of Love* she had seen no reason for Christ to enter into the equation:

Past iron Time there is an age of gold,
And hand in hand we will seek entrance there. T0781,v7-8

'It is rather difficult,' Henry remarks in 1908, 'to make any terms between Zeus & Christ' (ZJY 22a). Michael's faith had been with her all her life, as her entire canon of poetry proves; the fall into popery was not the Leucadian leap of her niece. She knew 'Eros cannot be a Christian' (MAS 177). [Henry, commenting on this, remarks 'Perhaps if you embrace the Boy this is true— *but all Love is not Erotic*' (ZKD 7a, ICT italics).] Christine White, despite her informed and interesting analysis of the rose imagery of Michael Field's poetry, is however surely way off the mark when she decides "Sappho is succeeded by the Virgin following Bradley and Cooper's conversion to Catholicism, but never entirely removed from the picture" (FSR 84). It seems unbelievable the two women would make such a connection, consciously or unconsciously; and one feels fairly certain that they would find the proposition unspeakably repugnant, were it to be offered them.

XII Fellows

> *I cannot let you go. There is love*
> *Of woman unto woman, in its fibre*
> *Stronger than knits a mother to her child.*
> Brangaena, THE TRAGEDY OF PARDON III iii

Alice Trusted, one of Michael's oldest friends (OCW 12-3), testified to "their passionate affection for one another" (OKE 126r). Gordon Bottomley (MFC 56) and his wife were friends of the last days. He recorded: 'life was one of their arts... this beauty of life was to be seen in their devotion to each other... This always struck me anew when either of them would refer to the other in her absence as "My dear fellow"; the slight change in the incidence and significance of the phrase turned the most stale of ordinary exclamations into something which suddenly seemed valuable and full of delicate, new, moving music. It seemed said for the first time...' (FMS 36-7). This fellowship is sketched in *A Japanese Print* (T1178, SZD); but is most evocatively conjured in *Balsam* T0891 (MAS) and *Nightfall* T0893 (SZD). Then in her last months, breaking out of the 'wattlefold', Michael penned a final great pagan celebration of their twinned life and love; in it, she claimed their place— in the Heavens rather than Heaven— as the *Dioscuri*. Fittingly, the poem was called *Fellowship*:

> *We cling and joy. It was thy intercession gave me right*
> *My Fellow, to this fellowship. My Glory, my Delight!*   T1721,v14-5

'We are to the world Michael Field... I shall have no pleasure in American readers, if they care more for Michael Field's name than his numbers' (OKG 11-2). So Michael in 1898, in a prophetic vision of what would be true a century later. And (almost certainly) Henry, writing a note at the end of BRUTUS ULTOR: '..in the present day, while the baser aspects of life are unshudderingly exposed, the obscure nativity of goodness is unvisited, and the honour of the human spirit uncredited and unsung. It has been my aim to penetrate the mysteries of womanhood that lie, unforbidden, in its taintless depths, and, by contrast of these *happy* (ICT italics) secrets with the experience vaunted by the materialist and the voluptuary, to unfold "To creatures stern sad tunes, to change their kind"' (XBU 78).

Their time in the courts of Earth is done, neither praise nor condescension can touch them now. Yet when all is said and done, ought not we to afford these two extraordinary women the courtesy of *listening* to their own testimonies? *Before* parading them in the public eye as "inseparable, incestuous and intense" (a review of *We are Michael Field* in Lambda Book Report, 1999)?— or describing them as indulging "an unabashed reconciliation of religion and lust" (AED xxxviii)? Could not Yopie Prins have avoided calling them "*sly* little scholars" (JYX 171), her careless if not wilful subversion of the clear Journal entry '*shy* little scholars' (ZJB 66b)? They who had hoped for fame have achieved instead a species of infamy at the pens of the faddists and new soap-box psychologists of the 'erotics of writing'. Female interest in their private lives, in the worst scenario they could possibly have imagined, has all but eclipsed that in their works (except as a peg on which to hang a thesis or a theory). How Michael Field, in celestial constellation, must hanker for a MALE academic (surely the ultimate accolade in their eyes) to afford in the 21st Century— as Michael once told Browning!— 'real criticism— such as man gives man' (ZCL 18r). Sadly, he has yet to appear.

Virginia Blain describes Michael Field as 'standing in the closet with their backs to the world and the door wide open' (FAV 138-9). One smiles and admires the neat phrase, but not the proposition. If anything, aunt and niece present more often as closet *straights* than closet *gays*, less *queer* than *strange*, in a very long tradition of English grotesques and eccentrics. Robert Fletcher more wisely stands back, observing "...'Michael Field' continues both to accomodate and to elude the interpretive control of 'his' readers" (FAV 178).

Even this one!

Invocation

Thee, Apollo, in a ring
We encompass, carolling
Of the flowers, fruits and creatures
    That thy features
Do express, and by thy side
Live their life half-deified:
Grasshoppers that round thee spring
From their mirth no minute sparing;
Hawk and griffin arrow-eyed;
Cock the gracious day declaring;
Olive that can only flourish
Where the fruiting sunbeams nourish;
Laurel that can never fade,
That in winter doth incline her
Lustrous branches to embraid
Chaplets for the lyric brow;
The white swan, that fair diviner,
Who in death a bliss descrying
Sings her sweetest notes a-dying:
These, all these, to thee we vow,
We thy nymphs who in a ring
Dance around thee, carolling.

The roses that for her are sweet,
The scent of new-mown hay,
The grand old chesnuts at whose feet
We watch the children play.

What bitter mem'ries ye may be
What mem'ries bitter & sweet,
Again beneath the chesnut tree
The little ones may meet.

The roses bloom in pinken spray
Mid briar thickets fair.
But she who made the summer day
For us, will she be there?

Oh what an' if the roses red
The hay about our feet
Should 'mind us of the Darling dead
For whom they once were sweet.

T0037   Emma Bradley developed a malignant breast cancer, and by July 1867
her condition was deteriorating rapidly. She and Katharine were now
living with her elder daughter's family in Newton Leys near Tissington,
a few miles from Ashbourne in Derbyshire. Katharine began a fragmentary journal,
and under an entry headed *Newton. Sunday morning July 7th* wrote: '...And on the
Saturday I went with her down to the hayfield; & she sat down under a chesnut tree;
while the children played under the hay-cocks, & I read to her; all wore the
semblance of happiness, & the sunshine was about us: yes we were happy, I at least
not realizing the truth that lay behind the bright semblance. Again too last week
another morning, she has been in the hayfield; & often in the evening; then the sun
light fell upon the bright green of the cleared field; & made all the sky look glistering
white above the western hills; ...' (OYB 4b-5a). In another entry she records 'And the
roses, & the gladdening voices of the children & the hayfield where she sits; ... how
all these things may become memories, to us memories bitter sweet' (OYB 4b). At
this time Edith and Amy were 5 and 4 respectively. The simple poem is known only
from the fragmentary journal; the first stanza stands alone, and the next following
date is *Sunday 14th* (OYB 5b). The remaining three stanzas follow in OYB 8a; the
bracketing dates are *Wednesday evening July 24th*, and *August 9th* (OYB 7b,8a).

Katharine 'tidied up' the piece— thereby sadly losing the old form *chesnut*, and the
poem's spontaneity— and gave it the title *Bitter-Sweet* (T0087). This revised version
was published in THE NEW MINNESINGER, TNM 29-30; sa *Rue and roses* (T0377).

You are five years old my Amy,
   Five years, yet a baby still,
A cradled babe, or a crownèd queen
   At the touch of yr. changeful will.

Yet in all yr. moods & yr. fancies,
   You cling, oh my Darling, to me
You are sent like some sweet little god-child
   My own little maiden to be.
I must sing you a song, my minstrel
   A song for yr. own sweet sake;
If my lips cd. but strike my heart-strings
   What melody they wd. make.
It is in my heart's love, my Amy,
   That I lay in yr. hands to-day
A book, that, tho' full of stories,
   Is not quite a book of play.
It is not "for old", my dearie,
   'Tis a book for best indeed,
To be dress'd in paper cover,
   & with washen hands to read.
You will never outgrow it, my Amy,
   Should you grow very gray & old:
You will find in the stories a beauty,
   And a truth that is not told.
Yr. own little children will love them,
   Just as you used to do,
At first they will plead for the picture
   And then for the story too.
And should my own little Amy
   All true to her plighted word,
In her woodland home, aye tarry,
   The one little nestling bird,
She will love on the book to ponder
   In the quiet evening glow;
My child, there are joys to the maiden,
   That the wife may never know.
And afar in the golden city
   At least so it seems to me,

The angels will have us remember
   What we learn'd at our mother's knee

But whether with crowd, or in desert,
   My little one's feet may stray,
This book will last till the day break,
   And shadows shall flee away.
Grow up with the Dane, my Darling,
   To your Saxon blood be true
If the North are warrior-fashion'd
   They are heavenly dreamers too
Oh browse on their beauteous legends,
   Drink deep of their dear delights;
Far away from the baneful glitter
   Of the one & thousand nights.
And a day will come when those half-closed lips
   That babble in rhyming play
Will ope to the touch of a Mighty hand,
   And a pow'r they must obey.
A day when the scatter'd tricklets
   Of music that come & go,
With a full & even current,
   In river of thought shall flow.

And far on in the golden sunset
   If I stay till the eventide,
I may die in the joy of music
   With my minstrel at my side.

T0046   This poem draft occurs in the fragmentary diary in which Katharine
            kept a record of the last days of her mother. It is of particular interest
            in providing evidence that Katharine did not write solely for Edith.
Amy was born 05 March 1863, but the context entries independently establish the
composition year to be 1868. The first section of the poem, to v40, follows an entry
Thursday March 5th Amy's Birthday (OYB 55-6a); other diary entries intervene
before the second section. This is headed *Amy's birthday (continued)*, the final
v41-64 closing with the date *Thursday March 26th* (OYB 62ab). One assumes that
Amy never saw the draft— or at least, not in time for her birthday. The poem
reduces to 16 quatrains, but the curious layout of the draft has been preserved. A
minor puzzle is— what *was* the birthday book? Thankfully not Middle Eastern Myths.

my minstrel: Amy's musical talents seem to have been early manifest (sa T1290).
aye tarry: If Amy indeed at this tender age expressed an aversion to marriage
                 (or at any rate, a wish to stay always at home), it becomes easier to
                 interpret Edith's later poem *So jealous of your beauty* (T0407),
                 written when Amy was 26.

Katharine Bradley
(Michael Field)
Rob.t Cav. 1885. 37 White Ladies Road, Clifton.

A Harris Bradley   This portrait purports to be a likeness of Katharine Harris Bradley, yet even Carta Sturge, who knew Katharine personally, has said "The engraved portrait I can scarcely recognise. It has not her characteristic expression or appearance at all" (portrait and text attached inside the front cover of a copy of Mary Sturgeon's <u>Michael Field</u>). The inscription *Katharine Bradley (Michael Field) about 1885* is in handwriting identical with that of Carta's text. In 'about 1885' Katharine would have been 39. It is hard to reconcile this stressed, middle-aged 'likeness' with the youthful portrait dated *1889* (front cover MAS). There is an admitted family likeness, but there were two other Harris Bradleys. One would prefer to think that this is a picture of Katharine's mother, 'severe as a gray summer evening' (H ZJP 72b) but the date at least, if reliable, precludes this. The second possibility would be Katharine's sister 'Lis': in 1885 she was 50, with only four years to live. The resemblance to her known portrait (MFC 26) is at least as strong as the resemblance to Katharine herself. If the portrait was bequeathed *unannotated* to Carta Sturge, such an attribution is a very real alternative.   (YCA 5: Bristol University Library Hlc).

42

On other earth to thee I kneel,
Earth that hath made no sod
For my Beloved, yet I feel
      As close to thee, my God
The sounds that fill this foreign air,
    Are new & strange to me
My comfort, that my English prayer,
    Will find its way to thee.
In a great city, far apart
    From home & household cheer
And that great desert in my heart
      That widens year by year
Oh yet I trust that inner call
That stirring at my heart;
That bade me from my home & all
      My kindred to depart.

T0055   Emma Bradley died on 30 May 1868, and by October Katharine was no longer in England: 'Paris Quai Voltaire 21. Oct 16th Today, my first Sunday in France' (ZJA 4b). She had arrived to meet a possible, but most unlikely, husband (see T0058). 'The one brother passionately devoted to a deaf & dumb wife, & renouncing all society for her sake, the other (*ICT: her prospective swain*) as passionately devoted to the memory of a dead wife. I see if I stay here I must endure hardness. Sometimes I think I must go home: but if health is given me perhaps it would be better to stay here. Oh my all precious mother, can you look down on yr. child now' (ZJA 5ab). It is at this point that the draft poem appears in her Paris Journal; the curious lineation of the original has been preserved, but an initiating double quotation mark omitted. Though the poem itself is undated, the next entries are for Monday, Tuesday 19th (*ICT: 20th*). Within a page Katharine is standing 'in the formidable French presence of M. Gérente. I shall never forget the mingled feelings with which I entered the home of the hermit artist.. ..He is a workman all through, not a touch of the amateur, of the contemplative about him: ..The way in which he spoke of the ..painful labour necessary to produce real works of art, almost saddened me' (ZJA 6ab). The Journal records her continuing doubts. 'Miss Gérente is very good to me; but there is a quiet firmness about her that I had not expected.. ..In all the Gérentes there is a touch of sternness, an absence of tenderness that brings strange shiverings about my heart. On Saturday night the long gathering storm burst & I had a good cry that softened Miss Gérente to me..' (ZJA 7-8). The following 'Tuesday morning (*ICT: 27th*) was my 22nd. birthday' and that day fortnight she was invited to dine with the artist. 'I sat on Alfred's right hand.' (one way of keeping control of the situation) 'I told him how much kinder his brother had been to me than he had, commencing at once to speak English to me: but with his sweet amused smile he assured me, it was a virtue on his part to speak French' (ZJA 21b). Virtue or not, a massive stroke (apparently) carried him off on the morrow.

A little flowret has come to me
That has grown neath English skies
And oh it is dear as the prison flower
To the captive's prison'd eyes

Ah why did he guard it that lovely stem
Shooting up thro' the prison floor
It told him tales of the outer world
And the sun that he saw no more

And the snowdrop tells me of one I love
Of one that I may not see
And oh it has brighten'd blue eyes whose light
Is more than the sun to me.

I love to think of the quiet spot
Where that flow'r of promise grew
All folded round by the fallen leaves
Of the long lime avenue.

I love to think of the pattering feet
That ruffled its autumn bed
And danced with joy when two parting leaves
Uncover'd its cowering head

And oh when I think of the merry eye
Bright lit with a sudden glee
At the thought that that ﺏﻮﺑ flower
Might travel across the sea

T0062   This poem draft persists in faded pencil sketches in the Paris journal.
           The source, and the internal evidence, make a composition date in
           the early spring of 1869 a virtual certainty. The text given here
appears to end on a pause, but it is the most complete that has survived (ZJA 55).
Of the two more important of the remaining three, one is on the front inner cover
(ZJA 1), the other on the facing page (ZJA 2). This latter has recognisable drafts for
stanzas 1 and 4 before the palimpsest-like superscription of a letter written in French.
Through this it is just possible to identify drafts for stanzas 2 and 3. But even in
fragmentary state the poem presents an unmissable picture, vivid and arresting, of
the circumstances that appear to have prompted its writing.

little flowret: The first sketches begin *A little snowdrop is come to me* (ZJA 1), and *A little snowdrop has come to me* (ZJA 2).

little: The adjective itself is legibly ambiguous; it could equally (one would almost say, more easily) be read as *white*. It does seem unlikely that the draft 'snowdrop' should be described as 'white' (what other colour is possible?), though of course this argument would not apply in the final form. However *both* words occur in the alternative stanza 5 (see below). Apart from the scansion problem, it seems even more unlikely that the child should be commemorated with *white* feet, whilst the word 'white', in the *white head* of the emerging bloom is both obviously different, and very clear. This seems to clinch the argument in favour of 'little' in stanza 1.

one I love: Stanza 5 makes it fairly clear that this is a child; at this point Edith would probably be 7, Amy possibly still 5. However the Paris journal contains a further scrap, even more fragmentary, of what is surely a related poem (ZJA 94b); and this seems to settle the matter in accordance with one's expectations:

> And thou knowest thou not all the longing
> That the flower awoke in me
>
> In the shady walk one morning
> Very early in the Spring
> Little Edith found a snowdrop   T0063, f2-3

Another fragment, T0064 (which in itself may be related to a different poem draft T0061), offers tantalising, idyllic glimpses of Katharine's little niece, and of Newton Leys:

> And you climb for the pendant catkins
> As I might for the clustring May
>
> All merrily every morn
> A scarlet haw, or a hedgrow spray
> Or a branch of the budding thorn
>
> I know a little maiden
> Who will start betimes today
>   ⸎⸎⸎   village schoolhouse
>   ⸎⸎⸎   half a mile away   T0064

The special interest of this fragment is that it is immediately followed by early sketches for stanzas 1 and 2 of T0062; this is the fourth known draft (ZJA 94a).

lime avenue: At Newton Leys (see T0156). In 1905 on the return visit, Edith wrote 'The landmarks are much disturbed between Alsop & New Leys— .. There is a labourer's cottage where there was only a Barn on the Little Winnets. No Horse-trough--- & as we approach no noble shady walk— the great drive, the home of the snowdrops & wood-forget menots gone; meagre trees left: the great hay-rick hidden from the road ..the large gray enclosure cleansed of the central manure-heap, & looking clean & decayed at once as a skull' (ZJT 89-90).

feet: The Journal inner cover has also a delightful preliminary version:

> I love to the (sic) *think of the little feet*
> *Pattering down that garden way*
> *Of the pause: of the search, of the sudden spring*
> *When that first white head was seen*

⸎⸎:   These words are illegible.

45

Written during the Communist revolt of 1871 when Notre Dame was momentarily threaten'd with destruction

Thy own fair city holds thy fairest thought,
Thy noblest offering! Notre Dame still glows
Gemm'd with thy grisailles,— blue so subtly wrought
'Tis garnish'd forth with emeralds, purpling rose
And scarlet from the daybreak,— Yet even those
Grand molten harmonies I smile to see
Let round with sweet memorial sanctities,
Dyed for immortal blooming, may not be
Kiss'd by to-morrow's sunlight. Love thou must
Find thee a surer monument, I swear
That yon firm towers should fall a crumbling dust,
There is a <u>time-proof</u> tenement will bear
Eternal witness to thee: only trust
Thy mem'ry's keeping to a spirit's care.

T0077   In June 1871, events in Paris turned Katharine's thoughts once more to
             Gérente; this poem, in its single autograph, survives only in the Oxford
             manuscript, OVB 2b. Modern enquirers into the early days of Michael
Field are heavily indebted to Ursula Bridge, who first uncovered the essential
biographical data on Gérente. Alfred's mother was English, a Miss Salt from
Birmingham, and Alfred had certainly visited Katharine's home-town— as well as
other parts of England (OZQ 124). He submitted work to the 1851 Exhibition, in the
category of ecclesiastical painted glass; and indeed won the Prize Medal for "A
window in the style of the twelfth century. In the figures, which represent the history
of Samson, and particularly in the ornaments, the style of the period is rendered with
extraordinary mastery and truth" (Reports by Juries, Volume IV OZQ 130). Apart from
his work in Notre-Dame, and other French churches, in 1854 he made "pour la
cathedrale d'Amiens la grande et belle fenêtre de la chapelle de Sainte-Theudosie."
In his last years he was apparently at work on five windows for Lausanne cathedral.
At his death in 1868 a French obituary charmingly records "La mort a été pour lui
plus clemente que la vie; elle l'a frappé à l'improviste et il n'a souffert qu'un instant"
(JFC 47, OZQ 147). An English obituary mentioned work "in various parts of
England, for example... S. Mary, Stafford" (JTE V 29, OZQ 128).

Edith would eventually find Notre-Dame (and the *grisailles*) wanting. In June 1892
she was in Paris with her aunt, and, after the obligatory visit to "the Morgue" (where
they saw corpses of three men), 'We go into Nôtre Dame— it is intolerable to be
there— It is a grand Dead House with infinitely less to teach us than the mean one
behind it. The cold ceremonies go on under the pillars & arches— Alfred Gèrente's
windows look crude— I feel I can never admire them again— that homage is as
dead, with its past on it, as those poor fellows by the Seine' (H ZJE 123-4). As for

The Crescent Moon

How faint a glow the early moon
    Gives to the evening skies!
O love, 'tis like the crescent light
    I saw within thine eyes,

When first I looked into their depths,
    With troubled heart, to know
If from so slight a promise e'er
    Love's golden prime could grow.

But e'en that faintly-gleaming moon,
    Across the blue, behold!
Her fair completion unfulfilled
    Hath limned in tenderest gold.

And with that little golden ring
    A sudden hope doth rise;
I look beyond the crescent light
    Of those soft-shining eyes,

And now that I may nearer gaze,
    Across their blue I see,
All limned in tenderest lines of love,
    My perfect bliss to be.

Katharine, when November 11th came round again that year, her only remark was peripheral. 'It is... 24 years since Alfred Gérente died. And I write to his little old maid sister to whom the beaks of her canaries twitter enough of life' (ZJE 144b).

grisailles: A technique developed in the 13th century for decorating clear glass with monochrome paintings, using a paste of ground glass admixed with iron or copper filings. On firing, the brown or black tones faded to shades of gray, as is implied in the name.

towers: The subjunctive is out of place; the sense is '*should* yon firm towers fall.'

T0094   Known only from its inclusion in THE NEW MINNESINGER, TNM 40-1; as with the majority of these poems it is impossible to date. It appears unlikely that it is Gérente who is still centre stage, since all the other such published pieces are gathered in the *Youth Time Songs* section of the book. If we discount persons unknown, it does seem that a case might be made for the 'blue' eyes of Edith. If this bold guess is correct, this may be the earliest discovered such poem (with the possible exception of T0062). Edith at most would be 13 at this time.

Midnight Thoughts of Morning

When I wake not to moon or stars,
　Or soft-cheek'd pallor of night;
When my weary and baffled eyes
　Feel after the restful light

And can find no relic of day,
　No promise of morning beam;
When the raven robe of the night
　Is woven without a seam,

Then I close up my dark-fill'd eyes
　In their dark, and tears, and tire,
And paint them, on spirit skies,
　The dawning of their desire.

Though the light of the eyes be gone,
　The heart in the East may be;
For faith looketh further on
　Into immortality.

T0104　　　Known only from its inclusion in THE NEW MINNESINGER, TNM 68-9.

The early years of Michael Field are but fragmentarily documented. We have it on Edith's testimony that she 'began to write' in 1872 (ZJY 40a). The family moved once again, probably in early 1873, to Park House in Solihull (see T0156, MAS). In 1874 the 12 years old Edith completed her first drama *THE IWL-DÛ* (OPJ 24b), and was at work on the equally outré *ATYS AND ADRASTOS*. 1875 was most important as the year in which Longmans & Green published Katharine's first book THE NEW MINNESINGER (subtitled POEMS OF ARRAN LEIGH). Though she was later to disown it, it contains little unworthy of her; her lyrics already show that sure grasp of prosody that would never desert her (for 'Arran Leigh' see footnote to T0153, MAS).

T0147　　　What might be a meditation on Luke XII 27-8, this is one of the final
　　　　　　　Devotional Poems of THE NEW MINNESINGER, TNM 161-2. Katharine
　　　　　　　chooses three 'lilies of the field' to sing 'in verse'. Basil Thyme, *Acinos arvensis* (also known as Basil Calamint), is a Labiate of calcareous soil similar to the dead-nettle, but with a blue-violet flower which is white at the lip. Shepherd's Purse, *Capsella bursa-pastoris*, a widespread member of the Cruciferae, is named for its flattened triangular fruits (siliculae). Poor Man's Weatherglass is another name for the Scarlet Pimpernel, *Anagallis arvensis*; a member of the Primulaceae, its flowers

The Least in the Kingdom of Heaven

The lily who can choose but greet?
The cowslip-scent is ever sweet,
   But dearer joy to me
It is in their old haunts to find
Those wayside flowers of humbler kind
   That few would care to see.

'Tis hard to sing of them in verse,
The Basil Thyme, the Shepherd's Purse,
   The Poor Man's Weatherglass;
Yet the rough-christen'd names they bear
(Untutor'd fancy's rude compare)
   Give pleasure as I pass.

And oh, meseemeth every year
More marvellous it doth appear
   How they their place maintain.
They break not into gloried hues,
When the soft heaven beseeching woos;
   They chalice not the rain;

They have scant beauty to desire,
Yet the great God doth never tire
   Of these poor wayside weeds.
A little waft of homely scent,
Breathing to Him their deep content,
   Is all the praise He needs.

And if He wearieth not of these,
If such dim-flowering things can please,
   The hope our spirit cheers
That our poor lives, obscure and dim,
May quietly bloom on to Him
   Through the eternal years.

close on the approach of bad weather. (A common brown seaweed, also known as
the sugar kelp or sea-belt *Laminaria saccharina*, is also sometimes given this name
since its fronds, limp under humid conditions, become dry and brittle in finer
weather. Not however, one imagines, what Katharine had in mind...).

The New Minnesinger

('Think of womanhood; and thou to be a woman.')

O Woman, all too long by thee
   Love's praises have been heard;
But thou to swell the minstrelsy
   Hast brought no wealth'ning word.
Thou who its sweetest sweet canst tell
   Heart-trainèd to the tongue,
Hast listen'd to its music well
   But never led the song!
The world, through countless ages roll'd,
   Hath given us but in part,
But in tradition faintly told
   The love-lore of thine heart.
Long hath the study been pursued,
   Nay, ere his brain began
Its toil and tent solicitude,
   It was essayed of man.
And all of it that he can con,
   With toil and study true,
He hath deep-mus'd and thought upon,
   Mislearnt, and learnt anew;
Till losing through confusèd will
   The grace, the touch divine,
His own too worldly-busy skill
   Hath wrought his art's decline.
Dear, Eden-dated, heavenly art,
   Ne'er doom'd of God to fall,
These woman-lips, so slow to part,
   Thy glory shall recall!

Yes, Woman, she whose life doth lie
In virgin haunts of poesie,—
How have men woven into creeds
The unrecorded life she leads!
What she hath been to them, oh, well
The whole sweet legend they can tell;
But what she to herself may be
They see not, or but dream they see.

50

Content with what they touch and feel,
As from a violet we steal
Its sweet heart-odour; thinking so
That we its inmost being know;
And never learn what to the flower
Hath been the springtide's op'ning hour;
What winds have whisper'd, what the dew
Hath spoken, how the heaven's blue
Smil'd promise, when the timid thing,
Leaf-folded, dream'd of blossoming.

Yet it were worth our while to know
How fare the flowers before they blow;
To learn the low-breath'd life that's past
In snowy may-blooms, shut so fast.
Mid soothings of soft shaded light,
Warm creeping through the curtain'd white,
What deep security! what calm!
What fragrance of close-petall'd balm!
But slowly do the leaves unfold,
And chang'd the flower when we behold;
As chang'd as maiden in her prime
From that dim, early-growing time
When, happy with herself at play,
Amid warm nestling hopes she lay—
Such blameless hopes! they did not shoot
Like older hopes from sorrow's root;
No sharpen'd blast of outer breath
Brought to their promise blight or death;
But op'ning in the very air
That wooed their buds, they blossom'd fair.
Ah, would she but to us rehearse
Her first girl-life in April verse—
A fairer spring-tide would be ours
Than e'er across the woodland flowers.

And those first dreams of dawning told,
While yet the sky is paly gold,
And she half-slumb'ring— will she then
Tell of that spirit-wakening, when
O'er her soft opal heaven is shed
Love's first faint flush of morning red?
Yes, will she to the world disclose,

Not the fair seeming and the shows,
The pretty masks that still she wears,
The wiles, the Eve-descended airs;
But will she ever give us part
Of the deep workings of her heart,
When suddenly she finds before
Its all unheeded, open door
A stranger, clad in pilgrim weeds,
Whose homeless state and simple needs
Ask courtesy and kindly care,
Which he wins of her unaware,
Meek suppliant! and then reveals
The lofty rank her roof conceals,
And urges secrecy, and lays
Constraint on all her guileless ways?
Her free, frank life she puts aside,
Careful her kingly charge to hide,
And guessing dimly thro' her fear
How the new durance groweth dear;
Tho' angry thoughts hot protest make,
Sore questioning why she should take
In her unquiet heart to rest
This captive, regnant, royal guest,
Who must be homaged, must be hid,
Till, conscience-goaded, conscience-chid,
Almost she wishes him away,
Almost she could her trust betray,
Then closer shuts the house, lest e'en
A peep of treasonous thought be seen.

And may we learn the bliss, the pride,
When she's no longer forc'd to hide
Her secret sovereign, but when he
May in full daylight thronèd be;
When with a very little thing—
The mother's kiss, the troth plight ring—
Her guilty wonderment, her dread
Of secret chamber'd thoughts, is fled.
No longer of her love afraid,
Her narrow prison-cell new made
To sainted chapel, now she ne'er
Need cease from service and from prayer;
Sweet worship there she offers:— praise,

Full pomp of rite on holy days,
And quietly, when none are by,
Pours out her heart's idolatry;
And feeds the lamp, and tends the flower,
Meek vigil keeps at midnight hour,
And joins with matin chimes the throng
She worships openly among.

And, when soul-summon'd, at the last
She bids farewell to all her past,
Oh, may we stand to see her start
On those strange travels of the heart,
When, growing restless, ill at ease,
In homely Ur of the Chaldees,
She turns, most Abraham-like, to go
To a far country he will show
Who is her Promise, Covenant, Call;
For whom she leaves her girlhood, all
The happy plains and pastures sweet
Fleck'd with the track of childhood's feet,
Fragrant with all the bliss that she
Hath known from earliest infancy;
Her goal, where he directs alone;
She leaves the lov'd, familiar, known,
For rose-lit rims of hills that gleam
On far horizons half in dream.

She goes, and God her path doth bless,
Her faith is counted righteousness.
She goes to pilgrim's fare and pain,
To woe and loss, and endless gain,
To doubt, misgiving, gladsome cheer,
High hope, and sudden blight of fear:
She goes, oh, not to heavenly peace,
Calm settlement, and toil's surcease,
But fierce, strange peoples to withstand
Even within the Promised Land:
She goes a worship high to hold
'Mong brazen bulls and calves of gold,
To break down many an idol show,
To suffer much, and much forego,
Nor haply, e'er her sun decline,
To sit beneath the promised vine.

Yet not for years in sorrow spent
Will she a moment's span repent
That Faith's fair prowess made her dare
Claim that untravers'd country, where
(As she sweet Canaan's conqueror knows)
Alone life's milk and honey flows.

Lone songs of girlhood, loftier lays,
Rich-noted, fuller-toned, to praise
The life new-margin'd, flowing wide
With a fresh water's mingling tide,
We ask of her; and then we call
For a new song most sweet of all—
A Song of Songs! but can it be,
O Earth, long list'ning Earth, that she
Hath hushed thy children's cries so long,
Nor given the world one cradle song!
Yea, even thus. All mothers know
Those brooding notes, those wailings low
That our new wearied mother Eve,
Her nursing daughterhood did leave—
Half sighs, and half caresses! still
Their faint, sad music seems to fill
Our childhood's air, as woodland breeze
Melodious with the minstrel trees;
But still poor broken lays, that bring
Scant glory to the love they sing.
That tell how woman's love doth make
Herself a child for children's sake:
Full of vain babblings, murmurings vain,
And snatches of too fond refrain;
But of that vaster love and deep
That lies about a baby's sleep,
That gives the heart prophetic fire,
Deep-passion'd prayers, and high desire—
Of these soul-reachings in no wise
We learn through earth's old lullabies.

O Woman, can she e'er complain
Of straiten'd lot in song's domain,
Having as dower of highest good
The whole wide realm of motherhood?
Having on human souls a claim

54

That through all ages is the same:
No newer love can thrust aside,
No sad soul-wand'ring e'er divide.
From the first promise and the pain
Her children ever hers remain;
Most hers, when children's children show
How far the sacred fire can glow,
And lips, new-bath'd in mother's bliss,
Return the primal mother's kiss.

Fain would we listen to her song,
Her tender nursling flowers among:
Voice of the turtle would we hear
The fragrant lily-fields anear.
Fresh from the wild woods, with the scent
Of purest life her being's blent;
And yet with all that nature sweet
Blooming, rich scatter'd, at her feet,
Scarcely one flower-bud will she sing
Of all its countless blossoming.
Unchronicled her native bliss,
All spoil of travel she must miss.
The poet learns at home his art,
Woos it and weds, and if he part,
'Tis but, as traveller's wont, to yearn
O'er the lost pleasures and return;
But she, heart-errant, doth not prize
The fair realms where her queendom lies;
Courts empery in higher place,
Asks broader paths, and ampler space;
And seeks among life's busy throng
A swifter cadence to her song
Than e'er can tune itself to lays
Sung by life's bracken-hinder'd ways.

And if, we ask it with a sigh,
The time, the happy time's gone by
When she, home-homag'd, must be known
By household gift and grace alone;
If she must sing of other theme
Than Love, or waking or in dream,
Yet must she harbour none the less
Care of her ancient blessedness.

Sage-sued, world-beckon'd, she must be
Full woman: lifted to a free
And fellow-life with man. No more
Must she creep dumbly as of yore
Adown the ages; but her word
Must, as man's echo, ne'er be heard.
How high soe'er her thought may reach
Still it must flow through woman's speech
In woman's fashion; only so
Can the twinn'd lives unhind'ring grow.
The woman's way— we count her blame—
Must be her glory-crown, her fame:
And far in after ages, when
She shares life's loftier toil with men,
Oh, never must she cast aside
Her early grace through growing pride,
Nor, foreign-cultur'd, leave behind
The native instincts of her kind!
Chosen by Nature's self to be
A consecrated ministry,
All needful knowledge to impart
In the fair scriptures of the heart,
Aye must she count her priestly name
Outhonours every earthly fame;
And whatsoe'er new gain she reap,
What realm encloseth, ever keep
All things subservient to the good
Of pure, free-growing womanhood.

T0150   If one excepts two of the mind-numbing BELLEROPHÔN pieces of
              problematical authorship, T0183 and T0184, this is probably (at
              270v) the longest poem ever written by Katharine. Even
Trompetenruf (at 200v) can only make second place. *The New Minnesinger* must,
then, be considered seriously. Angela Leighton, quoting the first eight verses of
stanza 2, describes it merely as a poem in which Katharine "declares her imaginative
allegiance to her own sex" (FAL 206), and it is true that 'modern-women of the
shirt-fronty kind' (M OCX 5o) will be disappointed of polemics and trenchancy. But
there is more to the poem than this. The old German poetical *Minne* translates as
love. This, as throughout her entire life, is Katharine's central theme: the great 'Lord
Love', the Stranger to whom she was ever in leash. Her complaint primarily is that
woman has not been treated seriously as capable of active love *in her own right* (in
this context see the slight T0553, but especially T0564). Her secondary theme is that
woman, as equal but different, *should not have to relinquish her essential femininity*
in order that her voice be treated with respect in a male-dominated society. The

second point she makes crystal-clear in the peroration:

> All things subservient to the good
> Of pure, free-growing womanhood.

Katharine knew that the struggle to lead a full life outside (and especially within) the woman's world of *kirche, küche, kinder* was to be one without forseeable conclusion. Much later she was to write to Isabelle Wedmore 'We women must all fight against having our lives frittered away' (OCY 125r). In the event, as with the parallel and later cause of gay rights, the first stirrings of recognisable rebellion (a woman's rights convention organised in New York in July 1848 by Elizabeth Cady Stanton and Lucretia Mott) were in America. Meanwhile, as Katharine would soon realise, a male *alias* could win a preliminary toe-hold. If as yet you can't beat 'em.

The poem is given pride of place as the opening piece in THE NEW MINNESINGER, TNM 1-13. No autograph is known, nor are there any surviving clues to the date or circumstance of its composition, but it is unlikely to have been written earlier than 1868 (stanzas 6-7 could be read in terms of the Gérente episode). The first stanza is set in linked quatrains, but the remainder continue to the end in the freer form of rhymed couplets.

Minnesinger:	'Love singer'— a German lyrical poet-musician (12th-14th centuries) akin to the troubadour and some minstrel-jongleurs, whose principal theme was the lovesong.
tent:	Probably aphetic for *intent*.
virgin haunts:	Christine White wilfully subverts the poem to her own version of a femininity that "concedes the reality of an attraction to men, *destructive as that is*" (italics ICT). "The virgin woman poet", she writes, "by virtue of her freedom from men, possesses the potentiality to be 'lifted to a free / And fellow-life with man'" (JTX 200). But this is not at all the *sequitur* intended by Katharine. The lines quoted come almost at the end of the poem (s11,v10-1), by which time the protagonist's virginity is but a memory, *Having as dower of highest good / The whole wide realm of motherhood* (s9,v3-4). By then— *children's children show / How far the sacred fire can glow*— she is in fact a grandmother! (s9,v11-2). Virginity, or rather, "freedom from men", had never been postulated as a prerequisite for equality; on the contrary, Katharine's thesis results in *twinn'd lives* (s11,v18).
A stranger:	Here the 'Lord Love' makes his first memorable appearance (sa T1155, and OCA 122r).
soul-summon'd:	Compare with *A.G.* (T0058).
Abraham:	Abram (an ancient Hebrew crumbly, by tradition early 2nd millenium BC) left Ur in Mesopotamia because "God" (allegedly) "called" him to found a new nation in a "promised land" (Genesis XII 1-2). This God later renamed him *Abraham* "father of many" with the covenant that his "seed"— he was now 100 years old— would inherit this land (of Canaan, between Egypt and Syria); apparently regardless of the irrefutably legitimate claims of the people already living there (Genesis XVII 1-8, XV 18).
brazen bulls:	Probably a reference to Jeremiah LII 20; sa Exodus XXXII 2-4.
promised vine:	But they shall sit every man under his vine (Micah IV 4).
milk and honey:	Fancied attributes of the "promised land" (Exodus III 8).
turtle:	Turtle dove (Song of Solomon II 12).

To Apollo— the Conqueror

Thy priestess, with the fillet round my tresses
That consecrates my lips to echo thine,
Claiming my temple brow & breast's wide shrine,
I watch thy sculptured form, while my heart guesses
The awful beauty of thine aureate life
Above thy foe dying in knotted strife;
The crimson in that frozen wave of scorn
That crests thy god-curved lips; the shadeless light
Of the clear brow, fronting the great slain night;
The locks, gold-dark as sheaves of dusky corn,
    Softening thy manhood's might.

Dower me with thine own lips! — Am I not bidden
The language from thy fair Greek mouth to take
To wing thy conquering arrows, till they wake
The heavy world & in its heart are hidden?
Thy hands, no more destroying, I have seen
With thrilling touch, like lute-strings sweet & keen,
Laid on my brow to dedicate & bless;
Coronis-like I dare not leave thee now;
No shade shall pass across thy sun-ripe brow
No white wing darken with my faithlessness,
    My God to thee I vow!

I feel within a joyful, onward-leaping
Like to a horse turned homeward, like the sea
That springs on to the far rocks joyfully.
The wind of inspiration downward sweeping
Lawlessly scatters all earth's thoughts aside.
In golden death, like dead leaves scattered wide.
— He stays with me.— Birth from his presence springs,
I am a mother to all beauteous things.
The moon, night's flower, the dark-leaved darkness breaks!
I am alone, but conquered, wedded, made
One with a vast divinity, arrayed
With what he gives & joyed with what he takes:-
    He called me. . I obeyed.

T0161   This extraordinary piece, written by Edith, shows a further broadening
of the young poet's horizons. The autograph in her hand survives
(just) as another isolated sheet in the same exercise book which
preserved *To A. Leigh*; it is in poor condition, with some gaps where the paper has
been lost. As in the earlier poem, it is dedicated to her aunt; undated, she signs it
Edith Cooper. For her who twined the "bay-wreath" for his priestess. The A.W.F.*
(OPJ 99o,100o).   *(*ICT: All-Wise Fowl, see T0153,MAS.)*

Luckily, a second copy of the autograph exists. Katharine made a fair copy in
another exercise book, turning it upside down and writing from the back; this time
the dedication includes a date, 1878, which would make Edith at most 16 at the time
of composition (OYJ 57a,56a). Katharine may have intended to copy several of
Edith's poems, for there is an overall title *The Poems of Isla for the joy of Arran Leigh*
(OYJ 57b). In this connection, there is a reference to the poem in a letter Katharine
wrote some years later '..I came across many of my P's dear early poems. Once
more I read the invocation "Dower me with thine own lips" .. after the mighty cares &
interests of the drama to go back to those early lyrics is like a gt. statesman's return
to his native village. He sees the village girl who first caught his fancy— & walks by
the quiet streams that made his musings musical;— he recognises the ineffable
charm of those fresh meditative days, but from the perplexities of home-politics, &
absorbing interests of foreign affairs can only give to early associations the tribute of
a kindly sigh' (OCA 174or). If such other 'dear early poems' did exist, they have
either not been correctly identified, or else apparently lost.

fillet:	Probably the said "bay-wreath"; see also the final note to T0763.
aureate:	Golden.
thy foe:	Since it is described as 'dying in knotted strife', this is probably the enormous serpent Python, parthenogenetic child of Gaea, which guarded the original oracle at Delphi. Apollo killed it for his mother Leto, or to found his own oracle there (sa *Tempe vale*, T0752).
Dower me:	The first two verses of this stanza seem to relate directly and unmistakably to Katharine's attempts to encourage her niece to learn Greek. In the event, Edith was to remain attached to her first love, Latin: Greek appears to have been one dead language too far (sa the final two stanzas of *An Invitation*, T0489).
Coronis-like:	Coronis ("crow") was another title for Athene, but this Coronis is undoubtedly the daughter of Phlegyas, King of the Lapiths (and hence a sister of Ixion). She caught Apollo's eye, as one does, and in the ensuing excitement became a mother. Her son Asclepius, famous as the founder of medicine, learned the arts of healing from both his father Apollo and the centaur Cheiron.
white wing:	In another version of the myth Apollo left a white crow to guard Coronis while he was away in Delphi, but apparently a mere god was not sufficient for the mother-to-be, and she took the opportunity to warm her bed with Ischys, son of Elatus. Apollo, enraged, cursed the crow (which has been black ever since): and Artemis, in sisterly outrage, shot Coronis full of arrows. In this version of the legend, Hermes cut Asclepius from his mother's body as she lay on the lit funeral pyre. Never a dull moment in ancient Greece (sa Edith's later retake of the story *One Sin*, T1010).
I feel within:	Edith's sensual imagery in the final stanza conjures up a picture which is not so much inspiration as impregnation. She would display a similar erotic extravagance of language in poems to all her future gods (see especially T0415, T0678, T1669).

Sleep & Waking

Why did'st Thou say she was asleep,
Lord, whom Thou knowest dead?
Was it not hardly said?
  Death is not like a sleep;
Sleep answers when one knocketh,
But at Love's need Death mocketh;
  Death is not like a sleep;
When for our sleeping ones we yearn,
Thou know'st a touch brings their return;—
  Our dead we overweep
Beseeching greatly to be fed
With crumbs, who might claim children's bread;
But the stern faces, once so fond to cherish,
Look as they would not care though we shd. perish.

Yet, Lord, Death is most like a sleep,
It is most like, to Thee,
Who can'st rouse quietly
  The rest that seems so deep.
Death answers when God speaketh,
Death yieldeth, when God seeketh,
  Death is most like a sleep,—
A sleep Thy lightest word can break.
Deaf to the "much ado" we make
  The dead we over-weep
Have heard Thy quick'ning Voice & live.
This is the comfort Thou would'st give,—
Let Death, Thy Voice can stir, as deep befall us,
That we from Death may trust Thy Voice to call us.

T0164 Known only from a single undated autograph (OVD 51-2), Katharine's
poem is directly based on a meditation on the tale of Jairus's daughter
in one of her exercise books labelled *Prayers* (OYE 43-4). This source is
compatible with a date around 1877-8. She quotes the text *Mark v. 25-43*, and
writes 'It seems to us so unlike sleep— so cruelly unlike... our dead do not seem to
hear us, do not awake to comfort us. It seems as if we might perish & they would not
care. Teach us, Almighty that when Thy dear Son spoke of Death as a sleep, He did
it to bring no false comfort, for that He never gave, but to bring the true comfort by
telling us the truth about death— that it was a sleep from which <u>God awakened</u>. ...
They are all awake & alive to Him.. .'

"As perfect music unto noble words"

Harmonia my sweetest Art or Aspirate in one,
The only air that suits my voice, let there be unison
Of noble music to the words I offer you to set,
And in your "linkéd sweetness", my dearest, don't forget
That you, my lady Dominant, at your sweet will may lead,
To any chord, to any key, may take at any speed.
I long to be <u>inverted</u>, <u>transposed</u>, <u>bound</u>, <u>figured</u>, <u>scored</u>;
"<u>The Mass in E</u>"; "<u>a service</u>" received of my adored.
And truly by the tremor I have seen in lip & eye,
The turns, the shakes, crescendos, in your voice, when I am nigh.
I dare to hope this Funeral March, my life, may change its style
To Wedding-March— March of the Priests far down the middle
    aisle
For only but the other night, when sitting by your side,
(Your open casement kept my head in handkerchief uptied
More than a week; but I forbore) what music must be read
Directing "Darling, very well", with answering smile you said,
As if responding to "Mama", but you meant <u>me</u>, I know,
<u>My heart was bound for two whole bars</u>; & then "<u>prestissimo</u>"
I thought the strings wd crack! O sweet Harmonia write <u>the rest</u>
That will restore the proper time to fitful beating breast,
You can "diminish" & "augment", can lovely grace-notes dare,
Tease with "false cadences", & dear "suspensions" sad "prepare."
But on this day St. Valentine gives you "the theme", his own,
And all its variations, dear, by you are subtly known,
Oh Love "the Theme" & yours the heart its changeful tale to tell
"Opus Magnum" the work will be that must be signed Brownell
<u>By you</u>,— the only 'signature' for every work of (He)art
That you may claim to sign.— I am the base & lower part
Henceforth of all that tunes your life, & you the High Divine
Enthralling sweet Soprano that guides & orders mine.

T0166   Unmistakably one of Katharine's 'frisks', an unrelenting succession of
         Cecilian puns addressed to a Ms. Brownell, an otherwise unknown
         musical *dominatrix* (v5,26). The single autograph (OYR 113) is undated
and impossible to assign beyond a guestimate ?1875-85; it was presumably written
one February (v23). The title alludes to Tennyson's <u>The Princess</u> (1847), which may
have inspired T0150. He affirms *For woman is not undevelop'd man, but diverse*
and hopes she may *set herself to man, Like perfect music unto noble words* (Canto
VII, 259-60;69-70). Harmonia was the daughter of Ares and Aphrodite.

The Halcyons

"And birds of calm sat brooding o'er the charmèd wave."

I

The storm-wind has heaped cruel snow on the breaker,
That sweeps in dread folds the white dead to the shore;
The hoar sea-blast no longer can wake her,
Who waited the dead she waits no more.—
A refluent wave round her bosom whitened,
A wave from the sea brought his cold corpse back;
With meeting of love bitter death-waves have brightened
                    Their wild track.

II

Dead love to love;— they may not be parted,
The chill, pressing waves have no power to part;
And even the whirlwind, careless-hearted,
Feels, as it passes, the throb of a heart.
Death with a ring of wild surf has wed them;
Dead lips to lips they have kissed in Death's sleep;
The scattered foam-flowers and the billows that shed them
                    Fade and weep.

III

The deep cold sky is rayed with the dawning;
The stars unchain their orbs from the night;
Like a dark flower fading, unloved of morning,
The darkness scatters its leaves in the light.
And white day broods on the white of ocean,
As the sea-bird broods on the ocean-breast,
And the winds lay the waves with a lulling motion
                    To their rest.

IV

Autumn stays her hands in their woodland reaving,
The cornlands stir not one brown-ripe stem;
While sleep's pale hand, still-fingered, is weaving
In the day's loose hair, night's anadem.
Her eyes take its rippling life from the river,

62

Her hand stills the plains of the heaving grass;
Through the air's deep calm the slight sunbeam-quiver
            Dare not pass.

V

Sleep lays her touch on the curling billow,
And smooths down its curves to a cradle-bed;
The love that sought love on the ocean-pillow
Can know no death, though white as the dead.
— Two fair birds rock on the waves together,
As close as the rocking blue can bring;
And the waters lift not one soft light feather
            From their wing.

VI

They sprang from their sad cold death, with the springing
Of pale sweet dawn from the chill fair foam;
And the sea round their strange new life is clinging,—
The ocean must be their new love's home.
And in winter the waves to rest are charmèd,
The halcyon's brood is their bosom's care;
While the wind and tempest by sleep are calmèd
            Everywhere.

T0181   One of the poems published in BELLEROPHÔN, BLN 141-3, and known
            only from that text; of unknown date and authorship, it is typical of the
            collection. The epigraph is a modified verse from Milton's *Hymn On the
Morning of Christ's Nativity* (s5,v8). In November 1897, following the discovery of
the body of Edith's father, Michael Field wrote *The Halcyon* T0815. Inspired by a
fragment written by the Greek lyric poet Alcman, this is a very different piece:

O love, o bitter, mortal journeying / By ways that are not told!
I would not sing, no song is sweet to me / Now thou art gone:
But would, ah would I were the halcyon, / That sea-blue bird of spring,
So should I bring / Fair sister-companies of fleetest wing / To bear thee on,
Thou being old, / With an untroubled heart to carry thee
Safe o'er the ridges of the wearying sea.   T0815

One has only to compare the simple elegance and *life* of this lyric with T0181, to
see the latter cardboard cantata for the stiff and sorry metrical exercise it is.

Halcyons: Ceyx and his wife Alcyone, daughter of Aeolus (see T1055), were
            drowned for *hubris*, and transformed to kingfishers. During 'halcyon
            days' (the week before and after the winter solstice) Aeolus provides a
            calm sea for the chicks to hatch in their nest afloat the rocking waves.
anadem: A garland or wreath for the head.

Love & Immortality

Thou lovest us to Death;
 Lord, I can vie with Thee,
I would die willingly
 For any friend.
Thou dost desire to spend,
To share with us Thine Immortality;
 It doth not weary Thee
Loving Thine own, to love them without end.
 Could I so condescend?
Lord, Thou surpassest me.

T0189 This autograph has probably only survived because the loose page was stuck (as in the case of T0164) into the back of an existing exercise book. It has the surtitle *Lord, open Thou my lips 1881*, as well as the footnote *New Year's Day. 1881* (OVD 53b). Nothing else is known.

Katharine takes a hard look at the *longueurs* and insipidity of the christian hereafter and not unsurprisingly finds the concept of a remorseless— or remorseful?— *interminable* love overpowering as well as incomprehensible. She seems to have overlooked the essential premise that the Stranger would be outside Time.

Frieda Girdlestone

F air Love that ruthlessly doth rend the heart
R efuses at all times to barb his dart
I nfixing its keen point with cruel pain
E mbittering; sometimes the boy will deign
D rop from his quiver the shaft's feather'd end,
A nd Friendship rises where those plumes descend.

T0192   Though of little intrinsic merit, this piece is interesting as the only
         known essay at an acrostic in the whole Michael Field *oeuvre*. It is
         undoubtedly by Edith, and has only survived as an enclosure in her
hand in a letter to Katharine's cousin, Frances Brooks (OCV 64o). The letter was
written by 'Katie' to 'My own dearie Coz.' on her birthday; Frances Bradley
Holinsworth was born on 06 February 1835. Someone has pencilled *Feb 1881* at
the top of the letter (OCV 63o), and if this is accurate, this also dates the poem.
Katharine says: 'I have been writing a Valentine to my temporary friend Carta* —
don't be jealous— & Persian° such a sweet bit of love-fancy to Frieda that I have
asked her to copy it for you' (OCV 63r). This Edith evidently did, and on the reverse
she adds her own message to Frances 'Warmest birthday greetings from the grey
Persian Puss. She would like to pat you with a warm paw!' (OCV 64r).
                        (*ICT: *probably Mary Charlotte Sturge, FES 165; °Edith.*)

Frances died 27 November 1898, and Frieda Girdlestone would make a sensational
entrance in the Journal some eleven months later, in connection with the mysterious
death of Edith's father in Switzerland in 1897. *La Girdlestone*, eyes down at a ouija
board, received a message from the Beyond (specifically Frances) for 'Catherine':
"you must go to North Italy at once & find George Globiatel & say to him that he
strangled darling James with a cord & drew him with a cord to the place where he
was found" (ZJN 118a). Whether sash, pyjama or plain umbilical apparently was not
specified. Edith's entry continues 'Frieda offers us the help of money & urges Ethel
Brooks* to rush over to us at once (Ethel writes she has no prompting to move in the
matter & Michael replies on a p. card "Take no notice of the Fiends. Order
suet-dumpling for dinner.")...'. Two days later 'Mary° writes. "If one cd. detach
oneself from it, the thing is full of the wildest humour. The thought of F. so stout, so
middle-agedly comfortable-looking, sitting down solemnly to wobble away at the
jerky foolish messages about Mr. George Globiatel fills me with joy unspeakable..."
(H ZJN 119b). Eventually 'On Tuesday came a card from F. saying a message
warning her her sister was ill had lied— The card was terrified & penitent' (H ZJN
120a).   (*ICT: *see T1195, fourth note; °the eldest daughter of Frances, MFC 59.*)

Alas for Frieda, but it must surely be doubtful whether Friendship ever rose quite so
enthusiastically after this crass episode. In 1999, Frances would have relayed her
"message" by Electronic Voice Phenomena.

plumes descend: See the second note to *Eros of the Summits* (T0993,SZD).

My Garden

I have a garden-ground,— oh not
To Solomon more dear
The lilied-land he called his spouse,
Than this sweet spot
   My God allows
To be my comfort here:
   A pretty plot
Of musk-mallow & sweet-briar rose;
Oh yet for all my care bestows
It will not bear the Mustard-Tree
That branches to Eternity!

"One thing this land will ever lack"
I cried in my despair;
And weeping left the wayward soil
[An exile from my fruitless toil]
Of her own self to bear:
   But, turning back
Through the dear fence to peer, I found
The Herb of Grace, while all around
Fruit-fragrance filled the air.
Now of my Garden boast I can
My Father is the Husbandman.

TO205   Apart from a fair copy in Edith's hand (OYF 65o), the other two
                  autographs are in Katharine's. One of these, enclosed in a letter, is
                  probably her first draft: it carries the footnote *Dean Prior Herrick's*
Home August. 82 (OCD 48or). In the same letter to her sister 'Lis' (in which she
enthused that she was 'full of Herrick') Katharine wrote 'In the afternoon Amy & I
went on pilgrimage to Dean Court, where Herrick lived:— not alas, at our Vicarage.
It is a dreary looking farm-house now, shut in with orchards' (OCD 46or).

Solomon: The Song of Solomon IV 12 *A garden inclosed is.. my spouse;*
Mustard-Tree: One of those amazing plants akin to the spaghetti palm and the
               treacherous ham bush: a metaphor for the kingdom of heaven,
               and prodigious growth (Matthew XIII 31-2). Edith was working on
               the drama that would become LOYALTY OR LOVE?; on September
               9th she wrote to Katharine 'I wonder if Et tu Brute is enlarging &
               springing up a mustard-tree in that dear big brain' (OCB 19,22r).
fruitless: The first draft has *bootless.*
peer: Edith has *peep*, almost certainly a transcription error.
Husbandman: John XV 1 *I am the true vine, and my Father is the husbandman.*

Sweetheart!
(before meeting)

Already to mine eyelids' shore
    The gathering waters swell,
For thinking of the grief in store
    When thou wilt say "Farewell."
I dare not let thee leave me, sweet,
    Lest it should be for ever;
Tears dew my kisses ere we meet,
    Foreboding we must sever:
Since we can neither meet nor part,
Methinks the moral is, sweetheart,
    That we must dwell together.

T0207   A fair copy in Edith's hand exists, on a leaf stuck into the back of one
        of Katharine's early exercise books (OYF 66o); but it seems fairly clear
        that this is another of the aunt's poems addressed to her niece. The
only other autograph, in Katharine's hand, is probably the original draft. It includes a
crucial locating footnote *Teignmouth. Sept. 1st. 1882.* (OVV 6b). The curious title,
present in both autographs, was omitted on publication in UNDERNEATH THE
BOUGH, where the piece appears as #2 in *The Third Book of Songs*, UTB 67. It was
reprinted in 1995 in the Leighton/Reynolds anthology "Victorian Women Poets" (ALR).

A letter to Edith dated August 31st confirms that Amy and Katharine were in
Teignmouth in late summer 1882, staying with 'The dear Uncle' at 13 Triangle
Place. 'We felt we had had enough of Dean Prior as we left it,' wrote Amy (OCF
40o, see T0205); near Tavistock they saw a working party of convicts 'Their faces
had no brutality in them— some looked quite nice' (OCF 45or).

The occasion of the poem seems to have been the imminent departure of Edith and
her father on an extensive trip to Cornwall, before her sister and aunt had returned
to Bristol. By September 9th father and daughter were already in Boscastle (at the
Ship Inn, letter to Katharine OCB 19), and Edith sent her sister a further letter from
Boscastle on the 12th (OCF 51). She also wrote to Katharine 'My darling Sim I have
health, I have energy, I have inspiration. ..Don't be sad. I charge thee, by thy Pretty's
lavender fur' Katharine wrote on the envelope *1st letter from my Pretty Persian Puss
Boscastle September 1882* (OCB 16-7). She would return to a theme of separation
in *Communion* (T0656) and *The Beloved* (T1115).

The Sands of Death

Death, men say, is like a sea
That engulfs mortality,
Treacherous, dreadful, blindingly
    Full of storm and terror.

Death is like the deep warm sand
Pleasant when we come to land,
Covering up with tender hand
    The wave's drifted error.

Life's a tortured, booming gurge
Winds of passion strike and urge,
And transmute to broken surge
    Foam-crests of ambition.

Death's a couch of golden ground,
Warm, soft, permeable mound,
Where from even memory's sound
    We shall have remission.

T0212   Of the four known autographs, two are in Edith's hand; neither is titled, but one has the note *Written February 27, 1883* (OVI 10a). The other two, both titled, are in Katharine's hand, and one of these also confirms the composition date (OVV 11). That the piece is by Katharine is probably but not certainly confirmed by her prose sketch (OYJ 10ab). She sent the poem to J. M. Gray, who liked it 'very particularly' but queried the word *gurge* (ZCC 2o). Katharine replied that she thought it had 'been used by someone, having authority. I will consult Edith' The letter continued 'But I want to thank you for so simply & wisely fulfilling the critic's office— relying on our not being of the irritable poetic race but craftsmen with a great yearning after perfection' (ZCC 118or). She managed to leave the question of authorship tantalisingly ambiguous, but it is worth remembering that the only other occurrence of this word in a Michael Field piece, is in *A crucifix*, known to be her work (T1464). The poem appeared in *The Academy* in October 1886 (JAC #753), and was published in all three versions of UNDERNEATH THE BOUGH, UTB 8-9. Sturge Moore included it in his SELECTION FROM THE POEMS OF MICHAEL FIELD, but omitted stanza 3, also probably because of the 'gurge' (SMF 56). The poem was reprinted in *The Broadview Anthology of Victorian Poetry*, one of the very last books of the twentieth century.

gurge: whirlpool
memory: The concept of a conscious afterlife is too farcical to be taken seriously, but were such possible, remission of all memories must be a blessing. In *Not Lethe*, Katharine would later take a different view (T1056).

Cowslip-gathering

Twain cannot mingle: we went hand in hand,
Yearning, divided, through the fair spring land,
Nor knew, twin maiden spirits, there must be
In all true marriage perfect trinity.
But lo! dear Nature spied us, in a copse
Filling with chirps of song and hazel-drops,
And smiled: "These children I will straight espouse,
While the blue cuckoo thrills the alder-boughs."
So led us to a tender, marshy nook
Of meadow-verdure, where by twos and threes
The cowslips grew, down-nodding toward a brook;
And left us there to pluck them at our ease
In the moist quiet, till the rich content
Of the bee humming in the cherry-trees
Filled us; in one our very being blent.

T0213   The two surviving autographs are in Katharine's hand, and it seems clear
         that she is the actual author. Both are dated *April 1883*, with the
         additional note *A memory of West Malvern* (OVC 7b,OVV 12ab). The
allocation is confirmed by an undated letter Katharine wrote to Amy sometime in the
early 1880's: 'The cowslip-fields will always be connected with West Malvern' (OCF
10r). The experience also made a lasting impression on Edith. On 23 April 1897 she
was writing with an acid pen about 'our friend', one wretched Blanche Palmer who,
amongst other failings, apparently did not know how to cull cowslips *à la mode*.
'Now cowslips need the greatest "chic" in their gatherer, combined with
one-thoughted poetry. I draw each stem up from the crimson heart of growth in the
midst of the leaves, & reject any stem that is not purple-stained from that sanctuary. I
only pluck free panicles with abounding flowerets, resistant to any wind in their
carriage. And I gather slowly, giving time for the upland suavity of their breath to
reach me' (*ICT: well, get her!*). But later: 'Cowslips always bind my Love & me close,
for their fresh clusters at Malvern memorably invited us years ago' (ZJL 52-3). All
this, apart from the text itself, hints that the episode may have a significance more
usually associated with the much later T0538; nor may it be coincidental that Edith,
at 21, had just "come of age." The lyric was eventually published in UNDERNEATH
THE BOUGH as #3 in *The Third Book of Songs*, UTB 67-8.

trinity: The sacred number (see T0295), the third person presumably subsuming
              the 'twain' into a single artistic identity. But even in 1883 this idea was
              not new; 'John Cooley' dates at latest from July 1882 (see MAS 47).
chirps: Both autographs read *twigs*.
humming: Both autographs read *hiving*.
in one: This single individual was to become 'veritable Michael' (ZCL 16o).

Fairies' Song

In the moony brake
When we laugh and wake,
And our dance begins,
Violets hang their chins,
Fast asleep—
While we laugh and leap.

Woodbine-leaves above,
Each a tiny dove,
Roost upon the bare
Winter stems, and there
Peaceful cling—
While we shout and sing.

On the rooty earth
Ferns of April's birth,
Brown and closely furled,
Doze like squirrels curled
Warm and still—
While we frisk our fill.

Hark! our ears have caught
Sound of breath and snort
Near our beechen-tree,
Mixing carelessly!
Sprites, away!
Fly as if 'twere day!

*   *   *   *

Silence! on the ground
Set the toadstools round.
Of these mortals twain
We to talk will deign,
Grave and wise,
Till the morning rise.

T0215   This fey piece, unexceptionably attributed to Edith (see T0216), is an
          interlude in the play FAIR ROSAMUND, *Another part of the Wood.*
          Moonlight. (XFR I.v, 159-63). Three autographs exist, this title only in

The Tree of Knowledge

Lord, Thy tree of knowledge fair
Languished in the Eden air;
For its fruit so poor & shrunken
We can scarce applaud the Giver:
Plant it by Life's brimming river!
When its fibres have well drunken,
Knowledge shall the more increase,
And the more abound our peace.

the fair copy in Katharine's hand (OWD 39b); the piece appeared in all three editions of UNDERNEATH THE BOUGH, UTB 12-3. In the play all five stanzas are interspersed with snippets of speech, at first only by Margery— a foster-sister to Rosamund— who 'Lies and watches the fairies dance and sing'. Stanza 4 announces the arrival of Sir Wilfred de Lacey 'leading his horse' (the horse has only a walk-on part). Their subsequent dialogue (the asterisks occur in UTB) delays the final stanza.

Doze: This becomes *sleep* in UTB.
twain: Margery and her armigerous swain.

T0218   Known only from two autographs in Katharine's hand, both dated *June 1883* (OVC 10b; OVD ii a, 14ab). Her individual and robust approach to a hackneyed myth is as delightful as it is refreshing; in March 1895 she would freshly crop it in *Adam & Eve*, T0699. The following January there is a whimsical preface to the 1896 Journal headed *Dreamland*, in which she again refers to the theme. 'Deliberately I said to Henry the other day— "Henry, let us go together into dreamland, & there be shut up." There is a world of noble spirits & enchanted nature, a world where one may listen all day long, or speaking feel the quiet in the air that comes when there are many listeners. And in this world of dreamland who is there one may not meet. Surely if there be any world the dead haunt for holiday— for doubtless the dead have their great practical affairs, "fareing on, fighting upward ("),— it is this. The sweet seasons are there & age & youth, & all the softness of flowing water. It is an Eden one attains by laughingly eschewing the Tree of Knowledge, & eating perpetually of the Tree of Life' (ZJK 5b).

Tree: *And the Lord God planted a garden eastward in Eden; .. the tree of life also in the midst of the garden, and the tree of knowledge of good and evil.*   Genesis II 8-9
fruit: According to the intellectual giants of fundamentalist Holy Writ, this was probably a grapefruit— hence Meredith's Great Shaddock Dogma of the primal slip (*The Ordeal of Richard Feverel*, published in 1859).
well drunken: This phrase is hyphenated in one autograph (OVC 10b).
abound: The other autograph also offers _redound_ (OVD 14a).

Youth's Defiance

Who hath ever given
Cupid's head white hair,
Or hath put our roses
Under the snow's care?
  If such fool there be
  We'll cry him God's mercie!

T0219 This sestet was written as a song for the minor character Walter, in Act
       I.i of the play THE FATHER'S TRAGEDY (XFT 13). It seems certain the
       piece is Edith's; in the postscript of a letter sent to Browning 07 June
1885 from Stoke Bishop Bristol (ZCL 25o), she writes 'The Father's Tragedy is all my
own with the exception of Emmeline's song' (ICT: T0242). One of her own two
autographs bears the further note Father's Tragedy Act I.i. Written 1883 & 4.
Published June 1885 (OVI 15a). 1883 (if not earlier, see T0160) seems the more
likely year of composition. Mary Sturgeon, in an at length discussion of the drama,
remarks "The play is.. the work of a very young mind, and one is not surprised that
its main feature is a vigorous and sympathetic study of youth" (FMS 131). The
(untitled) poem was eventually included in all three editions of UNDERNEATH THE
BOUGH (UTB 10; as #7 in The First Book of Songs). The title given here appears
only in an index of the manuscript book which has a fair copy in Katharine's hand
(OWD 30,5).

Edith's play concerns Robert III, King of Scotland (who is the 'Father' in question),
though it is his son David, Duke of Rothsay, who is the principal focus; Walter is
described as one of his 'boon companions'. At Rothsay's first entrance, returning
from a hunt with Walter and others, he says:

> Now is it not delightful to be young—
> The friend of every element? Old age
> Faints under heat, and trembles in the blast,
> Withers with cold, and aches with rainy air;
> But sun and wind and ice and storm to us
> Are Nature's boon companions.   While I think
> Of other blessings, Walter, do you praise
> King Youth with opening buds about his crown.

This is the cue for the song.

our roses: Edith's original play draft (OPV 6o) has a variant v3-4:
              Or hath put his roses / 'Neath the winter's care
such fool: When republished in UNDERNEATH THE BOUGH, this became
            such a fool.

Love growth

Methinks my love to thee doth grow,
    And this the sign:
  I see the Spirit claim thee,
  And do not blame thee,
Nor break intrusive on the Holy Ground
    Where thou of God art found.

    I watch the fire
  Leap up, and do not bring
  Fresh water from the spring
To keep it from up-flaming higher
  Than my chilled hands require
    For cherishing.

I see thy soul turn to her hidden grot,
    And follow not;
  Content thou shouldst prefer
    To be with her,
The heavenly Muse, than ever find in me
    Best company.

  So brave my love is grown,
  I joy to find thee sought
    By some great thought;
  And am content alone
  To eat life's common fare,
    While thou prepare
To be my royal moment's guest:
    Live to the Best!

T0221   Both autographs are in Katharine's hand, and precisely dated *Sunday
         night Oct. 7. 1883.* (OVC 12-3). The poem was published with other
         poems about Edith— but without its title— in UNDERNEATH THE
BOUGH (UTB 69-70). Even in 1904 she would still write 'Thankful I am to be the
handmaid of her art' (ZJS 204a). But one feels the art of each would have benefited
more if she had been no such thing. Mary Sturgeon's gloss on the poem 'Thus the
most gracious of her love-lyrics is that in which, after having fostered the younger
mind with infinite sympathy, making possible all that it became and achieved, she
withdraws herself to cede the higher place to her lover" is particularly exasperating in
its traditional *dummkopf* and *wunderkind* view of aunt and niece (FMS 83).

Henry Fawcett

O strenuous spirit, darkling hast thou shined!
  O light unto thy country, who hast lent
  Eyes to the dim hope of the ignorant!
Why the great form of Justice standeth blind
Thou dost make plain. From thy immurèd mind
  Thou, as from prison-walls, thy voice hast sent
  Forceful for faculty's enfranchisement,
And free commèrce of sympathies that bind
  Men into nations; even thy harsh divorce
From the familiar gossip of the eyes
  Moved thee to speed sweet human intercourse
By art's most swift and kindly embassies:
  So didst thou bless all life, thyself being free
  Of faction, that last bond of liberty.

T0248   A most artfully assembled sonnet, this is Michael (ZCL 17-8) in public
            mode— saluting a man who, for his championship of women's suffrage
            alone, must have been a personal hero: ".. a considerable number of
ladies who felt the deepest obligations to Mr. Fawcett.. followed his body to the
grave" (JSP #2942,1503a). From all accounts he was a good, great-hearted and
fearless man, loved and respected by the populace in general: that extreme rarity in
nature, an honest politician. He was 19 years in politics, being a Liberal MP for
Brighton, then Hackney. "He had no sympathy with legislation which had even the
semblance of making life less enjoyable. He would never subscribe to the doctrine
that the mass of the population is to be dragooned into being temperate and
well-conducted" (1509b). In 1880 he was made Postmaster-General: "the Post Office
enjoyed a rare popularity in the House during his administration; and even the most
bitter Irish Members would abstain from teasing questions, and would not block a
Post Office Bill except under what they conceived the direst party necessity" (1510b).
One major concern among many was the preservation of open spaces such as
Epping Forest. 'He walked, he rode.. he faced multitudes as boldly as any other
man.. We cannot even conceive of personal courage greater than that which
enabled Mr. Fawcett to skate over the frozen marshes from Cambridge to Ely, and to
endure for hours.. that tremendous speed.. over a floor that might be full of
death-traps, of which he could see no trace" (1510b). He died on the 6th November
1884 at the age of 51, and this poem appeared, with the footnote *November 10th*.
Michael Field, in *The Spectator* for 15 November 1884 (JSP #2942,1513b).

darkling: He was accidently blinded by his father, in a tragic shooting incident
            at the age of 25. The sonnet picks up on his blindness throughout.
thy voice: Verses 6-7 relate to his work on the franchise (his wife was Millicent
            Garrett, who campaigned for female suffrage over 50 years).

commèrce: He was Professor of Political Economy at Cambridge 1863-84, and a staunch free-trader. But verses 8-9 probably allude to his concern for the plight of the Indian poor; he spoke passionately on Indian finance committees, and became known as the 'Member for India'.

embassies: Verses 10-12 seem to refer to interests at the Post Office— telegrams, the telephone, and (in 1882) his institution of the parcel post.

faction: An independent thinker, he did not hesitate to speak out, even against the Liberals; he believed in and applied the radical teachings of Mill.

BELLEROPHÔN, the first collaboration of aunt and niece, was published by Kegan Paul in May 1881. The book was attributed to the joint authors 'Arran and Isla Leigh' (see MAS 40-1). May 1884 had seen the publication of their first major triumph, the two plays CALLIRRHOË / FAIR ROSAMUND— and with it the *début* of Michael Field. It was probably from about this time that Katharine irrevocably became 'Michael'.

The Stock Dove's Lament

I sing thee with the stock-dove's throat,
Warm, crooning, superstitious note,
That on its dearie so doth dote
    It falls to sorrow,
And from the fair, white swans afloat
    A dirge must borrow.

In thee I have such deep content,
I can but murmur a lament;
It is as though my heart were rent
    By thy perfection,
And all my passion's torrent spent
    In recollection.

T0266   This lyric was first published (untitled) in UNDERNEATH THE BOUGH, UTB 74, as #11 in *The Third Book of Songs*. All of these 'songs' were written by Michael for Edith, and we know the composition circumstances for this particular piece fairly exactly: *Sidmouth. spring 1885 April 13th* (OVV 28b). The two autographs are both titled and in Michael's hand. That April she was at 5 Clifton Terrace in Sidmouth (OCB 65), the rest of the family apparently in Weston; she was hoping that her sister would allow Edith to join her.

The 'Lament' was included in a letter she sent to her niece (OCA 90o): 'And see, my bonnie love, here is a branch of whortle-berry for our meeting— as the almond blossom meant desertion & farewell. Mother must have a heart of stone if after this she keeps you from me. What is it to me to be in the woods without my Pretty swinging on the boughs? It was sweet to watch the boy's pleasure picking anemones among the dried "acorn leaves" & our own dead beech-leaves. I wrote the Dove-Song a few days ago, but when you spoke of returning the French passage, delayed to see if I could add a touch... Coo.Cooooo- says the old Fowl— till His throat vibrates. Coo Coooooo' (OCA 90r). Edith wrote back: 'My own Deare, my Stock-dove, Sweet, very sweet is your call to me, I love it dearly & it does not coo in vain for me. I will come &, heaven favouring, we will indeed be happy! ... But wait a little for our dear little Pussie's sake *(ICT: probably Amy)*. She is getting better & parents want her to have a full week at Weston now this lovely weather is given to us. Let her have this full week & then I will come. They promise that. If we could but set her up for the spring! Kisses for the darling coral blossoms. My Deare & I have plucked them at Ludlow & Tintern. They seem a rosy pledge that we shall meet. I shall always keep them folded between the wings of my Stock-Dove's Lament (what a sweet voice she has!)' (OCB 69o,70o).

stock-dove: A dove like a small wood pigeon.
swans: According to an old tale, swans sing only before they die (sa v6).

Michael seeks a new name for his Lady

Sweet Heart, when God makes His own
A dear soul He writes a stone
With a fair new name, that He
Chooses for the blazonry
Of His jewel: Christ who knew
What was in men chose a few
And each child's soul of them christened
With a golden word that glistened
Keen, prophetic & complete:
My elect I too would greet
With a word that shall express
Our espousal's blessedness.
And in all my search I fail,
Till I stumble on the tale
Of the lover who kissed weeping
The fair girl her flocks a-keeping;
Who within his heart had room
For the tending of her tomb.
And, mid thronging chieftains, bled
For the boy she cherishèd,
Here by Ephraph's pillow brave
I my mighty love will grave.

Twice seven years I had to wait
For my perfect spirit-mate,
And I served with tears & pain
Her elected soul to gain;
But Time's barrier vanished quite
In the toil for my Delight.
Israel's fearful self am I
Timorous, yet defiantly
I can face the coming host
If I set thee hindermost.
While thine offspring,— in mine age
What so sweetly will assuage
As the children that express
All thy youth's far blessedness.
Dearer than the tribes my brain
Hath begotten are thy twain;

And my bliss in them shall be
Deeper than my bliss in thee.
One is born who shall prevail
<u>Till the earth & heaven fail</u>
And for ever by his state
From his brethren separate
Shall remain; whilst he thy youngest,
In thy art's conception strongest,
Doth possess me in such wise
I must have him 'neath mine eyes,
Feel him with my ageing thought;—
Should I lose him, there is naught
I can cherish: if thou leave me,
Rachel, of thy flesh bereave me,
Life hath nothing left behind
For my heart or for my mind.

T0269   This extraordinary poem exists only in two Oxford autographs; both
             appear to be in Michael's hand. One was obviously once in an
             exercise book, the leaves of which were later torn out, and their
order then confused; it exists now as two separate leaves, OYR 118or and OYR 110
(the final 20 verses). The other seems to be a fair copy (OVV 32-5). Both autographs
have the further inscription *Westone May:* OVV adds *1885.* The first, expository
stanza is centred in the Genesis story of Jacob; the 'new name' for Edith is to be
Rachel. In the second stanza Michael justifies and extends the analogy. It is here that
ambiguities arise. This hitherto unpublished, long overlooked and convoluted text
looks to be of key significance in charting the 'Genesis' of Michael Field himself.

writes a stone: Michael may be referring to the stone that Jacob 'set up for a pillar'
                 at the place of his dream of the ladder of angels, Genesis XXVIII 19
                 *And he called the name of that place Beth-el: but the name of that
                 city was called Luz at the first.*
fair new name: She may also have in mind the renaming of Abram, Genesis XVII 5.
blazonry: Identification, as with a coat-of-arms; display to all the world.
christened: Possibly a reference to John I 42 *And he brought him to Jesus. And
                 when Jesus beheld him, he said, Thou art Simon the son of Jona:
                 thou shalt be called Cephas, which is by interpretation, A stone.*
espousal: This, taken literally, could imply Michael and Edith were already
                 committed to each other in 1885: *possibly* dating from that April
                 (which would throw additional *retrospective* light on T0538).
kissed: Genesis XXIX 11 *And Jacob kissed Rachel, ...and wept.*
fair girl: Genesis XXIX 9 *And while he yet spake with them, Rachel came with
                 her father's sheep: for she kept them.*
her tomb: The shortest affair in history! However Michael has telescoped seven
                 chapters of Genesis. Rachel dies in childbirth, on the road to
                 Bethlehem, Genesis XXXV 20 *And Jacob set a pillar upon her*

	grave: *that is the pillar of Rachel's grave unto this day.*
Ephraph's:	Genesis XXXV 19 *And Rachel died, and was buried in the way to Ephraph, which is Bethlehem.* Ephraph, about a mile to the north, was probably an older settlement later taken up into Bethlehem.
Twice seven:	Jacob agreed to labour for his uncle Laban for seven years to win the hand of his cousin Rachel; but on the wedding night Laban palmed off a biddy who, as morning dawned, behold, it was his elder daughter Leah (Genesis XXIX 15-25). Esau must have been delighted at Jacob's overdue comeuppance for his own slimy tricks against his own brother (Genesis XXV 29-34; XXVII 1-41). Leah is credited with having 'weak eyes' (Genesis XXIX 17); she was placed on the back-burner while Jacob sweated another seven years to win Rachel (Genesis XXIX 30). Ha!
had to wait:	Michael equates herself with Jacob: she was *exactly* 14 years old on the day her elder sister married (27 October 1860); curiously, she 'had to wait' another *14 months* before the birth of Edith (12 January 1862). She may also be implying the 'tears and pain' of apprenticeship on the road to Edith's own 14th birthday in 1876. By then Edith was already writing (sa *Discipline*, T0241).
vanished:	Genesis XXIX 20 *And Jacob served seven years for Rachel; and they seemed unto him but a few days, for the love he had to her.*
Israel:	Genesis XXXV 10 *And God said unto him, Thy name is Jacob: thy name shall not be called any more Jacob, but Israel shall be thy name: and he called his name Israel.*
hindermost:	Jacob arranges a conciliation with Esau, who meets him with four hundred men (Genesis XXXII 6). Jacob, judging others by his own grubby standards, suspects a 'smiting' so puts his wives, handmaids and numerous offspring 'hindermost'. Leah and her children are of course placed *before* Rachel and their favourite son Joseph (Genesis XXXIII 1-2). The 'coming host' Michael personally anticipates are, presumably, underwilling publishers and overwilling critics— at least.
offspring:	Rachel eventually produced two sons.
children:	Edith's 'children' are presumably her earliest verses and dramas.
thy twain:	Genesis XXXV 24 *The sons of Rachel; Joseph, and Benjamin.*
my brain:	Perhaps a disparaging backward glance at THE NEW MINNESINGER.
One:	By 'One is born', Michael may be referring to their first great success CALLIRRHOË/FAIR ROSAMUND, or perhaps more likely Edith's THE FATHER'S TRAGEDY. But might not this 'One', who will be in a class apart 'from his brethren', be *Michael Field* himself? If so, her underscoring is surely a rallying cry that will not countenance defeat.
Till the earth:	In one autograph the underscoring is picked up again for the phrase *by his state / From his brethren separate* (OYR 110).
state:	Regardless of a private code, these two verses appear to return to *Rachel's* eldest, Joseph. Sold by his step-brothers into Egypt, his phenomenal administrative skills had won him the top post, Vizier to the Pharaoh (Genesis XLI 41-4).
brethren:	Genesis XLIX 26 *The blessings of thy father... shall be on the head of Joseph, ...the head of him that was separate from his brethren.*
youngest:	Benjamin, whose birth occasioned the death of Rachel (Genesis XXXV 16-8).
thy art's:	Michael may also imply Edith's 'youngest', surely BRUTUS ULTOR.
Should I:	Genesis XLIV 29 (Jacob, fearing the loss of Benjamin) *And if ye take this also from me, and mischief befall him, ye shall bring down my gray hairs with sorrow to the grave.*

'When thou shalt be old another shall lead thee'

Yea, I am growing old,
   Yet doth it grieve me
I by another hand should be controlled:
Whither I fain would go I know so well;
   The limbs self-girt
   Are never hurt,
Therefore to mine own pleasure leave me.—
     Thus I rebel;
   Till I discover
No stranger is about me,— not "another";
   'Tis mine own Lord
   Bindeth the cord.—
Dear Heart, I have no longing to be free;
Whither I would not do Thou carry me.

T0275   Known only from Edith's fair copy, an undated autograph in the black
          notebook 'The Heavenly Love' (OVD 47b). It probably dates from 1885,
          and may also have been written in Runham Vicarage. The title, and the
poem text itself, seem to relate partly to John XXI 18, the ominous and prophetic
words of Christ to Peter: ..*When thou wast young, thou girdedst thyself, and walkedst
whither thou wouldest: but when thou shalt be old, thou shalt stretch forth thy hands,
and another shall gird thee, and carry thee whither thou wouldest not.*

old: If the date is correct, Michael was about 39 at the time of this poem.
bindeth: There are in both text and title reminiscences also of Proverbs VI 20-2:
          *My son, keep thy father's commandment, and forsake not the law of thy
          mother: / Bind them continually upon thine heart, and tie them about
          thy neck. / When thou goest, it shall lead thee; when thou sleepest, it
          shall keep thee; and when thou awakest, it shall talk with thee.*

Noon

Full summer and at noon; from a waste bed
Convolvulus, musk-mallow, poppies spread
The triumph of the sunshine overhead.

Blue on refulgent ash-trees lies the heat;
It tingles on the hedge-rows; the young wheat
Sleeps, warm in golden verdure, at my feet.

The pale, sweet grasses of the hayfield blink;
The heath-moors, as the bees of honey drink,
Suck the deep bosom of the day. To think

Of all that beauty by the light defined
None shares my vision! Sharply on my mind
Presses the sorrow: fern and flower are blind.

T0292   On 24 August 1886 Michael wrote to John Miller Gray from The
         Parsonage, Wemyss Bay: 'When we are dull, we recall "what we were
         doing this time last week", which is perhaps the best & simplest way of
thanking you for making that Edinburgh week so memorable to us' (ZCC 116r-7o).
Later in the same letter she adds 'The copies of Noon & Beloved we ask you to
accept...' (ZCC 117r). Nothing else is known about the poem, no autograph has
survived. Bearing in mind that *Beloved* (T0244) seems to have been written in 1884,
one cannot be over-dogmatic about time of composition, but summer 1886 must
naturally be the latest date: and Michael the probable author— the bee reference in
v8 is further circumstantial evidence. (Edith was to write another *Noon*, the snake
poem T0996, in 1901). The present poem was first published in UNDERNEATH THE
BOUGH as #18 in *The Fourth Book of Songs* (UTB 103-4), and though omitted
from the second 'revised and decreased' edition, it reappeared in Mosher's American
text. It has also been collected in three anthologies, most recently in 1994 (ARL).

81

A Branch of Lilies

A branch of lilies, with their stems upright
And crowding heavenward, lies in the moonlight,
With leaves that are not shut at all by night.

Fulfilled of peace and passion to the rim,
Each flower glows ardent as the seraphim,
Tranquil as Abraham, when God talked with him.

Surely they listen what the Spirit saith:
No soil is on their senses: with such breath
The angel spake— There shall be no more death.

T0293   When Michael sent this poem with others to John Miller Gray in August
1886, for possible submission to the editor of *The Academy* (ZCC 3b),
he misread the title: '... please note the title... is <u>a</u> <u>branch</u>, not a <u>bunch</u>
of lilies' (M ZCC 118r). In October he wrote again. "The "Branch of Lilies", however I
think you should not publish there but in a volume. It requires <u>poems</u> to come before
it, not rude journalistic prose, to create the mood of mind necessary for its
appreciation" (ZCC 9b). Michael seems to have submitted her ramus to the editor of
The Spectator, for it was there that the poem first appeared in print, in August 1888
(JSP #3137). The circumstances of its composition seem to be identical with those of
Primrose Leaves, T0294 (qv); as with that piece, there is also an autograph in Edith's
hand (OVI 107b). Lilies were to prove a constant theme (sa T0990,2-3 and T1618).

seraphim: See T1253, note 4.
Abraham: See T1050, note 6; Edith's copy has *talked to* rather than *talked with*.
There shall: Sturge Moore (and Edith) italicised the final phrase (SMF 76); it is of
course a quotation from the wonderful consolatory verse Revelation XXI
4: *And God shall wipe away all tears from their eyes; and there shall
be no more death, neither sorrow, nor crying, neither shall there be
any more pain: for the former things are passed away.*
Would it were indeed so.

In October 1886 both Edith and Michael wrote to Robert Browning to tell him they
were writing songs and poems based on the surviving fragments of Sappho's work
recently collected and annotated by H.T. Wharton. Michael was quite excited 'We
have written about 30— nearly enough for a tiny volume; to me they have given the
most genuine delight of my life' (ZCL 73r). On 04 April 1887 they sent the 'tiny
volume' to him to see; 'Edith while indexing & arranging the Sappho poems for you
(after more than a year's silence...) suddenly became lyrical' (ZCL 89o). This seems
to imply that most of the pieces were actually written by Michael, who, after all, had
a keen interest in Greek. The two surviving Oxford manuscripts are fair copies (both
in Edith's hand). Browning returned the poems with his delighted comments a week
later (ZCL 91o). The 'tiny volume' became LONG AGO.

(Long Ago V)

Οἶαν τὰν ὑάκινθον ἐν οὔρεσι ποίμενες ἄνδρες
πόσσι καταστείβοιοι, χάμαι δέ τε πόρφυρον ἄνθος

As on the hills the shepherds tread
A hyacinth down, and witherèd
    The purple flower
Is pressed to earth, and broken lies,
Its virgin stem no more to rise
    In summer hour;
And death comes stealing with the dew
That yester evening brought anew
A fresher growth and fragrant grace,
Ere footsteps crushed the grassy place:

So underneath thy scorn and pride
My heart is bowed, and cannot hide
    How it despairs.
O Phaon, weary is my pain;
The tears that from my eyelids rain
    Ease not my cares;
My beauty droops and fades away,
Just as a trampled blossom's may.
Why must thou tread me into earth—
So dim in death, so bright at birth?

T0312   The two autographs are, as usual, in Edith's hand (OVF 9,OVG 6). The
               Sapphic fragment is #94 in Wharton's memoir: *As on the hills the*
               shepherds trample the hyacinth under foot and the purple flower [*is*
pressed] *to earth* (VSW 121). The final three verses show the influence of Browning
(ZCL 91r,95or). There is an interesting Journal echo in May the following year, when
Michael writes 'Nature becomes dumb to me from the moment she grows green. We
shall have no more communion till she summons me to her death-bed. They have
hurt & trampled the hyacinths; but one day last week in a field of vetches I saw them
growing safe. They formed a blue mist round the trunk of an oak, the russet shoots
of the young wood a little taller than they' (ZJB 7b). Yopie Prins remarks that "What
Bradley 'saw' is mediated by her reading of Sappho"— which is possible, even
probable, but scarcely *obligatory*— Michael would almost predictably have written
the identical comment if she had never read a line of Sappho. An empathy with
nature permeates all her work. Prins also states that Michael 'saw' "not a field of
vetches but the name of Michael Field, who revives the figure of the hyacinths and
makes them speak through Sappho's text when nature falls dumb" (JVP 33 141-2).
One can imagine Michael reading this and exclaiming 'Oh, did I really see all that!'
The poem was published in LONG AGO (LAG 8).

(Long Ago IX)

. . . Ἔμεθεν δ' ἔχεισθα λάθαν
  . . .Ἦ τιν' ἄλλον
[μᾶλλον] ἀνθρώπων ἔμεθεν φίλησθα

Thou hast not parted from the sun,
  Thou art not dead,
Numbered with fickle ghosts as one
  By Hermes led.

Thou still hast breath and memory,
  Can'st seek and yearn;
Yet wholly thou forgettest me,
  Or I discern

The truth— thou lov'st another more,
  Assuageless pain!
Betake thee to Oblivion's shore!
  Wilt thou profane

Love's wine by drinking twice the draught
  Of that red tide
We lifted to our lips and quaffed
  When side by side?

To thee let Lethe's drowsing wave
  Its solace give!
I, one bright memory to save,
  Will weep and live.

T0313   Browning had a one word comment for this piece, 'Ingenious' (ZCL
            91r)— presumably for its pairing of two Sapphic fragments, #21 Me
            thou forgettest, and #22 Or lovest another more than me (VSW
74,5). The surviving autographs are OVF,OVG 10, and the poem appears in LONG
AGO at LAG 14-5.

Hermes: See note to T0281.
forgettest: The same fragment #21 Ἔμεθεν δ' ἔχεισθα λάθαν is used alone
            as the germ for Long Ago XXXIX (T0359).
Lethe: One of Michael's favourite tropes, used perhaps most familiarly in
            T0538. She was to write extensively on this theme in 1902 (see
            especially Not Lethe, T1056).

(Long Ago X)

Τί'με Πανδιονις ὦ 'ραννα χελίδων

Ah, Procne, wherefore dost thou weary me?
Thus flitting out and flitting in,
Thou show'st the restlessness of one love-slighted:
And yet, Pandion's daughter, thou did'st win
Thy Tereus. Though he loved too well
      Dumb Philomel,
Tease not the air with this tumultuous wing!
Hast thou no passion for unbosoming?
      Such misery
Befits the breast that love hath ne'er delighted;
Thou to thy Thracian boy wert once united . . .
Ah, lovely Procne, wherefore weary me?

T0314   There are the usual two autographs in Edith's hand, OVF and OVG 11;
         the epigraph is the Sappho fragment #88 *Why, lovely swallow,*
         daughter of Pandion, [weary] me? (VSW 115). Wharton's 1895 edition
quotes in reciprocation v1-2,7 of the Michael Field realisation; the poem itself was
published in LONG AGO, LAG 16.

A case could certainly be made for Michael's authorship; she seems to have had a
special interest in this bloodthirsty myth (outlined in the third footnote to *Nests in
Elms*, T0878). Her unpublished 1901 verse cycle *Sonata Philomela* devoted a sonnet
to each of the three protagonists (T0983-5), and in the voice of verse 8 of the
present lyric there is an interesting pre-echo of the opening of a late poem— surely
hers— *O little Chow, hast thou no tryst to keep?* (T1232).

flitting:	Here is a vivid depiction of swallow flight.
Pandion:	King of Athens, father of the two sisters Procne and Philomela. He died of grief after learning the fate of his daughters and grandson.
Dumb:	There is confusion here with Ovid's version of the myth, in which it is Philomela, not Procne, who loses her tongue; considering the legendary beauty of the nightingale's song, always a less than convincing alternative.
Tease:	Originally *Rove* (OVF 11).
Befits:	Originally *Is for* (OVF 11).
Thracian:	Tereus, according to Graves, 'ruled over the Thracians then occupying Phocian Daulis' (Greek Myths, 46a). Some say he was a son of Ares.
lovely:	A trial of *restless* was eventually discarded (OVG 11).

(Long Ago XXX)

Πόλυ πάκτιδος ἀδυμελεστέρα, χρύσω χρυσοτέρα

Thine elder that I am, thou must not cling
To me, nor mournful for my love entreat:
And yet, Alcæus, as the sudden spring
Is love, yea, and to veiled Demetia sweet.

Sweeter than tone of harp, more gold than gold
Is thy young voice to me; yet, ah, the pain
To learn I am beloved now I am old,
Who, in my youth, loved, as thou must, in vain.

T0333   There are two autographs in Edith's hand, OVF 37 and OVG 43, but surely this is Michael's work. The epigraph quotes the Sappho fragments #122-3 in Wharton's memoir: *Far sweeter of tone than harp, more golden than gold* (VSW 137); sa T0671. In May 1902 Michael recorded in the Journal 'Last night I read to Henry from "Long Ago" "Thine elder, tho' I am" &c. The way from that to "Penetration" (*ICT: T0982, written in May 1901*) is very long— is in veritable time 13 years' (ZJQ 75b). This implies a composition date in 1888, but the 'small lyric cry', like the rest of the first series of Sappho elaborations, could not have been written later than April 1887 (ZCL 91o,2or). It was published in LONG AGO, LAG 49 and reprinted in Sturge Moore's SELECTION, SMF 35.

Thine elder: An echo from Sappho fragment #75 *But if thou lovest us, choose a younger bed-fellow; for I will not brook to live with thee, thine elder as I am* (VSW 106). Angela Leighton has remarked that "Michael Field dares, almost for the first time since Sappho herself, to write love poems addressed by an older woman to younger girls" (FAL 211); yet in this poem (v3) it is quite clear the addressee is a man.

Alcæus: A Greek lyric poet who was born in Mytilene around 620 BC, and died perhaps 580 BC; like Sappho herself, he was greatly esteemed— and, as in her case, only fragments of his poetry have survived.

Demetia: Sturge Moore makes the reasonable assumption that this is a reference to Demeter (the mother of Persephone, see T0877), and emends the text accordingly. The further allusion *sudden spring* of v3 seems to make this a certainty. The coinage may be unique to Michael Field. Edmunds (or Ballantine) inventively substitutes *December* (VJE).

in vain: If the author is indeed Michael, this could be a memory of Gérente.

T0343   The epigraph is Sappho fragment #71 in Wharton's memoir: *I taught Hero of Gyara, the swift runner* (VSW 118), and we know virtually everything about the composition of this delightful lyric. In a postscript to a letter that Michael sent to Browning on 4 April 1887 he tells him 'Edith, while indexing & arranging the Sappho poems for you... suddenly became lyrical, & yesterday & to-day has written <u>I taught Hero of Gyara, the swift runner</u>... she

Ἥρων ἐξεδίδαξ᾽ ἐκ Γυάρων τὰν τανυσίδρομον

Ye think I only teach my songs
To bridegrooms & my maiden throngs,—
Only to these! Oh, foolish thought!
Hero of Gyara I taught,
The swiftest runner: in his veins
Is my victorious fire; it reigns
Supreme in his tense muscles, then
It flashes in his speed, & men
Applaud as round the pillars he
Sweeps like a god imperiously.

Song is not only for delight,
It has a movement & a might
That urge to famous deeds, & brace
With vigour those who war & race.
Great is the man within whose breast
The golden muses are confessed:
He shall be crowned with holy bay,
With fame that never drops away,
And to the cherished goal be brought,
Who by a poet has been taught.

especially wants to know whether scholars think the passage implies that Hero was
one of Sappho's pupils in poetry; whether at least one may dare to adopt this
interpretation?' (ZCL 89or). Edith it seems had forgotten the romantic tale of the
priestess of Aphrodite in Sestos— and, for that matter, *Much Ado about Nothing*.
Browning broke the sad news; Michael's reply is of interest in itself. 'I fear Hero's
being a girl will destroy Edith's poem on the swift runner: yet I should like to re-write
it of a girl-athlete whose limbs were possessed by the fleetness & grace of Sappho's
metres; but I suppose, save at Sparta, women took no part in "the games". The
subject is beset with difficulty, yet whatever points to the bracing influence of Sappho
on her scholars— or— generally— of poets on the world is of value' (ZCL 93o,4o).
But neither aunt nor niece took the matter further; the piece never made it into
LONG AGO, and survives only as a single autograph in Edith's hand (OVF 50).

Hero: A female name ultimately derived from that of Hera, the wife of Zeus;
        Hero (or Heron) of Alexandria was however undoubtedly male.
swiftest: Browning preferred "wide-striding in the race." In answer to Michael's (and
        Edith's) original question he replied "If you like, a scholar of Sappho, but a
        graceful runner" (ZCL 92r).

(Long Ago XLIX)

Ὄτα πάννυχος ἄσφι κατάγρει

When my dear maidens lie
   Each on her bed,
When all night long sleep holds
Their eyes, and softly folds
Their busy hands that ply
   The wheel, or spread
The linen on the grass,
While hours of sunshine pass:

Thus when they lie and dream
   Of happy things,
The golden age reburns;
When youth to slumber turns
Beneath the Cynthian beam
   Again it brings
To life such bliss and glow
As vanished long ago.

Ah, once to lie awake
   Seemed sweet to me!
Now I who even have prayed
That night might be delayed,
Yea, doubled for my sake,
   Sigh wearily,
Watching my maids, where they
Together breathe till day.

T0361   Edith's fair copies are at OVF 81 and OVG 71, with a variant stanza 3;
the Sapphic fragment is #43 *When all night long (sleep) holds their
(eyes)*, VSW 89. This poem (as also T0366) has draft annotations by
Browning (OVF) and seems to have been written within similar parameters to those
of T0357. It was published in LONG AGO, LAG 81-2. Their friend Henry Havelock
Ellis described it as "superlative" (OKC 72r).

reburns: Suggested by Browning instead of *returns;* his further suggestion of
yearns for *turns* in the next verse was however not taken up (see p97).
Cynthian: Of Artemis; the goddess is said to have been born (just before her twin
sibling Apollo) near Mount Cynthus on the island of Delos; the 'beam' is,
by extension, moonlight (sa T0321, notes 1,6).

(Long Ago XLIII)

Ἀμφὶ δὲ [ὕδωρ] ψῦχρον κελάδει δι᾽ ὔσδων
μαλίνων, αἰθυσσομένων δὲ φύλλων
κῶμα καταρρεῖ

Cool water gurgles through
The apple-boughs, and sleep
Falls from the flickering leaves,
Where hoary shadows keep
Secluded from man's view
A little cave that cleaves
The rock with fissure deep.

Worshipped with milk and oil,
There dwell the Nymphs, and there
They listen to the breeze,
About their dewy hair
The clustered garlands coil,
Or, moving round the trees,
Cherish the roots with care.

There reign delight and health;
There freshness yields the palm
To musical refrain;
For never was such calm,
Such sound of murmuring stealth,
Such solace to the brain,
To weariness such balm.

Even a lover's pains,
Though fiercely they have raged,
Here find at last relief:
The heart by sorrow aged
Divinely youth regains;
Tears steal through parchèd grief:
All passion is assuaged.

T0366   The autographs are at OVF 93 and OVG 58-9; the epigraph is fragment
#4   *And round about the cool [water] gurgles through apple-boughs,
and slumber streams from quivering leaves* (VSW 66). Wharton
comments very reasonably that "the breeze, αὔρα, [ICT: rather than ὕδωρ] seems
more likely to have been meant" (VSW 67). Prins also provides a characteristic gloss
(JVP 33 135-6: see T1032). The poem was published in LONG AGO, LAG 68-9.

(Long Ago LXI)

χελύνη

There is laughter soft and free
'Neath the pines of Thessaly,
Thrilling echoes, thrilling cries
Of pursuit, delight, surprise;
Dryope beneath the trees
With the Hamadryades
Plays upon the mountain-side:
Now they meet, and now they hide.

On the hot and sandy ground,
Crumbling still as still they bound,
Crouches, basks a tortoise; all
But the mortal maiden fall
Back in trepidation; she
Takes the creature on her knee,
Strokes the ardent shell, and lays
Even her cheek against its blaze,

Till she calms her playmates' fear;
Suddenly beside her ear
Flashes forth a tongue; the beast
Changes, and with shape released
Grows into a serpent bright,
Covetous, subduing, tight
Round her body backward bent
In forlorn astonishment.

With their convoluted strain
His upreaching coils attain
Full ascendency— her breast
By their passion is compressed
Till her breath in terror fails;
'Mid the flicker of the scales,
Half she seems to hear, half sees
How each frighted comrade flees.

And alone beneath the pine,
With the serpent's heavy twine

On her form, she almost dies:
But a magic from his eyes
Keeps her living, and entranced
At the wonder that has chanced,
As she feels a god within
Fiery looks that thrill and win.

'Tis Apollo in disguise
Holds possession of his prize.
Thus he binds in fetters dire
Those for whom he knows desire;
Mortal loves or poets— all
He must dominate, enthrall
By the rapture of his sway,
Which shall either bless or slay.

So she shudders with a joy
Which no childish fears alloy,
For the spell is round her now
Which has made old prophets bow
Tremulous and wild. An hour
Must she glow beneath his power,
Then a dryad shy and strange
Through the firs thereafter range.

For she joins the troop of those
Dedicate to joy and woes,
Whom by stricture of his love
Leto's son has raised above
Other mortals, who, endowed
With existence unallowed
To their fellows, wander free
Girt with earth's own mystery.

T0371   Apollo, a son of Zeus by the Titaness Leto, inherited his father's
          deplorable habit of copulating in bestial attire with ingenuous virgins;
          however, not even Zeus went through two successive transformations
to that end, herpetological at that (sa the eighth note to T0415). The epigraph is
Sapphic fragment #169 *a tortoise* (VSW 161) and the autographs OVF 109,OVG
93; the poem appears in LONG AGO at LAG 111-3. One of the last of the cycle,
and definitely Edith's work, it appears to have been written in June 1888 ('I have
sung.. the love of Apollo for Dryope..' H ZJB 9a). The original idea looks back to the
1886 first visit to Browning (H ZCL 222r): 'after you had shown to us the photograph
of your son's statue of Dryope. Think of this when you read it.' (Letter to Browning,
February 1889; H ZCL 156o). The Brownings were delighted (ZCF 26;ZJB 60a,94a).

Birds in an Autumn sky

Wheel, wheel, ye birds, about the cheerless sky,
    Above the vapours, the rose winter-bloom
Facing the sunset; in clear circles high
Rise with a shrill, preluding muster-cry,
        Since not for song but flight
        Ye curve and spread
In such harmonious clusters overhead!
The gale with a sea-strength doth doom
Your woods; ye have no nestward care.
        Why should ye stay?
The mist is full of burden and decay,
The passing of the forest-leaves, the soft
Drip of the hedgerows; from the oak
The acorn severs: with victorious stroke
Winnow the cumbered air, rise, eddy, sway—
The sap is in your pinions— press aloft
        Through the illimitable gray,
        Compass sky-regions bare!
        Soon as I find
That life's soft bowers lie ruined in my sight,
        Prompted as ye,
        Ah, if I might
Rove with as confident tranquillity
Athwart the uncommunicating wind!

T0376   The single autograph, in Michael's hand, is dated *Nov 11th 1888* (ZJB
         44b); the poem was first published in March the following year, in *The
         Contemporary Review* (JCR LV 444). Arthur Symons thought it
"admirable" (ZCM 223o) and in November 1893 there was talk of a reprint. This
came to nothing, but Michael's remarks in a letter to J. M. Gray are interesting:
'Maliciously I would suggest Love's wings are wondrous swift. (*ICT: T0195*).. as a
far finer lyric.. I am always raised to laughter by the admiration lavished on <u>Birds</u>. ...I
do not think there is a note in it of real Michael— do you?' (ZCD 195-6).

eddy: Originally *circle*.
Soon as I: The bouncy final six verses seem to have been the contribution of Edith
             (they are added in the Journal in her hand, ZJB 45a). The original draft
             has a quieter, more appealing, 7 verse envoi:
                 Ah, if I may, / When life's soft bowers lie ruined in my sight /
                 So will I fare / And, even as ye, / Elate & free /
                 With ample wing for travel undefined /
                 Rise on the uncommunicating wind.

When thou to death, fond one, wouldst fain be starting,
    I did not pray
    That thou shouldst stay;
    Alone I lay
And dreamed and wept and watched thee on thy way.

But now thou dost return, yea, after parting,
    And me embrace
    Our souls enlace;
    Ask thou no grace;
Thou shalt be aye confinèd to this place.

    *   *   *   *   *

Alone, alone I lie, ah, bitter smarting!
    Thou to the last
    Didst cling, kiss fast,
    Yet art thou past
Beyond me, in the hollow of a blast.

T0401   Mary Sturgeon, writing in 1922, referred to "several psychic experiences which incontestably occurred to Edith Cooper, the most impressive being the vision which appeared to her as her mother was dying. Edith, who was helping to nurse her mother, had gone into another room to rest, as it was not believed that the end was near. She afterward told her friend Miss Helen Sturge that in the moment of death her mother's spirit passed through the room and lingered for an instant beside the bed on which Edith was lying. The event is recorded explicitly in a poem published in *Underneath the Bough* (first edition)." She then quotes T0401 (FMS 25-6). That Edith convinced herself of this visitation is borne out by her entries in the Journal at the time: 'I felt her round me and at my lips in an embrace that was like Pentecostal flame— It made me stronger than death... I felt her press me against the heart of her being' (ZJB 98,9b; sa ZCL 199-200). One can see why Miss Sturgeon seized on this poem as relevant to the occasion, even the row of asterisks (which in practice she omitted) suggest the flitting of a ghost; she would have been wiser however to look at the text more carefully, especially verse 6. The facts are otherwise; this is not *Edith* writing on *August* 20 1889 (the day of her mother's death); as the autograph confirms, it is *Michael* writing two months before, on *June* 20 1889 (ZJB 80b). Edith herself picks up on verse 6, in a comment on one of her own fair copies: 'She has parted from us, & returns: we grow together; the threads of our lives re-mingle— How can we part? (Sim's "true report")' (H OVI 25a). It seems Michael is "reporting" a brief and late remission in her sister's terminal illness. On June 8 she writes 'Our Darling Mother pronounced <u>better</u> by the doctor & with a bitter, rebellious cry receiving the news of Life' (ZJB 77a); the dated poem follows in her hand within three pages. The first publication was, as indicated by Mary Sturgeon, in UNDERNEATH THE BOUGH, UTB 48-9.

Solitary Death, make me thine own,
And let us wander the bare fields together;
   Yea, thou and I alone,
Roving in unembittered unison forever.

I will not harry thy treasure-graves,
I do not ask at thy still hands a lover;
   My heart within me craves
To travel till we twain Time's wilderness discover.

To sojourn with thee my soul was bred,
And I, the courtly sights of life refusing,
   To the wide shadows fled,
And mused upon thee often as I fell a-musing.

Escaped from chaos, thy mother Night,
In her maiden breast a burthen that awed her,
   By cavern waters white
Drew thee her first-born, her unfathered offspring, toward her.

On dewy plats, near twilight dingle,
She oft, to still thee from men's sobs and curses
   In thine ears a-tingle,
Pours her cool charms, her weird, reviving chaunt rehearses.

Though mortals menace thee or elude,
And from thy confines break in swift transgression,
   Thou for thyself art sued
Of me, I claim thy cloudy purlieus my possession.

To a lone freshwater, where the sea
Stirs the silver flux of the reeds and willows,
   Come thou, and beckon me
To lie in the lull of the sand-sequestered billows:

Then take the life I have called my own
And to the liquid universe deliver;
   Loosening my spirit's zone,
Wrap round me as thy limbs the wind, the light, the river.

T0409　　　Two of the three known autographs are in Edith's hand, and one's instinct is that this untitled piece is indeed her work. The text in her own fair copy book has the note *Written July 26, 1889* (OVI 45-6), a date confirmed by the Journal draft (ZJB 88-9b). The following year she copied the piece into a book apparently intended for her sister (YFA 44-5); the problem, as often, comes from consideration of that same Journal draft— which is incontestably in *Michael's* hand, and followed immediately by drafts (still in *Michael's* hand) for the closely related T0411-2 (ZJB 89-2). It is of course *possible* that Michael "wrote up" a draft by Edith, and then produced her own elaborations; Michael Field in Avernus is no doubt grimly amused. It is also difficult to assess how much the piece owes to the fashionable morbidity of a decadent aestheticism, how much to a genuine *Todeswunsch*. It certainly reads very much in earnest, and affords an interesting comparison with (surely Michael's) *The Sands of Death*, T0212 and the equally robust *Praise of Thanatos*, T0487. It appeared in all three UNDERNEATH THE BOUGH editions (UTB 38-9 as #8 in *The Second Book of Songs*). The only other publication until now was very recent, in the Broadview Press anthology 2000.

One of the two other poems written about this time *I would never ask to die* (T0411) elaborates the theme, and the hope to *Enter into solitude*; this material was then reworked into the closely related T0412, which opens splendidly:

I would not die	No hope to brood
To meet a goodly company;	Where harpers wing on wing intrude,
I was ever, ever shy,	Or bold saints with trumpets rude;
And have loved to live retired,	Where four beasts from turning eyne
That I might con	Watch my strange ways:
Some mystery scarce pondered on.	But in concealment of deep rays
Oh, this I have desired!	May some recess be mine!

The poem then rather loses its way before a closing stanza which restates, but cannot compare with, the grand sweep of the final stanza of T0409:

Endowed by thee,
Death, let me enter privacy,
Unmorose and fellowly
To mix, with the free pleasure
Of stars and springs
And magic, unfamiliar things,
My beauteous leisure.

thy mother:	See T0487, the note *Thanatos*.
plats:	Plots, or patches of ground.
dingle:	A dell, a small closely-wooded hollow.
chaunt:	Chant, song.
zone:	*In the specific sense of a girdle, but more aptly confines, or boundary.*

Low down on the sky
Deep-sea-waters flowing by,
Far off, at the even-tide
Lights into the light-house climb.

On high in the dark,
Stars are lit up spark on spark,
   By gold seraphim
Running on through spaces dim.

Love warns!— Mariner
Thee from wreck our lamps deter;
Love guides— thank the rays
God has trimmed to point thy ways.

T0425   This draft, in Edith's hand and almost certainly her work, is isolated on
a final page at the back of the 1888-9 Journal (ZJB 128a); it bears
neither title nor date, but appears to have been written in late October
1889. The same Journal page offers, just two lines below, another quatrain in Edith's
hand— not obviously of the same text, but possibly an aborted offshoot:

All together & each in a dream
The sea-gulls move with the tide,
The great high-tide that leaves
Behind it the whole of the sea.   T0426

On the 10th they had 'started to Scotland' and Edinburgh for a fortnight (ZJB 109a).
Their business in Edinburgh was with visiting the sites associated with their work on
THE TRAGIC MARY, but the 19th found them in St. Andrews 'our little city' (H ZJB
111b). Let Edith pick up the tale in her own words, in a Journal entry dated *Thursday
October 24*: 'Last night on the shore I & my Beloved One walked together— She is
as close as God when I am worthy of her Companionship. We listened to the
continual, pouring voice of the sea. Tawny light was in the sky, wreathed storm &
clouds that "dove-like sat brooding". The sand was streaming with the advance of the
tide, & over the reflective channels we saw the little ancient city making an horizon of
towers. One by one the lighthouses sparkled & the stars rose. It is beautiful to know
as one looks at the human lamps on the waters that they are kindled by <u>love</u>, by
man's sympathy for man; it makes one feel that the stars are not lighted otherwise.
As I thought this the near & far— yea, the very far— became indivisible; she & I
grew all the closer' (ZJB 113b). Edith's prose, if not often her poetry, reflects her true
feelings for Michael. They left for Edinburgh the next day.

light-house: 'We bade farewell to our lonesome beach, its white waves— saw the
light spring up on the Inchcape rock' (H ZJB 113a).

96

ὅτα Πάννυχος ἄσφι κατάγρει. 76. 81

When my dear maidens lie
    Each on her bed;
When all night long sleep holds
Their eyes and softly folds
Their busy hands that ply
    The wheel, or spread
The linen on the grass,
While hours of sunshine pass.

———

When thus they lie and dream
    Of happy things,
The Golden Age returns; *would "returns" be too bold? or*
When youth to slumber turns *"youth for slumber yearns"*
Beneath the Cynthian beam,
    Again it brings
To earth a bliss & glow
That vanished long ago.

———

But I am torn by pain,
    I am awake,   *lie*
Broken by longing wild,
And cruelly beguiled
By hopes & passions vain;
    I burn and quake
With loneliness, while they
Together breathe till day.

———

Autograph of *(Long Ago XLIX) When my dear maidens lie*, T0361
Hand of Edith Emma Cooper, circa 1887-8. Note Browning's pencil annotations; for
the published text (page 88) the final verses of s2 would be altered, and s3 almost
entirely recast.   OVF 81   Bodleian Library MS Eng.poet.d.58 fol 81r. (x0.58).

97

Marriage of Bacchus and Ariadne

Tintoretto

The Ducal Palace at Venice

Dark sea-water round a shape
Hung about the loins with grape,
Hair the vine itself, in braids
On the brow— thus Bacchus wades
Through the water to the shore.
Strange to deck with hill-side store
Limbs that push against the tide;
Strange to gird a wave-washed side
Foam should spring at and entwine—
Strange to burthen it with vine.

He has left the trellised isle,
Left the harvest vat awhile,
Left the Maenads of his troop,
Left his Fauns' midsummer group
And his leopards far behind,
By lone Dia's coast to find
Her whom Theseus dared to mock.
Queenly on the samphire rock
Ariadne sits, one hand
Stretching forth at Love's command.

Love is poised above the twain,
Zealous to assuage the pain
In that stately woman's breast;
Love has set a starry crest
On the once dishonoured head;
Love entreats the hand to wed,
Gently loosening out the cold
Fingers toward that hoop of gold
Bacchus, tremblingly content
To be patient, doth present.

In his eyes there is the pain
Shy, dumb passions can attain
In the valley, on the skirt

Of lone mountains, pine-begirt;
Yearning pleasure such as pleads
In dark wine that no one heeds
Till the feast is ranged and lit.
But his mouth— what gifts in it!
Though the round lips do not dare
Aught to proffer, save a prayer.

Is he not a mendicant
Who has almost died of want?
Through far countries he has roved,
Blessing, blessing, unbeloved;
Therefore is he come in weed
Of a mortal bowed by need,
With the bunches of the grape
As sole glory round his shape:
For there is no god that can
Taste of pleasure save as man.

T0462   Edith's original draft in the 1890 Journal follows her brief notes on the
picture; the date is *August 1* (ZJC 56ab). Stanzas 2, 5 of this sketch
were to be recycled as eventual stanzas 4, 2; and the original stanzas 3
and 4 (below) were replaced by others more immediately relevant to the painting.
There is also an Oxford draft, mostly in Michael's hand, with a variant stanza 5 in
Edith's (OVJ 66-8). Edith at one time made notes on *Titian's* Bacchus and Ariadne
(OYJ 22). The final version of T0462 was printed in SIGHT AND SONG, SAS 82-4.

Ariadne had been left, /Voiceless, of her prince bereft;
Looking out across the plain /With one vision on her brain
Of a sail that flew: when black /On the distant vessel's track
Rose a form which claimed her breath. /Was it loss-effacing death
'Mid the salt stream of the sea? /She forgot how ships can flee.

Theseus went: now someone came /From the waste & bowed like flame
Toward herself in his desire, /Life was in her blood like fire.
Desolation, barren waves /Had they brought the joy that saves?
Earth with its appeal, its green /Mystic energies was seen
Wooing her, as its young god /Through the ocean-water trod.

Ariadne, daughter of Pasiphaë and Minos, king of Crete, fell for Theseus when he
came to kill the minotaur; she gave him the magic clew which enabled him to thread
her father's famous Labyrinth. She then fled with him but was later abandoned on
the island of Naxos— where Dionysus, returning from a trip to India, found her
asleep on the shore and forthwith married her (a formality usually dispensed with by
his father). His bridal gift was a crown which was placed among the stars (sa T0727).

samphire: The plant *Crithmum maritimum*, which grows on rocks by the sea.
mendicant: Beggar.

The Eternal Passer-by

Come, mete me out my loneliness, o wind,
    For I would know
How far the living who must stay behind
    Are from the dead who go.

Eternal Passer-by, I feel there is
    In thee a stir,
A strength to span the yawning distances
    From her grave-stone to her.

T0473   A brief poem almost certainly originating with Michael, but with written evidence of revision by Edith. It dates from Sunday 23 November 1890 (ZJC 119ab). It was eventually published as #34 in *The Fourth Book of Songs*, UNDERNEATH THE BOUGH (UTB 118-9, and both later editions). The title appears only in an index of an Oxford manuscript, where the poem is collected within the wind group *Broad Wings* (OVJ 153). Sturge Moore greatly admired it, and reprinted it in his own anthology under the title *Mete me out my loneliness* (SMF 33 sa 15). The subject of the poem *might* be an unknown woman: it *could* be Emma Bradley, who was born in November 1812— but on balance it is *most likely* to be Emma Cooper, perhaps remembered at this time because of All Souls Day (though more than a little late, even for this). The Journal draft of the lyric and its related untitled sketches T0472,4 are of particular interest but not over-helpful. T0472 (ZJC 119a) stands in its own right as a first cousin to the poem:

> *Eternal Passer by— O Wind / Blow, blow!*
> *That I may learn how far are those that go / From those that stay behind.*
> *Make me more lone / And with the stir / Of thine interminable moan*
> *Span me the distances from her grave-stone to her.*

On the facing page (ZJC 119b) is T0473, with its original title *The Dead: in Absence*. Then follows T0474 (with its curious pre-echo of T0569):

> *We were lovers together side by side / The terror that we must part*
> *A nightmare before us, until she died / And I gathered her to my heart.*

Some four years later, Michael would write the fine poem *Freedom* (T0648) which develops these sentiments of companionship— and here we know for sure that the unknown woman is her sister. Would the word *lovers* inflame Christine White and her followers to the assumption of an unconventional relationship here too?

stay behind: In the Journal draft, v3/4 are in Edith's writing; the original reads
                  How far the living are who stay behind / From those who go.
to span: Michael's first draft reads:
                  A strength to measure forth the distances

The Grave of Schliemann at Colonus

ἵκου τὰ κράτιστα γᾶς ἔπαυλα,
τὸν ἀργῆτα Κογωνόν.

Sleep at Colonus, sleep as to the hum
Of Homer's chaunting; with the golden beam
Of crocus on thy grave, lie down and dream;
    And may the small, gray nightingale be dumb,
No cry from widely roving runnel come,
Cephissus tumble not in winter-stream,
That unto thee the Muse, her mighty theme
Again unfolding, may rehearse the sum
Of great Achilles' wrongs,— to thee recall
    That woven hymn of which a lovely fall
Caught on a comrade's voice so thrilled thine ears
One day in youth thou hadst no power to speak,
Except to pray to God with bitter tears
That by His grace thou sometime should'st learn Greek.

T0485   When this elegy appeared in *The Athenæum* on January 24th 1891,
         attributed to Michael Field, it carried a footnote *Written under the idea
         that Dr. Schliemann would be buried at Colonus* (JAT #3300, 121a).
In effect his burial (on the 4th) had been "in the highest part of the Athenian
cemetery, as Schliemann had himself requested, directly opposite the Acropolis..."
(JAT #3299). The original draft of the piece, in Michael's hand with some *variae* in
both hands, is dated *New Year's Eve 1890* (ZJC 129b). Dr. Heinrich Schliemann,
the discoverer of Troy (1871-3) and excavator of Tiryns and Mycenae (1874-6), had
died on 26 December 1890. One of the larger-than-life Victorians, he was perhaps
the world's first great populariser of archaeology. Yet A.S. Murray, when consulted
by Michael at the British Museum, remarked "The sonnet is too good for Schliemann
just as Colonus is too good for his bones. He was too rough a customer for such a
place.... Slymann as he used to be called in Athens" (ZKF 44-5).

Colonus: A village close to Athens, famous as the birthplace of Sophocles.
No cry: The first draft reads at v5-6 *From leaping April fount no laughter come,
            /No noise from Cephissus' low-creeping stream*. Murray remarked:
            "There are no April founts leaping about Colonus that I remember.
            Things get pretty hot & dry by then as I know quite well. Indeed the
            April dust of Athens & its neighbourhood is often unbearable." The
            published version seems Edith's response to this criticism (ZJC 129a).
Cephissus: A stream or small river arising in the Pentelikon, which flows past
            Athens into the bay of Phaleron, just east of Piraeus.
comrade: Hermann Niederhöffer, a drunken miller; it was 1837, and Schliemann
            was 15. For the whole episode in Schliemann's own words, see page 7
            of his *Ilios: The city and country of the Trojans* (1880).

Unconsciousness

He with the Gentle Ones is hid from sight:
We may not follow. He hath dwelt with woes
So dread, he lays his confidence in those
Men shrink from, who remember and requite.
O comfort him, sweet daughters of the Night,
For fear of whom man's thought doth softly tread;
Within your grove let him be deeply led
To reconciliation and repose.

T0486   Here is a Michael Field poem which is wide open to conjecture. At present nothing is certain either as to author, or date of composition, or the subject matter. It *seems* to be of a piece with the Schliemann elegy and the other Greek poems of late 1890. If "He" is an actual person— which seems probable— his identity is unknown; no autograph has survived, nor Journal nor letter reference yet been detected. All that can be said is that the piece must have been completed by 1893, the date of publication of UNDERNEATH THE BOUGH (in which it appears as #24 in *The Second Book of Songs*, UTB 54-5).

Gentle Ones: Presumably the Eumenides, a propitiating name for the Erinnyes, or Furies. Often invoked to enforce curses, they were in effect the Goddesses of Vengeance (Dirae), exacting punishment especially on offenders against blood kin. They pursued, and drove into madness, both Orestes and Alcmaeon, each of whom murdered his mother; also Meleager, who killed his uncles. Often thought of as an avenging horde of hideous monsters, they have alternatively been described as three winged huntresses with scourges and sickles, and given descriptive names (Alecto, Tisiphone, and Megaera). Athene placated them after the acquittal of Orestes, by granting them a sanctuary in a grotto of the Areopagus in Athens. It is here that they were worshipped as 'the kindly ones' (Eumenides), and offered milk and honey in water. Which all seems more than a little suspect.

daughters: There is a further confusion here with the Fates (the Moerae or Parcae). The Erinnyes were born of Gaea (the earth) from drops of blood scattered at the castration of Uranus; hardly an auspicious childhood, or one likely to engender a sweet nature. It is the Fates who were the daughters of Night. Again a trinity (see second note to T0824), they have also been described as the daughters of Zeus and Themis, or even of the more ancient progenitor Necessitas, the Goddess of Destiny. Nyx (Night) sprang from Chaos, and is credited with several other daughters apart from the Fates (sa Hesperides note to T1375). Although the Fates carry out the decrees of Zeus, some say that even he is subject to their plotting.

Winds to-day are large and free,
Winds to-day are westerly;
From the land they seem to blow
Whence the sap begins to flow
And the dimpled light to spread,
From the country of the dead.

Ah, it is a wild, sweet land
Where the coming May is planned,
Where such influences throb
As our frosts can never rob
Of their triumph, when they bound
Through the tree and from the ground.

Great within me is my soul,
Great to journey to its goal,
To the country of the dead;
For the cornel-tips are red,
And a passion rich in strife
Drives me toward the home of life.

Oh, to keep the spring with them
Who have flushed the cornel-stem,
Who imagine at its source
All the year's delicious course,
Then express by wind and light
Something of their rapture's height!

T0496   The Journal draft of this untitled poem is in Edith's hand, and includes
two variants of a fifth stanza (ZJD 14ab). The other draft (OVJ 155)—
in Michael's hand, and within the *Broad Wings* set— has only these
first three. The piece, possibly Edith's work, was written in the first week of February
1891; it is unmistakably recast from Michael's earlier poem *The sources of the
spring* (T0493). It was published as #23 of *The Second Book of Songs* in
UNDERNEATH THE BOUGH, UTB 53-4.

cornel-tips: The cornel (or dogwood *Cornus sanguinea*) is a deciduous shrub with
conspicuous red twigs, common in southern England in hedgerows and
thickets; decoctions of the bark were apparently used to cure dogs of
mange. Its hard wood was used for butchers' skewers, and that of its
south European cousin, the Cornelian cherry or cornel-tree *C. mas*, for
staves and javelins (sa twelfth note to T0353).

103

To fields where now the forests fail
  The nightingale comes back,
To the soft footsteps of the wood so clinging
  As if there were for singing
    One track.

The poet, as the nightingale,
  Must haunt the olden track,
Must sing of Love where Love first heard his singing,
  Though there's no bringing
    Love back.

T0499   A delightful lyric with a bleak conclusion that only Michael could have
          written; the only autograph that has survived is her original Journal draft
          'August 1st Yesterday I made in the train this little song' (ZJD 61b). In
another ten years she would return to the theme with the surpassing *The Woods are
still* T1073. The poem was published as #30 in *The Fourth Book of Songs,* in the
original UNDERNEATH THE BOUGH, UTB 116. It was never titled, and never
reprinted in the other two editions.

footsteps: The draft reads *current*.

(Cupid's visit)

I lay sick in a foreign land;
  And by me, on the right,
A little Love had taken stand,
  Who held up in my sight
A vessel full of injured things—
His shivered bow, his broken wings;
And underneath the pretty strew
Of glistening feathers, half in view,
A broken heart: he held them up
Within the silver-lighted cup
That I might mark each one, then pressed
His little cheek against my chest,
And fell to singing in such wise
He shook the vision from my eyes.

The National Census for 5 April 1891 records James R. Cooper, widower, and his family living with two servants at The Durdans, Wray Park Road, in Reigate Surrey (they had moved on the 3rd of March); 'Katherine' and Edith are described as 'Dramatist   Author'. In August came the fateful visit to Dresden when Edith had her first near brush with Thanatos (see page 14); within weeks she is irrevocably to be reincarnated as 'Henry.'

T0504   This cloying and cringe-inducing piece (contrast for example with the austerely grand *Eros* of 1897, T0821) is only of interest as a record of that crucial episode in Dresden. Here Edith wrestled with scarlet fever (in between intermittent bouts fighting off the amatory assaults of the nurse, Schwester Christiane). Edith's fair-copy book records *'Written by Sim* "im Krankenhaus" Dresden, September 2, 1891 exactly reproducing a vision of my delirium the night of Monday, Aug 26°'*. The text follows on the facing page (OVI 77-8). The Journal includes Michael's account: 'P's vision Written down Tuesday Morn Aug 26° A little Love comes to me & lays his little cheek against my heart. He shows me in a vessel his broken wings, his broken bow & arrows, his broken heart. And then he sings--- In the vessel it looked such a bright, feathered smash' (ZJD 98b). It was probably also Michael who wrote at this time *A Hospital Garden* (T0503), where—
One may pick up a wood-dove's feather / Beneath the tall plane-trees. T0503,v5-6 She even (perhaps in pique at Cupid's presumption) brought Edith a hygienically-suspect gift of two such feathers (ZJD 99b). (*ICT: *See T0288, first note; °?24; *?25.*)

Cupid's visit appeared in the April 1892 issue of *The Academy* (JAC #1042), but the title may not be authoritative. At any rate it was lost when the poem was included (with T0503) in UNDERNEATH THE BOUGH the following year, UTB 112-3.

broken wings: Both drafts are in Henry's hand, and read *bleeding wings* (OVI 77b).

105

But now behold the royal bird at play;
           He can no more delay;
Leda, though skilled with scroll & plait to bind
           Her locks, to-day
Has left them loose to caper with the wind:
     And some there be miraculously fair:–
           He may no longer scan her;
     One wing flapped as a banner,
     Close by her ear he seizes
     The whimsical, wild hair,
     And snaps, & tears, & teases;
     His breast inflated with the glee
           Of pecking to satiety.

Leda with love's obeisance holds aside,
           Till he is satisfied,
Her head, & keeps her fingers spread between
           The stalks that hide,
Amid the river-flowers of rank, coiled green,
     The cradle that is just a cygnet's nest;
           The other hand relaxes
           Grip of the throat that waxes
     So ardent in its straining
           Compliant to Love's Zest
     She pleasures in love's gaining
His will too poignantly to guess
That her cramped limbs are in distress.

T0511   Michael Field wrote on this subject at least three times (T0369,512-3).
           This untitled Journal draft seems to have been a preliminary attempt
           at *A Pen-drawing of Leda*, T0512. The metrical layout is significantly
different, but the language is unquestionably more graphic and sexually vigorous.
Dated 31 October 1891 (ZJD 134a), the author is probably Michael. In a letter to
John Gray, dated Nov 1891, she writes: '.. I am being held with delight by..
Sodoma's Leda series.. What can Michael do but write, write madly of them' (ZCD
106or). An (unconnected) remark by Henry on 08 November is also curiously
relevant: 'How beautifully true womanhood speaks its best language in the midst of
male entreaty & anguish!.. to have a Sydney *(sic)* at one's feet!' (ZJD 135a).

Leda was the wife (and daughter) of Tyndareus, King of Sparta. One day, fresh from
his Spartan games, she was wandering (as one does) beside the river Eurotas when

To H.H.E. on his marriage

or an epithalamium!

May a common lot befall
Ye whose happy lives now twine together;
Ill they fare who know not all
Stress & fluctuation of the weather.

Heaven in varied cloud will burst;—
Well it is forsooth Heaven's clouds shd. vary,
And the tempest do its worst,
And at whiles the sun himself be chary.

Though ye fail in harvest glee,
And warm hours of August's golden tressing;
April on her part will be
Prodigal in rich, distressful blessing.

Lovers of the light & wind,
Never lay your bliss upon achieving;
Think not of the sheaves to bind;
Breathe the scent the furrow is upheaving.

Follow freedom on the breeze,
The sure path yon flock of birds has taken;
Watch the sunset through the trees,
Sweet will be your sleep when ye awaken.

surprised and trodden by Zeus, all got up as a swan. It is little wonder the fortunate
girl laid an egg or two: in the circumstances the parentage of her clutch is disputed.
The four chicks fledged as Helen and Clytaemnestra, Castor and Polydeuces.

T0517   Known only from an autograph in Michael's hand, this Journal sketch
          has the footnote *Dec. 18th. 1891. The poor bridegroom's bridal eve.*
          (ZJD 150a). The wedding of Henry Havelock Ellis, editor, physician and
sexologist, was a civil one; Henry's hilarious account has already been published
(WAD 192-3). His bride Edith M.O. Lees, a friend of Rudolpho, 'was married in an
ulster' (ZJE 59a). Michael Field wrote other epithalamia, notably *Long Ago XLVII*,
T0345 for 'Pen' Browning; and *Marriage-Vows*, T0668 (also T0666) for the union of
Bertrand Russell and Alys Pearsall Smith. One couple (the Baynes) allowed
publication of their tribute *I sing / A wedding-day so wise*, T0750, some 29 years
later in a 1925 issue of *The London Mercury* (JLM V12 296).

Will not my Love look fair?
— For she has a gown
As lustrous as the lovely coat
Of the lady-cow—
The burnished darkness, the damask mote,
That mingle, I know not how,
In a black-green myrtle & brown;
With a cherry-knot underneath the chin,—
The limpid, water-tints of her skin
And the pencilled, springing hair—
O will not my Love look fair!

O will not my Love look fair,
And will she not win applause
'Neath the brim of her summer hat?
Meseems it will behove
That satin green bows bunch round a pat
Of the dead carnation clove,
Sombre red on the ebon straws;
That the magical, amber eyes below
In clear relief may their lustre show
And quick-ravished youth ensnare
My love will be dazzling fair

T0536   At the end of the second week of February in 1892 Henry had noted in
         the Journal 'I choose at Vickers' my Lady-Cow velveteen dress for
         Milan!!' (ZJE 46b). Then another week later Michael wrote 'Last night
came home my Love's new clothes. What a deep interest attaches to clothes from the
first skin-coats to the latest gossamin— And my Love has a gown as lustrous as the
mail of the lady-cow,— a burnished darkness— & in relief are knots of colour that
glitter as the cherry. All this to frame the limpid water-tints of her complexion; & the
pencilled springing hair' (ZJE 49a). Her poem, with the footnote *Written Sunday
night toward eleven Feb 21st 1891* (sic), follows on the facing page. There is one
other fair copy in Henry's hand in an Oxford autograph (OVI 84b-5b), but the piece
was never published in the lifetime of Michael Field. Henry's note in the same fair
copy book on another 'dress' poem of Michael's, the better-known *My love is like a
lovely shepherdess* (T0408, sa T0877), to the effect that 'dear Mother-One.. thought
it would make me vain' (OVI 43a) may afford a reason. But Henry's much later
admitted sin was the defensive armour of pride, not the gossamin show of vanity.

lady-cow: An old name for the 'lady-bird', one of the familiar brightly-coloured
               spotted beetles (as the common *C. septempunctata*, brilliant red with

108

In Memoriam
Anne Clough— died February 27, 1892

All women, honour her! By the glad hours
Ye owe her, by the joy, the ripened powers,
By youth renewed, by all ye have laid by
Through her for age, let not her memory die:
She gave you to the Muses; grant it true
Ye once were slaves, thus she enfranchised you.

seven black spots) of the extensive family *Coccinellidae*. The name apparently dates from the Middle Ages and is in allusion to the Virgin Mary— curiously, as she is traditionally described as immaculate.
That mingle: Henry's fair copy reads *Commingle*.

T0537   This tribute was published in the *The Academy* issued 05 March 1892 (JAC #1035 p230a); it would still be absent from the canon but for the subscript *Michael Field*. No autograph exists, and no known Victorian Periodical Index lists it; the current writer only discovered it during months of a semi-methodical trawling of the Colindale bound volumes many years ago. It still gives him pleasure as being the one positive, if only slight, advance in Michael Field scholarship personally achieved. No other poems were discovered at that time, but it would seem likely further such minor published pieces will yet be found.

Anne Jemima Clough was the first Principal of Newnham College, Cambridge. Michael of course had been one of the first Newnham students, coming up in Michaelmas Term 1874 "for how long is not clear" (private communication from Newnham, dated 27 November 1991). "J.L.", in a College obituary in the same issue of *The Academy*, wrote "Anne Clough was born on January 20, 1820, one of four children, and the elder sister of Arthur Hugh Clough, the poet. ...Much of her early life was spent in America, at Charleston, and in Canada; but she returned to England and to her birthplace, Liverpool, when she was about twenty years old. ...she began a (girls') day school in Liverpool; ...It was largely through her efforts that lectures were started for ladies in Manchester and Liverpool; ...in 1869, Cambridge University started its higher local examinations for women; and in 1871 Mr. Henry Sidgwick and others invited Miss Clough to come to Cambridge and manage a house for five girl students who wished to attend university and college lectures. Out of this ...(has) gradually grown up our college of 140 students and our three halls... In.. character... her large mindedness, her silent devotion to duty, her entire unselfishness... her delightful sense of humour... In private life few women were more fascinating than Miss Clough; for she had travelled much, she had known all sorts and conditions of men, she had read all kinds of books..." (JAC 229-30).

Michael Field honoured Miss Clough, and through her Newnham College; the reverse cannot be said. In 1994 the College was offered a Michael Field Scholarship in perpetuity, contingent to readings of the poet's work. The offer was turned down. One wonders what the wordly-wise Anne would have thought of such pusillanimity.

Love rises up some days
From a blue couch of light
    Upon the summer sky;
He wakes, and waking plays
With beams and dewdrops white;
His laugh is like the sunniest rain,
    And patters through his voice;
He is so lovely, tolerant, and sane,
    That the heart questions why
It doth not, every hour it beats, rejoice.

Yet sometimes Love awakes
On a black, hellish bed,
    And rises up as hate:
He drinks the hurtful lakes,
He joys to toss and spread
Sparkles of pitchy, rankling flame,
    He joys to play with death.
But when we look on him he is the same
    Quaint child we blest of late,
And every word that once he said he saith.

T0562   There survives a single undated autograph in Henry's fair copy
         book (OVI 90-1); bracketing pieces indicate the most probable
         composition year was 1892, possibly late summer. The poem was
published in UNDERNEATH THE BOUGH, as #26 in *The First Book of Songs* (UTB
24-5); it shows her wrestling with the contrary emotions most typically aroused by
Berenson (see SZD 49). The very antithetical structure of the poem is identical with
that of T0569. But it *may* be significant that her other, published, Berenson-provoked
pieces (including T0569) were grouped together in *The Fourth Book of Songs*.

patters through:	Henry's autograph reads *patters on.*
doth not:	Originally *does not.*
On a black:	Originally *In a black.*
Quaint:	In the autograph this is scored out and replaced by *Bright.*

T0564   One of the last pieces in UNDERNEATH THE BOUGH (UTB 131-2):
         there are two extant, undated autographs, one in Henry's hand in
         her fair-copy book (OVI 92b). It seems likely however that the
piece is by Michael, since the other autograph is a corrected Journal draft in her

I would not be a fugitive
Far in the past amid the olden,
Fond times men labour to recover,
But in the age, ah, verily the golden,
When first a girl dares to become a lover.

How sweeter far it is to give
Than just to rest in the receiving,
Sweeter to sigh than be sighed over,
Sweeter to deal the blow than bear the grieving,
That girl will learn who dares become a lover.

The songs she sings will have the glee,
The laughter of the wind that looses
Wing and breaks from a forest cover;
Freedom of stream that slips its icy nooses
Will be her freedom who becomes a lover.

What Eden unto Eve the tree
Of Life to pluck, to eat unchidden,
Then as a hostess to discover
To man the feast, himself a guest new-bidden,
Now she at last dares to become his lover!

hand; surrounding entries place it in the second half of November, 1892 (ZJE
148ab). Tennyson had died on October 6th, leaving the Laureateship open, and this
may well have been the ultimate unlikely trigger for the poem. 'Bernard writes that
the reason there have been no women-poets is because they have not dared to
woo.' Her interim response was T0561, after a robust rebuttal: 'a fair number of
females in England are capable of wooing' (M ZJE 141b). Women-poets, she says,
can attain/... only if they love in vain (T0553). One speculates uncharitably on a
possible ulterior motive of the 'Doctrine'— but Henry did not rise to the cherry.
Leighton, unaware of all this, discusses the present poem at face value (FAL 225-6).

to give: For Henry's view see the fifth note to T0353.
The songs: Michael's first draft of stanza 3 opens:
                 When she sings in her song will be
                 The joy of the wind when it looses   (ZJE 148a)
To man: The draft of these final verses originally read:
                 To man life's feast, himself a guest new-bidden,
                 Now she herself dares to become his lover!   (ZJE 148b)

My love was like a dormant chrysalid
　　Which thou didst lay
In thy heart's casket, that it might be hid
　　From the cold light away.
Warmly it wintered in its prison-room;
　　Thou wouldst not let it die.
　　In April bloom
　　It opened to an azure butterfly,
With wings that languished for the beds of broom,
And the soft joys that come of liberty.
　　Thou wouldst not let it free,
　　And it lay there
Dead of its fostered yearning's young despair,
　　When thou didst lift the lid.

T0589　　　There is no known autograph, nor any other reference by which the
　　　　　　piece can be dated; it makes a single appearance in the original
　　　　　　version of UNDERNEATH THE BOUGH, UTB 102. This in itself means
that it must have been written before the publication date in July 1893. If the subject
is Berenson (as would seem to be the case, from the inclusion of the poem in *The
Fourth Book of Songs*), then the author is presumably Henry. This supposition gains
credence in her application of the identical trope some seventeen years later. The
occasion was a meeting with McNabb in 1909, when she timidly advanced the
ground plan for what would be her final completed drama, IPHIGENIA IN ARSACIA.
McNabb was surprisingly enthusiastic about a pivotal appearance of St. Matthew,
making suggestions of his own which seem to have overwhelmed her: 'To attempt to
say all this in poetry! Father, under the weight of it I feel like a buried chrysolis *(sic)*
— as if I should be always bound tight & never get my little wings' (ZJZ 167b).

Strange as the metaphor was, and it obviously describes the emotion, not the
beloved, Henry would receive an even stranger classification from Ricketts in her last
days of almost total immobility: 'Fay's eloquence is formidable... I am like one of
those creatures, half-vegetable, half-sensitive with animal-life that sway in the great
under-waters of the sea, always stretching out toward the invisible light, desired &
adored. This picture seems to me full of most sincere tragic sorrow. Could Henry be
presented with greater pathos or a more weird grace?' (H ZKD 27a).　sa T1684.

chrysalid:　　The pupa (or protective case containing it) of a butterfly or moth, in
　　　　　　which complete metamorphosis into a winged, sexually mature
　　　　　　insect occurs.
broom:　　　Common Broom *Cytisus scoparius* is a leguminous shrub with
　　　　　　golden yellow flowers, common to verges and clearings.

The lady I have vowed to paint

The lady I have vowed to paint
Has contour of a rose,
No rigid shadow of a saint
Upon the wall she throws;
Her tints so softly lie
Against the air they almost vie
With the sea's outline smooth against the sky.

To those whom damask hues beguile
Her praise I do not speak,
I find her colour in the smile
Warm, on her warm, blond cheek:
Then to the eyes away
It spreads, those eyes of mystic gray
That with mirage of their own vision play.

Her hair, about her brow, burns bright,
Her tresses are the gold
That in a missal keeps the light
Solemn and pure.   Behold
Her lashes' glimmerings
Have the dove's secret springs
Of amber sunshine when she spreads her wings.

T0591   'All these verses were written in praise of Amy Bell, & the soft, strange
            lines of her face and skin': thus Michael, in the midst of sundry drafts
            of the poem, in early April 1893 (ZJF 38b). The gender slip *blond*
(v11) is curious. Amy Bell, an old friend of Michael's from at least April 1885 (OKD
17), was "something in the City"— or at least, the Stock Exchange (H ZJG 84a)— and
the commission seems to have arisen during the course of a visit over the Easter
weekend. 'On the afternoon of Easter Day I go to Porchester Terrace... Monday
morning The stockbroker in one bed, the poet in the other, we brood' (M ZJF 37b).

The following year in July both aunt and niece were on a second visit, and it appears
Henry was also asked for 'a study all to herself— rather more elaborate than in "The
lady I have vowed to paint"— she has so many race-strains in her, Dutch, Spanish,
Anglo-Indian, theatrical, military &c &c &c— that she is difficult to fix as a type. I
must try another time' (H ZJG 84a). But there is no evidence that Henry ever did.
This tribute however made it into print, in all three editions of UNDERNEATH THE
BOUGH, UTB 102-3.

On a Portrait by Tintoret in the Colonna Gallery

An old man sitting in the evening light,
Touching a spinet: there is stormy blow
In the red heavens; but he does not know
How fast the clouds are faring to the night:
He *hears* the sunset as he thrums some slight
Soft tune that clears the track of long ago,
And as his musings wander to and fro
Where the years passed along, a sage delight
Is creeping in his eyes. His soul is old,
The sky is old, the sunset browns to grey;
But he to some dear country of his youth
By those few notes of music borne away,
Is listening to a story that is told,
And listens, smiling at the story's truth.

T0599   There are drafts and fair copies of this suitably italian sonnet in at least eight manuscripts, all of them at Oxford, and only one in the hand of Henry (OVL 15b). Her autograph bears the alternative title *A Portrait by Tintoret*, which is repeated in a corresponding typescript (OVM 44b). An early fragmentary pencil draft in Michael's hand probably establishes her as the actual author (OPF 46a), but the preliminary notes on the painting are all by Henry, in her own tiny travel notebook (OYN 38-40). The only sure date <u>*May, Rome 1893*</u> occurs on drafts in a notebook labelled 'Italian Poems' (OVK 3a). There is no doubt however that the sonnet dates from their six-week Italian journey in April-May 1893. In a letter from Rome dated Monday May ?9 to John Gray, Michael writes 'I wonder if you remember a picture by Tintoret (Colonna Gallery) of an old man sitting somewhere open to the sunset.— He is playing on a spinet— & the notes bring a train of memories to his face that make sunset there' (ZCD 171r). Drafts in another notebook suggest she may have begun work on the sonnet in earnest on Tuesday May 16 (OYL 21). The poem was first published in *The Dial* (Vale Press, 1896 sa VRS 11) before inclusion in WILD HONEY, WDH 133; this led to reprints in a 1908 review of WILD HONEY (JNY, August 1st), and in Sturge Moore's selection, SMF 104.

Tintoret: Jacopo Robusti (c1518-94), a Venetian painter who was also known as Tintoretto; the painting *Portrait of Old Man playing a spinet* is in the gallery of the Palazzo Colonna, Rome. SIGHT AND SONG contains two other poems based on his works (T0462 and T0510).

hears: 'Edith says the old man <u>hears</u> the sunset' (M ZCD 171r).

thrums: See also first note to T1061; in 1901 Michael endured distressing aural experiences of a spinet that were less than synaesthetic. Henry quotes her letter to Francis 'Don't you ever go to hear the harpsichord chatter its teeth; but go, if you can, to Bayreuth' (H ZJP 33b). Locard's article (JCF 1977) illuminates and enlarges.

On the death of a blind beggar in S. Martin in the Fields

Blind & a beggar, yet I shed
A tear on learning he was dead,
Nor can I through long years forget him,
His setting, & his terrier, & his can
Around him eloquent this tranquil man
Set us a musing on our lot:
I see him not,
And I regret him.

T0606 An undated scrap in Michael's hand, known only from a Journal autograph; from the context it was written in the interval 5-17 March 1894 (ZJG 12a). One stifles a yawn when reading the late, worthy elegy *Esther* (T1708) concerning *Pretty, Devonshire, apple-cheeked Esther, / Who came to London and learnt the ways of sin*, — presumably at her local Evening Institute (how much more attention-grabbing Hardy's *Ruined Maid* !)— yet this spontaneous unmoralising picture wakes an immediate response. In 1902 Michael would write a similar, memorable, tribute to a sempstress (T1042). The key event of 1894 occurred in January, William Rothenstein's introduction of the two artists Charles Ricketts and Charles Shannon (see *Compensation*, SZD 52-3). This was the year they also met Alice Meynell and Bertrand Russell; but the friendship of 'the Poets' and 'the Painters' was to be of lasting consequence.

setting: Presumably a reference to the *façade* of the famous church; the autograph is illegible at this single word. Other possibilities are *matting* or *netting*, but *setting* makes the most sense. Its probability seems strengthened by the exact echo at the start of v6, a technical weakness often apparent in Michael Field drafts.
eloquent: The sense demands a pause at this point.

T0618 [See over] An unpublished picture of an unknown woman; both autographs are in Michael's hand. Sailor hats seem to have been a women's "fashion" at this time (is *nothing* sacred?). This draft, from the 1894 Journal, is probably the most satisfactory; it is dated *Tuesday, June 5th* (ZJG 58b). Neither of the Oxford manuscripts, which show significant variations in punctuation, bears a date (OVO 7b, typescript OVM 12b). So who *is* this woman whom we must indict with such a millinery misappropriation malfeasance against mariners? The Journal for June 1894 gives no further clue. It is true that Henry would obtain such in 1896 'Then we buy... a flax-blue sailor-hat with black velvet & quills for me' (ZJK 55a — a rear-admiral's tile, no less). But Henry (or rather her face) must immediately be ruled out; Michael would have found it physically impossible to 'defy its snares.' One possibility is 'Hiatt's young bride'; Hiatt Baker was a classmate at Clifton (ZJH 158a) who married in October 1895. 'Her black sailor-hat with roseband almost suppresses her hair— of a colour not defined, but

Negative Beauty

Set against the crumbling wall
Of a black-oak, carven stall,
With no sun on it at all,

Beautiful exceedingly
Is her olive face to me
In its blank serenity.

Oh, to see her forehead's crown!
But a sailor-hat, drawn down,
Cuts it off: her hair is brown,

Sombre; but one needs no glint,
Breathless at the temples' tint
Where the eyebrows cease to print.

Then— white, bossy lids, their strange
Dominant, voluptuous range
Over eyes that never change.

Beautiful the narrow flow
Of the iris' indigo
Undisturbed by flash, or glow.

Beautiful the mouth's defect,
The sucked underlip, the checkt
Curves, the chin by shadow fleckt.

Through the patter of the prayers
The face haunts me, unawares,
Rising, I defy its snares.

stealing into one's admiration to waylay it. The eyes have a chastened brightness— it is morning in them, but autumn morning; & the white & red of her skin are like the white & red of late roses at sunrise. She is a lady among barbarians—' (H ZJH 171a). One must remember this was written *over a year after* Michael's poem itself.

Sombre: Michael discarded an earlier draft of stanza 4—
Sallow hair! We first catch hint
Of what charms us in the print
Of her eyebrows, temples' tint,   (ZYG 58a)
sucked: The Oxford autograph and typescript both read *suckt.*

Tiger-Lilies

Lilies, are you come!
  I quail before you as your buds upswell;
  It is the miracle
Of fire and sculpture in your brazen urns
    That strikes me dumb,—
Fire of midsummer that burns,
  And as it passes,
Flinging rich sparkles on its own clear blaze,
Wreathes with the wreathing tongues and rays,
Great tiger-lilies, of your deep-cleft masses!
    It is the wonder
    I am laid under
   By the firm heaves
And overtumbling edges of your liberal leaves.

T0624   Michael wrestled with the subject matter of this paean to *Lilium tigrinum*
in June 1894, ending up with four distinct metrical versions. The first
sketch, titled *The fire of summer on the brazen urns of tiger-lilies*
(T0621), appears in an Oxford manuscript OKF; this also has the sketches and final
draft for a longer second attempt (T0622). The third, longest version (T0623), in
Henry's hand on a loose leaf, was enclosed in one of the Journal volumes; its
existence indicates she may well have had a late hand in assembling the material. As
far as T0624 is concerned, we have Michael's Journal drafts, undated, but in a
context June 14-22 1894 (ZJG 66ab); a single Oxford autograph, again in her
hand, includes the full footnote *June 17th. Fourth Sunday after Trinity* (OVO 10b).
The poem was printed in the September 1895 issue of *Atlantic Monthly*, JAM #76
370; and finally in the American version of UNDERNEATH THE BOUGH, UTD 90.

Lilies: The first version begins, rather tamely:
           No poet must surmise what flowers are like
           But watch them in their rising spike on spike   T0621
     This becomes:
           Lilies — are you come /I quail before you,
           I adore you, /It is not your strong odour lays me low
           It is the way you throw / Your leaves back in the air...   T0622
     The text in Henry's hand begins:
           Tiger-lilies, are you come? /.. /Such conflagration
           Made flesh within your petals strikes me dumb.   T0623
Fire: A variant (ZJG 66b) at v7 reads:
           Smoulders, spirts, lightening as it passes
           Black orange sparkles on its own clear blaze
heaves: Henry's draft ends:
           Till on the last curled heaves /Of your refulgent leaves
           It streams forth lucid on the air.

The Depths of the Grass

Look, in the early light,
   Down to the infinite
Depths at the deep grass-roots;
   Where the sun shoots
In golden veins, as looking through
   A clear pool one sees it do;
   Where campion drifts
Its bladders, iris-brinded, through the rifts
   Of rising, falling seed
   That the winds lightly scour—
Down to the matted earth where over
   And over again crow's-foot and clover
   And pink bindweed
   Dimly, steadily flower.

T0634   The Journal is the sole source of a longer poem with the identical title (T0633); the text was later recast in the present form, and published in the American version of UNDERNEATH THE BOUGH, UTD 86-7. Both surviving drafts of T0634 are in Michael's hand, one dated _Early July 1894_ (OVO 15b). The (undated) Journal drafts for both versions follow an isolated block of Henry's prose which is clearly their common source. 'The grasses on the hillside are a deep sea— Between their frothy heads & the acquamarine spaces of mere herbage one can see down perpendicular into windless depths, where clover & crowfoot dimly yet steadily flower, at the bottom of an underworld. Here & there in the mid-deep campion floats its sea-weed bladders, & the light shoots down in golden veins that stripe the shade & tarry as they do in water. What peace about the drowned flowers! What secrets in this ocean a scythe can sweep away & turn to bare land!' (H ZJG 71a).

campion: Probably the Bladder Campion or 'White Bottle', _Silene vulgaris_: the 'bladders' or 'bottles' are the strongly inflated calyces.
iris-brinded: Rainbow-striped; _brinded_ is 'mighty jargon' for _brindled_.
crow's-foot: If a 'true' crowfoot, the only likely candidate is the Ivy-leaved Crowfoot, _Ranunculus hederaceus_, a creeping plant with white flowers; the commoner yellow-flowered _R. acris_ and _R. arvensis_ would seem too tall to be seen _Down to the matted earth_.
pink bindweed: Unmistakably _Convolvulus arvensis_.

T0635   Michael made several copies, but this poem was probably largely written by Henry. The earliest sketch, bound in with one of the manuscripts of the play QUITS (OPD), is unquestionably in her hand. Two others are

July

There is a month between the swath and sheaf
    When grass is gone
    And corn still grassy;
    When limes are massy
    With hanging leaf,
And pollen-coloured blooms whereon
Bees are voices we can hear,
    So hugely dumb
This silent month of the attaining year.
The white-faced roses slowly disappear
From field and hedgerow, and no more flowers come;
    Earth lies in strain of powers
    Too terrible for flowers:
    And, would we know
    Her burthen, we must go
Forth from the vale, and, ere the sunstrokes slacken,
Stand at a moorland's edge and gaze
    Across the hush and blaze
Of the clear-burning, verdant summer bracken;
    For in that silver flame
    Is writ July's own name—
    The ineffectual, numbed sweet
    Of passion at its heat.

dated *July 10, 1894*: an Oxford autograph in Michael's hand (OVO 16b), and a fair copy in Henry's hand isolated in the final pages of the 1894 Journal (ZJG 146b). It was first published in *The Pageant* in 1897, then the American version of UNDERNEATH THE BOUGH (UTD 87) the following year, before its eventual appearance in the *Mane et Vespere* section of WILD HONEY (WDH 105-6). *Mane et Vespere* contains two other 'month' poems, *September* (T1208) and *October* (T1292); and the Michael Field canon also includes *February* (T0584) and *April* (T0842). But none of these poems are otherwise related.

no more: The Journal version, probably by oversight, omits the *no*; Henry's draft includes a sustained flower passage which became redundant:
        Month of the springlike summer bracken / Across the moorland silverly rejoices / With light through which the foxgloves rear; / And creamy honeysuckle hides each thorn. / July is just the noontide of the year, / Self-poised, forlorn, / Full of passions far too great / To let themselves abate, / And that one sees / Burning in the eyes of marigolds / The blood of poppies, & the purple splendour / With crimson of sweet-peas.   (OPD 23).

The Grand Mogul

Your rose is dead,
    They said,
The Grand Mogul— for so her splendour
Exceeded, masterful, it seemed her due
By dominant male titles to commend her:
    But I, her lover, knew
That myriad-coloured blackness, wrought with fire,
Was woman to the rage of my desire.
  My rose was dead? She lay
Against the sulphur, lemon and blush-gray
Of younger blooms, transformed, morose,
Her shrivelling petals gathered round her close,
    And where before,
Coils twisted thickest, at her core
A round, black hollow: it had come to pass
Hints of tobacco, leather, brass,
Confounded, gave her texture and her colour.
I watched her, as I watched her, growing duller,
    Majestic in recession
    From flesh to mould.
My rose is dead— I echo the confession,
  And they pass to pluck another;
While I, drawn on to vague, prodigious pleasure,
    Fondle my treasure.
O sweet, let death prevail
Upon you, as your nervous outlines thicken
And totter, as your crimsons stale,
I feel fresh rhythms quicken,
Fresh music follows you. Corrupt, grow old,
Drop inwardly to ashes, smother
Your burning spices, and entoil
My senses till you sink a clod of fragrant soil!

T0637   In May 1907 Henry would write 'I choose my flowers by the way they
           die— I adore the lavish death-beds of the poppy & the rose. It is against
           the lily that she festers' (ZJW 120-1, sa T0407). But it is unquestionable
that this piece is Michael's; the first draft, in her hand, is precisely dated *Wednesday*

July 11th 1894 (ZJG 79ab,82a). Oxford has one fair copy in Michael's hand (OVO 17b), also two typescripts. The poem was first published in Mosher's American edition of UNDERNEATH THE BOUGH as #12 in Book 5, UTD 85-6. It has remained popular and been reprinted several times, as when George Macbeth included it (with T1090) in the 1963 *Penguin Book of Sick Verse*. Its most recent appearance (2002) was in *Victorian Literature 1830-1900*.

Chris(tine) White has written an extraordinary but arresting analysis, choosing to read the poem as a description primarily of a *woman* seen as a *rose*— rather than (surely) the Michael Field makar approach of a *rose* seen as a *woman*: "The speaker is ungendered, so this poem is not straightforwardly or simply readable as a lesbian poem, but the text pursues a celebration of a woman who has been loved for a very long time, and whose aged appearance has made no difference to the love, even when compared to younger, more perfect, more alive blooms: ..." (FTP 158-9). She stops short of identifying this as a love poem from Henry to Michael, but to describe the piece as a "celebration of the female body" seems wayward.

Grand Mogul:	Emperor of Delhi, and most of Hindustan; the last such was dethroned in 1857. All the drafts and typescripts carry this title, but it was not used in the published text; the original sketch affords a simpler, and possibly better, opening statement: *"Alas", / They said / "Your rose is dead"! / She lay— / Whose myriad-coloured blackness wrought with fire / Had maddened my desire—* (ZJG 79a). Since no rose called 'The Grand Mogul' has proved traceable (though there was once a 'Mogul' plum), this may be another apposite coinage of Michael's: an impression almost substantiated by the apologetic nature of the later inserted verses.
they pass:	At some point Michael considered *then pass* (ZJG 82a).
O sweet:	In one Journal draft, these final eight verses are all indicated to be italicised (ZJG 79b). The Oxford autograph and both typescripts have *Sweet* for *sweet*, and *Death* for *death*.
burning:	The draft, and all three Oxford versions, read *mummy*.

Walter Pater
(July 30, 1894)

The freshness of the light, its secrecy,
Spices, or honey from sweet-breathing bower,
The harmony of time, love's trembling hour
Struck on thee with a new felicity.
Standing, a child, by a red hawthorn-tree,
Its perishing small petals' flame had power
To fill with masses of soft, ruddy flower
A magic roadside in thy memory:
And haply when thy life ebbed on the air,
And the sweet things that thou hadst clung to passed
From sense, the goodly places of thy land
Were shining on thee, and the world grown fair
As seen of thee in vision, lay at last
A veritable wealth within thy hand.

T0644   In a Journal note Michael recorded: 'On Monday, July 30th Walter Pater dies' (ZJG 100a). She seems immediately to have started work on a sonnet to mark the occasion, and ended up with four separate versions. Three of them (T0643-5) survive as newsprint clippings pasted into the Journal (ZJG 102a); the fourth (T0646, unpublished) was a joint effort, over a week later *Joyously finished by Field & Logan Pearsal Smith in sight of the sun-dial Saturday, August 11th 1894* (ZJG 102b). The committee predictably produced a camel. Of the three versions to see the light of day in different organs of the press, the one reproduced here is probably the most satisfactory; it has proved impossible to identify the source of the clipping. (Michael behaved in a similar impulsive matter at the death of Browning, sending off variations on a theme to different editors, apparently with every post— and with equal success: see T0434.)

Walter Horatio Pater was "the first of the aesthetes", with a mind transparently sensitive to beauty; it was therefore his misfortune to be a rather ugly little man in his own person. Some wit dubbed him "the Caliban of letters". In 1860 friends decided that something, at least, had to be done about his face; a moustache was prescribed, to which he meekly acquiesced. For the rest of his life he hid behind a soup-strainer of Bismarckian proportions (sa MFC 61). His doctrine, "Art for art's sake" — the sufficiency of sensational experience in itself— appealed to a kindred spirit in Michael Field. Indeed, in the October following Pater's death, they borrowed his phrase FOR THAT MOMENT ONLY as title for a collection of prose pieces which aspired to capture such instances. Berenson the previous year had suggested to Henry that she should write brief sketches (the French *croquis*, ZJF 104ab).

Pater died at the age of 54, of heart failure following pleurisy and rheumatic fever; he is buried in Holywell Cemetery, Oxford. The obituary sonnets centre on what was apparently the seminal experience of his life. This he clothed in the guise of fiction (writing of "Florian Deleal") in <u>The Child in the House</u>, a piece which appeared in *MacMillan's Magazine* in August 1878. The relevant passage deserves an extended quotation: "I have remarked how, in the process of our brain-building, as the house of thought in which we live gets itself together, like some airy bird's-nest of floating thistle-down and chance straws, compact at last, little accidents have their consequence; and thus it happened that, as he walked one evening, a garden gate, usually closed, stood open; and lo! within, a great red hawthorn in full flower, embossing heavily the bleached and twisted trunk and branches, so aged that there were but few green leaves thereon— a plumage of tender, crimson fire out of the heart of the dry wood. The perfume of the tree had now and again reached him, in the currents of the wind, over the wall, and he had wondered what might be behind it, and was now allowed to fill his arms with the flowers— flowers enough for all the old blue-china pots along the chimney-piece, making *fête* in the children's room. Was it some periodic moment in the expansion of soul within him, or mere trick of heat in the heavily-laden summer air? But the beauty of the thing struck home to him feverishly; and in dreams all night he loitered along a magic roadway of crimson flowers, which seemed to open ruddily in thick, fresh masses about his feet, and fill softly all the little hollows in the banks on either side. Always afterwards, summer by summer, as the flowers came on, the blossom of the red hawthorn still seemed to him absolutely the reddest of all things, and the goodly crimson, still alive in the works of old Venetian masters or old Flemish tapestries, called out always from afar the recollection of the flame in those perishing little petals, as it pushed gradually out of them, kept long in the drawers of an old cabinet. Also then, for the first time, he seemed to experience a passionateness in his relation to fair outward objects, an inexplicable excitement in their presence, which disturbed him, and from which he half longed to be free. A touch of regret or desire mingled all night with the remembered presence of the red flowers, and their perfume in the darkness about him; and the longing for some undivined, entire possession of them was the beginning of a revelation to him, growing ever clearer, with the coming of the gracious summer guise of fields and trees and persons in each succeeding year, of a certain, at times seemingly exclusive, predominance in his interests, of beautiful physical things, a kind of tyranny of the senses over him. ...Also, as he felt this pressure upon him of the sensible world, then, as often afterwards, there would come another sort of curious questioning how the last impressions of eye and ear might happen to him, how they would find him— the scent of the last flower, the soft yellowness of the last morning, the last recognition of some object of affection, hand or voice; it could not be but that the latest look of the eyes, before their final closing, would be strangely vivid; one would go with the hot tears, the cry, the touch of the wistful bystander, impressed how deeply on one! or would it be, perhaps, a mere frail retiring of all things, great or little, away from one, into a level distance?"

The original red hawthorn is said to have grown near the Archdeacon's residence, close to the King's School in Canterbury; here Pater was a pupil 1853-8.

And haply: In the version which made it into *The Academy* (T0645, JAC #1162), the sestet reads:

> And haply when the tragic clouds of night
> Were slowly wrapping round thee, in the cold
> Of which men always die, a sense renewed
> Of the things sweet to touch and breath and sight,
> That thou didst touch and breathe and see of old
> Stole on thee with the warmth of gratitude.

A Woman's Prayer

O Time, thou passest on to reap,
    I greet thee on thy way;
Pass to thy work; but let me keep
    Thine hour-glass for a day—
Thine hour-glass for my very own;
Leave me with that and life alone,
Then, while my spirits still are blithe,
Turn back, and slay me with thy scythe.

T0660   An unpublished octave known only from an Oxford autograph in
Michael's hand, and a typescript. The autograph has a date *Sept
1894* (OVO 31b), and the typescript the additional footnote *Written on
the banks of the Rother* (OVM 36b). The Journal is silent on the circumstances of its
composition. However *An Ayrshire face* (T0658), which precedes it in OVO, is known
to date from September 12 (ZJG 125a). Hence this piece could have been written in
the last days of the holiday before the return to Durdans at the end of the month. On
the 27th they were at Ambleside, and it could be significant that someone has
corrected the typescript Roth*er* to Rotha. There are several rivers called Rother, but
only one river Roth*ay*, and this indeed is in Westmorland. A Journal entry in
Michael's hand for September 15 'I go forth to the garden & the sun dial' (ZJG
128a) *may* be an extremely tenuous indication of the original inspiration. As is to be
expected, 'Time' as a subject occurs elsewhere in the canon (notably in T0523-4 and
T1143, as well as the prose piece QTM of 1890).

Turn back: A note on the autograph also suggests *Return*.

A Letter

He pleads with me— <u>write</u>, & I send a letter
To a steam-ship, a greeting on the sea,
And an answer comes that I write prose better
Almost than the Masters, that may be,
But the irritating thing to me
Is that I have not a single friend
Who, deep in his heart, would not find it sweeter,
If a packet of post-cards from S. Peter
Were duly promised, my life should end,
Than that we should meet, as friends meet / see
One another in a gallery,
Or at lunch, or a club, with all the colour
Of lighted faces, & flash of dress;
But to me it's so infinitely duller,
I care for their letters so much less
Than for all they can give to eye & ear.
My friends!— the glory when they appear,
Oh made, just I myself should have made them
Wit & beauty to match. I must upbraid them
For this the cruellest of their blows
That if my death meant a heavier mail,
With masses of humourous detail,
I mean of course from this Master of prose
They would not be sorry my life should close.

T0663   In late November 1894 Berenson was travelling from America back to
Paris. On the 9th he wrote to Michael that he would be sailing on the
New York on the 21st: "If you wish to perform an act of charity write
me a nice letter addressed "Steamer New York, Southampton"— no later than Nov
26th." (ZCE 154r). She complied, and it was his reply on the 28th from Bradley's
Hotel that sparked this sketch. "Michael, in your letters you are one of the fine
prose-writers of English. Would you could be persuaded to realise how well you write
<u>prose</u> English" (ZCE 155or). The single Jounal autograph is undated (ZJG 136b).

better: '... I would rather he had said "Dear Mick, Your letter just sets me
              longing for a sight of you"' (M ZJG 134b). Fat chance!
cruellest: Worse was to come the following year: 'He does not say <u>Write to me</u>,
              he says <u>Write to her</u>' (M ZJH 9b). *(ICT: Mary Costelloe)*
humourous: sic. The autograph has an astringent coda: *For me, I don't want my
              life to close / Till some heads, now blond, are grown bald or grey, /
              Till the light of some eyes has passed away, / And tongues, eloquent
              now, have no more to say.*

To give my spirit rest
  I laid a stone on love,
   I left love to decay,
  Within my heart the boast
That I would overlive & turn it into clay.
But from that hour I withered as one crazed,
   I wandered as a ghost;
                I said:
<u>These are my hands, my feet, my breast</u>
As one may claim the body of a friend
From recollection; but life served no end.
  O agony! — One day
  The stone was raised:
I only heard some thunder far away
  The roll of flames that burst:
    I was no more accurst!
I felt my hands, I felt my feet could tread,
And through my breast a sheen of fire was spread,
      Life of the dead,
        O Love.

T0688   In the first week of January 1895 Berenson had sent a portrait of himself to Durdans: Henry, with a last vestige of clear sight, observed 'He looks a fearful little fright in a light sporting-coat, and an American felt cap over clipped hair' (ZJH 6b). Michael sent back a brusque letter '... And now I want you and Mary to sail out of our lives as if you were dead' (ZJH 12b). There was a brief silence, then in February Berenson wrote again: "People don't separate easily when they have got so much from each other as I from you & you from me" (ZJH 15b). The effect on Henry was emotionally devastating. 'I half read the letter, & then before I knew what was come to me I was sobbing slowly as if I should almost die of it, & yet my brain had grasped that joy was the fact beneath this despair. I have never cried for joy before— all morning I cried from time to time. Joy generally comes as a summer day after a day of tempest— not with the long reluctance of the spring after winter' (ZJH 15a). One of the uncertain blooms of this spring was the present poem, here in what appears to be its eventual form, in an undated fair copy in Michael's hand (ZKF 110o).

Winter Lyrics: A small verse-cycle seems briefly to have been considered. In the index of one of Michael's notebooks it is entered as *Winter Lyrics V*, but the entry is deleted, and the lyric does not appear (OVN 1b).

I laid a stone: This is the original first verse; Henry's first draft (T0676) in possibly two stanzas, untitled and undated, is marked <u>not passed</u> (ZJH 16a). There are other drafts, in Michael's hand, in an Oxford manuscript (OQT 42-4). That this habitual rumination by the aunt over her niece's work could extend even to such a fraught piece as this, is perhaps the single most extraordinary— one had almost written tacky— aspect of their lifelong collaboration. Such emotional symbiosis was to plumb a bizarre nadir in T0706.

I left love: A tie in the fair copy would convert v2-3 into a single verse.

Come with me down to this grot,
Out of the splashing rain,
Out of the clinging wet
Of the beanfield, the slippery stones:
Here is the cleft, & here
Are the mossy steps that lead
Down to the mouth of the well.
See, there are seats of stone
Where the drawers of water may rest,
Dry, for the ivy-tod
Overhangs them, & spreads
Its weft half over the sky.
There let us rest, &, oh,
Snuff the air, for the bay
Is filling the cleft with incense poured from her leaves.

Stand on the lowest step
Of the mossy stairway, turn
Your eyes from the hollowed dark
Of the well, in its stony cave,
To the limpid light overhead;
And listen! What feathery sound
Creeps down through the ashes & falls
Light as a leaf on the floor,
Slips as a gleam through the grass!
Now, from the rain outside,
One large, fugitive drop
Splashes an ivy-trail;
And now a breeze is astir—
Listen, how still it is!
Here one feels not a god
Haunting the place, no passion
Stirs in one's heart to build
An altar, to breathe a song:
Here one needs not to pray—
All things are coming to pass.

Up, for the rain is over,
The sun burns hot through the clouds;

The time of refreshing is gone;
Up again by the stairs
Into the beanfield, & out
To the glow of the road, the whoop
Of the peasant driving his mule,
The shriek of the bells aswing
In the convent church by the steep;
How one is kept from them all!
—Kept afar by a peace
Prolonged in one's heart, a sense
Of solitudes bringing to pass
All the desire of the soul.

TO707   The scene is the Well of Santa Rosellia. In April they set off on what was to be their longest (and final) trip to Italy, meeting up with Berenson and Mary Costelloe at Fiesole, and staying over at his rooms in the Villa Kraus. On 01 May, while he was in Florence ('One adores him— one despises him, & the two states slope into each other when one is not in a positive mood' H ZJH 70a), they went with Mary on a late afternoon walk. 'She takes us along stony tracks & walls & by barking dogs to a wheat-field which we enter. There is a cluster of trees in one corner— a covert, low down on the ground. All of a sudden we stop by these trees & a flight of steps descends far below them into a cleft— we follow the steps down & find ourselves between rock-walls in a scooped grotto, with a seat round it, & a foot below, reached by a few more steps, a well is seen through a hole at the side. The coolness is awe-inspiring, transcendent, dark— a Presence— more than that, a Dweller there in the Shade, who grants a welcome. ..It is a Sacred enclosure.. Nowhere in Italy have I come on a spot as classic, as essentially Virgilian. Close to the steps an old man of seventy was digging.. The well is Etruscan the old peasant admits, but there is no name older than Santa Rosellia' (ZJH 70ab). The present piece was apparently begun after a second visit that Saturday morning (04 May): 'In ten minutes the rain begins, but we continue walking toward our Virgilian grotto.. We reach the grotto into wh: the rain hardly shoots at all...it only smacks the bay-leaves & then runs down the sides of the rock & among the stems of butcher's broom & cotyledons of ivy, with a feathery sound, the motions a bird makes pluming itself. The earthy moss-smell is mixed with the hieratic incense of the bay in a most delicious manner. My Love & I are happy, with the good unseen divinity surely close by us as we sit on the shelf of stone round the grotto' (H ZJH 77-8). It is probable that Michael, as often, 'made up' this material of her niece; but the final vivid images in the beanfield seem entirely her own.

The piece, unpublished till now, exists in two autographs. The text given here is the fair copy, which has a note *Fiesole Copied at Asolo May 25th* (OVN 13-4). The presumably original draft in the first 1895 Journal differs only marginally, and carries the extended epigraph *Copied at Asolo Saturday May 25th 1895 Saturday morn. Henry chewing camphor pills* (ZJH 103ab). Both texts are in Michael's hand.

ivy-tod: Ivy bush.
incense: The draft splits the verse: *Is filling the cleft with warm / Incense poured from her leaves* (ZJH 103a).

Edith Emma Cooper (1862-1913)   Henry photographed at Asolo by 'Pen' Browning in a truly awesome hat, the creation of Mme Veréna (Edith Sitwell, eat your heart out). The year was 1895, Henry was 33. Michael extracted it from 'an unsuccessful tea-group' (this is a modern enlargement x1.85), and memorably described it as '..beyond praise. It is Henry in the world, half grande-dame, half fascinating demon.' She continues, 'His toilette is Apolline in rightness, his curved lip is half ironic, half roguishly mocking & his eyes are shooting forth those glances that give his eyes their myriad names— black spa, amber, green— as the inner jewel burns' (ZJH 116b,25a). The Blackfriars print is misallocated on the back *Miss Bradley "Michael"* in an unknown hand; there is no question that this is Henry.
(Blackfriars Archive YSR - BKF 8.87).

130

Lady! all simile I lack
To say your eye-brows are— how black:
Rejecting ravens, & the strip
Of black upon the orchid's lip,
Rejecting thunder & the sloe
I fail, I let sweet fancy go.
But Love, disdainful of this fuss
And strife concerning Erebus,
Thus, mockingly, repairs my blunder,
Can it provoke a poet's wonder
The eyes that I have filled with light
Threw all around them into night.

T0718   One of a scant handful of pieces in which Michael celebrates the beauty of a girl other than her niece. This poem is known only from a single autograph. On 18 October 1895 Michael recorded in the Journal 'Kathleen sends me her portrait— I reply'; then follows immediately the untitled poem (ZJH 172b). The girl is Kathleen Fitzpatrick, sister of Lucy 'Lion' Fitzpatrick. The sisters make a first appearance in the Journal in April 1894: '"Lion" & Kathleen— or, as we named her, "the Quail"' (H ZJG 35b). In the autumn of 1895 Lucy married Robert Phillimore, and on 22 June 1896 both sisters were received at Paragon: 'Mick puts the unmarried beauty on her right & pays to her all the honours, with many jibes at the bride, who grows wildly leonine, falling on Kathleen with lawn-shaking roars. Poor bride— something is wrong— ...tears are held in the austerity of her expression just as water in ice' (H ZJK 96a). The following December, on a return visit to the Fitzpatricks (ZJK 187-90), Kathleen lent Michael 'a thick-spotted veil'— with the surely unique outcome that Michael would write a second poem about Kathleen, *Clothed for an hour in Beauty's veil* (T0773):

> ... The spotted talisman I bind / Across my eyes, my hair; /
> And even kiss the magic thing / Where thy sweet breath awhile did cling.

Although Henry appears to have been untroubled by this special attention to Kathleen 'with her brilliant almond eyes & the arcs of her shining eye-brows' (H ZJK 189b), she initially took a positive dislike to Lucy: '—she is rude & ignoring to me, & takes carresses *(sic)* off my Love with a liberty that exasperates me. I hate her untidy mind, her race-socialism (she is Irish)— her voice, her shillalah eyes.. her charm for my Love' (ZJG 84b, sa T0789). After 1900 neither sister appears again in the Journal.

Erebus: Erebus is the covered pit or cavern first encountered by the spirits of the dead as they enter the kingdom of Hades; but Michael is surely concluding her splendid parade of *chiaroscuro* similes with a reference to Erebus as *Darkness*, son of Chaos and the brother of Nyx (Night).

(Dithyramb for Pylades)

Every stream that hides in rock,
Heart of wood or udder soft,
With repletion gurgles, flows
Down the hillside, down the plain:
Grape-sap, nectar of the bees,
Flame from stones, a surge of milk
Follow, running, where I tread.

Then there is a clustering sound
Underneath the clustered leaves;
And the woodland creatures spring
Sudden from their deep retreat:
Tigers with loud boom descend,
Swift and yellow
And mute-footed;
Panthers, teasing, speckled, gracious;
And the troops of hoof-foot satyrs,
Free at last from fear and cunning,
Free from shadow, free from silence,
Snakes in coils about their horns,
And the wild-vine round their fleeces.
Old Silenus follows after,
Pricking each long ear for secrets
Told by brook and hill and woodland,
As he passes on his beast,
Hung with fir-cones of the forest,
And the wreaths that twine in shade.

Through the cities next I pass,
And the silent houses waken;
Footsteps beat the marble threshold,
And the breezes swell round bosoms
Bare and heaving with a candour
Once inviolable— now
Yielded to the sun and breeze.
Women gather, maids or wedded,
Rushing forth from old seclusion,
Free as showers of April rain,
Through the valleys, through the pine-stems,

Singing, dancing for their pleasure,
Not for pleasure of another,
But because their breath is singing,
And their feet the dance itself.
Mine a glory drawn from covert
By the rapture of my spells,
Drawn from under dale and mountain,
    From recesses of the city,
    From recesses of the wood,
By my power the caves of ice
In the old man's heart are riven—
Then his crutch becomes his thyrsus,
Then his silver locks are serpents
Tossing in a spring-tide wreath.
We are revellers, for revel
Strikes the sky from our array;
We are revellers, the ground
Shakes behind us, red with leas,
Strewn with foliage and the shreds
Of the rended flock and herd.
We are just a feast to look on;
We are terrible to know—
Every withy hides a spear-point;
Every voice rails high, and Pan,
Leader of our dread parade,
Blowing from his pipe, defeats
Courage in a mortal's blood.

March! Let fly your jests like arrows,
        Slay with laughter,
        Slay with hatred,
With the tongue and with the voice.
March! Our pleasure is a passion
    Keen to strive and keen to conquer,
    While audacious to enjoy.
India, ho!— The world before us!
All the plains and timeless deserts
That are African and Asian,
All the meadows of the West,
And the steeps of Italy.

I have passed one lonesome figure
By the surf-edge of the ocean,

With a salt and sterile drearness
In the eyes that gaze to sea:
But, unprompted, flashing forward
As no wing of bird can flash,
I am near her, I have called her,
And her lips breathe toward my breathing,
And the light from off her face
Is the glow of my own triumph,
As I draw the love within her
Out from modesty to truth.
Now my spells have wrought a kingdom
Now is Ariadne crowned;
Side by side, above the tigers,
Side by side and gaze on gaze;
Forth we press, our powers behind us,
We the bounteous, we who live.

Evoe! Hark the word that rouses
Tigers' fierceness,
Women's madness,
Cheers and jubilee of satyrs,
Execration in our foes,
Turbulent felicity
In our ranks and in our hearts.
Evoe!— for the earth is waking,
As the sun can never wake it;
As alone victorious passage
Of its life-blood into living
Can arouse and fire its kingdoms.
Evoe! Frantic, beat the cymbals,
Satyrs, beat your little drums!
Down with impetus of dances,
Down on India, with your serpents,
With your wine-cups and the garlands
Round your weapons and your brows.
Overwhelm the world with singing,
Light it with one flow of torches,
Laugh across it, clang against it—
Evoe!— for the world is ours!

T0727   The dithyramb, a song or hymn in honour of Dionysus, reached its peak
around the 6th century BC with elaborate spectacles at Corinth. Lasus of
Hermione supplied the words, which were accompanied by reed flutes

and a circular dance of up to 50 men and boys. Henry rather fancied herself in this line of composition (see especially Henri Locard's fascinating article JCF 1979), and the present example comes from Act III of THE WORLD AT AUCTION (XWA lxvii-lxxiii). The original draft of the play, in Henry's hand, is now in the Fitzwilliam Museum; it carries the date *December 19th 1896*, with a note that the play was *Begun Nov 12 1895* (YVE 149b). However work had already begun on the scenario in 1894 (ZJG 144b), and it is probable that Act III (and the dithyramb) were drafted by 10 December 1895: 'Henry has read to me wonderful Third Act of The World at Auction this morning—..' (M ZJJ 43a, sa 30a). On 31 December 1895 Henry wrote:' ...I have done the first version of both Act III & Act IV— The Bacchic Chaunt has given me joy— it seems like triumph in unrhymed lyrical verse to wh: I have always felt drawn. It sang itself out of me with no more effort than the spider's web unravels out of the spider' (ZJJ 54b).The Cambridge manuscript version of the dithyramb (YVE 94b-104) contains passages that were cut from the published text, with some necessary rewriting at the excisions. Henry asks the Chorus to chant 'with rapidity, almost violent' (YVE 94b). The scene is set in 'a Triclinium of the Regia' at twilight; it is the Spring of AD 193. The wealthy Roman senator (and short-lived Emperor) Didius Julianus is on stage. The words of the song are given to a Chorus: *Voices sing to the flutes while Pylades rhythmically interprets the Canticum*. In a further stage direction Henry advises: *Between each strophe the flutes play on, unaccompanied by the voices, and Pylades executes a dithyrambic dance*. As the Act proceeds there is stage action between the later strophes (stanzas), the final one being repeated. (There is no space here to detail all the manuscript cuts, but three of the most interesting ones are given below; for a closer look at Pylades see T0772).

fleeces: Here follows the first of the excised passages—
>*Dryads follow them consenting;/ Robes and fingers white as foam*
>*Whirl around the tambourines,/ That like tossing buckles clang,*
>*While the cone-sheathed spears & pikes/ Shoot aloft & shake adown*
>*Ivy on the ivied tresses/ Fauns come frisking, skipping gaily,*
>*Trimmed with horn & pelt & tail/ Of the lonesome, highland goat;*

Silenus: Bald, snub-nosed and pot-bellied, Silenus had the ears and tail of a horse. He is rumoured to have been the tutor of the young Dionysus, and was often pictured, rather the worse for wear, riding a donkey. Under coercion he told Midas the secret of life: the best thing for a man, is not to be born at all— the next best thing, to die as early as possible. *In vino veritas*, but Solon is the more likely philosopher.

waken; Here a vivid image is unaccountably lost—
>*Distaffs drop with reckless sound/ Somewhere by the hidden fountains;*

itself: After the maids and matrons there was a passage of young men—
>*Youths are slower to assemble,/ Till Silenus pours his goblet;*
>*Then the eyes that see it stream/ Flash in concert each with each.*
>*Out of boys I draw the wisdom/ That is heyday life's— tho' hid*
>*By stale knowledge of the school:*

crutch: An unfortunate verse, only too easily misconstrued by the ribald.

Ariadne: Abandoned by Theseus on the island of Dia (Naxos), she married, or was carried off by, Dionysus. After her death he placed her wedding garland, the *Corona Borealis*, in the night sky. These events are celebrated in at least three other Michael Field poems (T0462, T0571 and T1117).

Evoe!: See the fourth note to T0415; or, as John Case put it in 1586, 'Those drunken euohes and howlinges' (*The Praise of Musicke*).

India: Henry later was to work on an extraordinary poem, *A God's Jest* (T0970), in which an enraged Dionysus enmeshes and suffocates an Indian king (and his elephant) with tendrils and leaves of a fast-growing vine.

135

Unity

They twain by Ostia's gardens, being spent
With a long journey, feeling need to win
New strength for a new voyage, far from din
Of the world's turmoil, in a window leant
Together and alone; and, with the scent
And flower of many roses flowing in,
Perceived the rule of the great peace begin
That has its towers beyond the firmament.

Love, were it possible that thou and I,
Being one day together soul to soul,
At shore of some wide waters, in the flush
Of roses tingeing them, might so draw nigh
That we might feel of our accord the hush,
Binding all creatures, of God's pure control!

T0757   In November 1895 Berenson and Mary outraged by their disrespectful reception of the latest Michael Field play (SZD 57). The rift was to last until the *rapprochement* at Richmond in 1901, by which time the culprits were married. But Italy was lost for ever. The first drafts (OVJ 116b) and five other autographs of *Unity* survive, all but one (OVL 18b) in the hand of Michael. Only one is dated; here the poem falls in a group of <u>Lyrics 1896</u>, and has the precise footnote *Fourth Sunday in Lent March 15th* (OVN 49,53b). The poem (as is fitting from its subject, an italian sonnet) was first printed in *The Commonwealth* in the issue dated May 2, 1897 (OYV 66). Here, as in the autographs, it was split 8,6; it was only on publication in WILD HONEY (WDH 167) that the octave and sestet were united. This was not the only variation (v.i.).

Unity: In the autograph book *Perpetua* which Michael wrote for her niece, the sonnet is the opening poem, and is headed *A Dedication* (YFB 2b).

twain: The Journal is unhelpful; one might guess at Berenson and Mary, but the estrangement was possibly still too recent. It could have been the honeymooners (Ronald and Helen Bayne) whose wedding was celebrated in T0750. There is no shred of supporting evidence either way. (It is however curious that Amy took the 78 year old James to Italy that June, and here the first three verses would appear especially appropriate; but the sonnet date seems unassailable.)

Ostia: A seaside resort about 3 miles SW of the ancient Ostia Antica (once the port of republican Rome on the Tiber, but now about 4 miles upstream).

tingeing: WILD HONEY has the less comfortable *tinging*.

accord: Some drafts read:

        That of our accord we might feel the hush   (OVJ 116,OVN 53)

The Art of Love

Ah, Dearest, thou dost cleave to me
    Even as Ruth to Naomi;
Yet, seeing great Love has grown in art,
At Death there is no need to part;
Nor shall one sue for burial where
    The other crumbles into mould:
Past iron Time there is an age of gold,
And hand in hand we will seek entrance there.

T0781 There are two autographs, both in Michael's hand, with the footnote *Liphook January 12th 1897* (ZJL 7b,OVQ 2b); the Oxford manuscript has the additional note *My Merle's Birthday*. Henry (the Merle in question) recorded in the Journal their arrival at Liphook— a market town in East Hampshire some 8 miles NE of Petersfield— on the 7th of January (ZJL 6b). They had taken up a tea-break residence in Hertford Cottage; Michael elaborating 'We have fled from Reigate, as from a land of abortions, drains & damp' (ZJL 6a). On the 12th itself, Michael made another Journal entry: 'At prayers they speak of having to give an account of our talents to the Lord as if we were little errand-boys who must return correct change. I hustle Henry out of the room, demand a Bible, & read from <u>the Book of Ruth</u>.. .' Michael then quotes Ruth I 14-8, as well as The Song of Solomon II 9,14. 'After this perfect "religion", Henry settles in the rocking-chair, with his toes to the fire, & scribbles at the 3rd Act of <u>A Race of Leaves</u>' (ZJL 6b-7a).

Merle (the blackbird *Turdus merula*) and mavis (the song-thrush *Turdus musicus*) appear in literature from at least 1450; 'Merle' seems to have been a pet-name for Henry that January. It also occurs in a footnote to a Journal draft of *Beauty liberating*, T0784 (ZJL 8b), and an early draft of *Power in Silence*, T0790 (ZJL 17a).

Their time at Liphook was certainly a happy one: 'What games we have by our bed-room fire at night! We lie on our bed, read proofs & poems, & stick roses in our ears' (M ZJL 7b). They were back at Durdans on January 18th. '"Let us be thankful for the things we haven't!" I say to Henry in ribald devotion, as he slowly dresses in the ash-chill of an east-wind, his face still transparent, & something of the scorched wire about his lips— "That we haven't large wens, & don't live in the suburbs of big cities" responds the little Boy' (M ZJL 10a).

Ruth: This story, in the magnificent cadences of the King James bible, is one of the great classics of fidelity: *Intreat me not to leave thee.. for whither thou goest, I will go*. Did Michael see herself as the widowed Naomi, with Henry as the equally widowed, and devoted, daughter-in-law Ruth? What is certain is that Henry received a 'little copy of <u>Esther & Ruth</u>' on the 13th, as well as this poem on her birthday morning (M ZJL 7b).

Death: Ruth I 17 *Where thou diest, will I die, <u>and there will I be buried</u>: the Lord do so to me, and more also, if ought but death part thee and me.* Michael herself underscored in the Journal the passage indicated.

The Beauty of Gratitude

"How shall my heart be lightened?" Menna, knowing,
Answers, "O king, thy sick heart to refresh,
To twenty maidens I will give a mesh
Of net for raiment, and will set them rowing
Adown the grassy waters of this cool,
Bird-fluttered inlet." So it comes to pass,
As the king gazes idle from the grass
To the plashing oars and dazzle of the pool,
Voluptuous gladness fills him unaware.
Fair are the virgins: yet a fairer sight
Than those fair limbs, fair breasts, fair shading hair
Is Nebta's face when her new malachite
Drops in the stream and at the king's command
The chief magician lays it in her hand.

T0799   By contrast with T0798, this poem, the fifth and last of the Egyptian
         Sonnets, is almost unknown; this is the first reprinting since its original
         publication in WILD HONEY, WDH 89. Not a strict sonnet, perhaps
better described as an Egyptian quatorzain, it was written by Michael in April 1897—
a note on an Oxford autograph adds *Begun on way to British Museum, finished at
Lyme* (OVP 6b). They were at Lyme Regis from the 9th, and on the 12th Henry wrote
in the Journal 'Michael works at a sonnet'; an early draft in her hand follows
immediately on the facing page (ZJL 34ab). The poem provides a vivid and delightful
picture which culminates in a baffling sleight of hand.

Gratitude: *Gratitude* is also the title of perhaps one of Michael's last poems
              (T1430, qv).
Menna: Curiously, at some point Michael changed, or allowed to be changed,
              the names of the protagonists. *Menna* was originally *Zasa*, and
              Nebta was *Aila* (ZJL 34b).
king: The Journal draft has *King* throughout, and *Magician* in v14.
To twenty: Here it reads *I will give twenty maidens a gold mesh.*
unaware: As in all the autographs; WILD HONEY has an obvious printer's
              error *unawares.*
malachite: A pleasing green mineral (basic copper carbonate).
Drops: In a footnote the Journal draft also suggests
                   Drops, &, obedient to the King's command,

138

Eros

O Eros of the mountains, of the earth,
One thing I know of thee that thou art old,
Far, sovereign, lonesome tyrant of the dearth
Of chaos, ruler of the primal cold!
None gave thee nurture: chaos' icy rings
Pressed on thy plenitude. O fostering power,
Thine the first voice, first warmth, first golden wings,
First blowing zephyr, earliest opened flower,
Thine the first smile of Time: thou hast no mate,
Thou art alone forever, giving all:
After thine image, Love, thou did'st create
Man to be poor, man to be prodigal;
And thus, O awful god, he is endued
With the raw hungers of thy solitude.

T0821   Henry's father, James Cooper, went to Switzerland with his younger
daughter Amy on 12 June 1897; aged 79, he wandered off on an
evening stroll and never came back; his body was not discovered until
25 October (for a fuller account see SZD 62-4). Michael was to write an extended
chain of sonnets on this event over the next two years. The present poem is one of
Michael's *The Longer Allegiance* cycle (and indeed published as such in WILD
HONEY as # VII, WDH 143), this english sonnet can easily stand on its own without
the Riffelalp subtext. There are at least five autographs, and all agree on the
composition date *Wednesday Nov 24th.. 1897* (OWG 29b). This source and two
others carry the additional note *(before the valuer)*. Later, Henry would also use the
title for one of her DEDICATED poems, T1203.

The present poem was not always *Eros*. For a time the title was *Love* (OVQ 26b), or
even *The Mighty Love* (YSL uf). It is addressed to the Stranger in his most terrible
aspect. Angela Leighton agrees: she comments "No baby philanderer with bow and
arrow, 'Eros', here, is the older, Homeric god of love, associated with the
germinating force of life itself. Such love is no more than a tyrannical and lonely
'drive', a lust to live, as ancient as the universe... Man... is explicitly made in the
'image' of Eros rather than in the image of God... In the end, the characteristic of
Eros is not a warm ripeness of the senses, but rather 'raw hungers'... This is the
bleak side of Michael Field's creed of pleasure" (FAL 238-9). Leighton wishes to
distinguish Eros *from* God; it could equally— and perhaps more convincingly— be
argued that for Michael, Eros (Love) *was* God. But Leighton's gloss of v12 "a
creature of both unfulfillable and wasteful desires" is apt, and as Sturge Moore rightly
remarked in an undated (1908) letter, *"Love, thou didst create / Man to be poor,
man to be prodigal"* is magnificent' (ZCF 219r). It is therefore not surprising that he
included this noble sonnet in his own selection, SMF 60.

Parting

Lo, even memory must give up its dead!
Where he has walked we must not walk again,
Nor pause by garden borders where he led,
Nor seek his flowers; we must unknot the pain.
For, if we look not on our memory's corse,
Sweet sculpture of our memory will abide;
The eyes, the lips will take their human force,
Life's lovely images keep by our side.
Anew in the young sunshine we shall meet,
By paths, belovèd, where thou hast not been;
Thou, being by, shalt make the strangeness sweet
Of the long, silver river and the green;
And all our passion grow a child to cling
About the freshness of thy welcoming.

T0863   As the new year began, Michael wrote in the Journal 'I have put away
         my dead in Durdans— It is unsanctified, & unclean, & cannot be
         renewed or blessed to us any more until we have proved our willingness
to give it up.' The first poem draft follows within a page 'so mild a day, & every bird
thinking of its mate'; it carries the footnote *Sunday January 8th 1899* (ZJN 7a,8a).
At least five other autographs are known, four of them at Oxford. The sonnet was
properly included within *The Longer Allegiance* cycle as # XXIII, when eventually
published in WILD HONEY, WDH 159. Two other Michael Field poems at some time
received the title *Parting* (T1433,1503).

memory: With a capital letter in the drafts; also *Belovèd*, in v10.
garden: 'On Christmas Day *(ICT: 1898)* I went round beloved Durdans Garden
           & felt detached from it— the anguish allayed & vague as it becomes
           before final parting' (H ZJM 138b). As 1898 closed, Michael wrote
           'Columbus did not discover America by carefully wrapping himself in a
           great cloak. Our harbour must be the open sea' (ZJM 139b).
corse: corpse.
river: The Thames; and the *green* at Richmond, Surrey. On 27 December
           1898, Henry wrote out a letter received from *The Artists*: ".... There is a
           house at Petersham old-fashioned with garden, near here, close to the
           river, & near the most beautiful park in the world" (ZJM 138a

Low Sunday

Honouring this lesser feast my shrines I spread
With the unfragrant violet, and rehearse,
Plucking the small grape-hyacinth for thyrse,
My exultation that, tho' earth's low bed
Hath never been of flesh untenanted,
Forever taking leave, bowed by Time's curse,
Bowing to doom, for better and for worse,
Deep married to their breath men hath the dead.
Without them were no god, no crownèd king,
No feast, no fair procession; they abide.
Bosomed by them the petals disappear
Frail on the wind; they are with every spring:
Though something keep us from them, though they hide,
May be forever hidden, they are near.

T0883   There are no problems here with the author. There are at least five
autographs, all in Michael's hand, save for Henry's WILD HONEY
fair copy (OWL 157b). All are dated *April 1899* (OWG 20b); but
whereas Low Sunday in 1899 fell on the 9th, the earliest (Journal) draft was not
recorded until *Thursday April 13th* (ZJN 55b). From the beginning one of the
sonnets of *The Longer Allegiance* cycle, the piece moved from XLII (OVQ 65b) to
XXXVII (OVR 42b) to its final position at XXIV on eventual publication in WILD
HONEY, WDH 160. Two years later Michael referred back to the poem 'I read my
Low-Sunday sonnet to Henry', before reworking the theme in an unpublished sonnet
Octave, T0979 (ZJP 54ab). On Low Sunday in 1912 however, Henry found fault with
the earlier poem: 'The sonnet in <u>Wild Honey</u> is a little unreal because a little devious
from the Truth' (ZKC 41b).

Low Sunday: The first Sunday after Easter Sunday. It was particularly dear to
Michael, who described it as 'my own little feast-day— precious &
humble', remarking further 'For ever & ever let those who love me
honour & keep this day' (ZJN 54b). Take notice, out there.

Honouring: The Journal draft opens with a badly cobbled octave:
> Ah, feast of mine, for thee my shrines I spread
> With the unfragrant violet, & rehearse
> (The small grape-hyacinth my humble thyrse)
> My exaltation, nothing 'minishèd
> By tale of empty tomb discredited,
> My exaltation that, despite Death's curse,
> Throughout all time, for better & for worse,
> Deep married to their breath, men have the dead.

     A draft Oxford MS. shows several further attempts before arrival at
the final version (OVU 33-5).

thyrse: See the fifth note to *Sanctuary*, T0879.

Vale!

There are, so strange it seems, there are who say
That distance gives intenseness to farewell.
Ah, no! If she should leave me for a day,
A year, without her life has lost its spell.
The withering senses shudder as they lose
Their warm possession; and it is all one
If for far voyage or a simple cruise,
Just where the stream is ocean, she is gone;
And if, but from my side, she disappears,
There follows her a piercing *vale* shout
From lips, from eyes, ah, most of all from ears
That starve and hope: nor time, nor narrow space
Can give ease to the senses left without
The appeal, the dear temptations of her face.

T0888   On 16 May the move to Paragon was accomplished, and this poem
may have been the first to be written in their new home. Two of the four
known autographs have the footnote *August 13th Richmond Sun-room*
(OVU 38b) and a third is in an exercise book following a page with the single word
Richmond (OVR 44ab). On the Bank Holiday weekend (5-7 August) they had taken a
break at Wye, where they reflected on their fresh habitat. 'We see our new home in
perspective as we walk— it is good to see it— its simplicity, its harmony, its river-lit
charm. And we are grateful for these gifts in spite of our clear sight of its
disadvantages— its steepness, its unpopularity with servants, its age & infirmity. We
find its little garden is like a rich bit of carpet in our hearts. This home of ourselves—
not of our past— is close & extraordinarily precious to us' (H ZJN 90a). On the 13th
itself the Journal affords a hilarious picture of one of their first "at homes": 'Yesterday
Amy & I were in Richmond all morning— at noon Mr. Thelwall came— that faithful
chip of the Clifton past, giving the pedigrees of all his friendships & a few <u>mots</u>— A
Catholic lady once quoted "sufficient unto the day is the evil thereof— as Lord Byron
says" As soon as he is gone Mr. Lupton brings his daughter— his fierce eyes in her
face— & asks her to recite. Recitation always alarms my laughter—it holds its sides
with panic— When the panther drew closer to the recreant Indian Civil Servant, who
had betrayed the heart of his comrade's chosen One, a volcano of terror & laughter
all but opened from the depths of me. I expected Michael to rush into the room with
the family bowie-knife.' Henry continues 'Today in the gray autumnal heat we have
both written for the first time— Michael a sonnet to me on Farewell--- I am proud
indeed that the little white Sun-Room has heard my praise before that of any god—'
(ZJN 93ab). Vale! (*ICT: Farewell!*), which possibly began as a farewell to Durdans,
thus became another tribute from aunt to niece. The poem was published in WILD
HONEY, WDH 168 and became one of Henry's special favourites (ZKD 90a).

There are: One autograph has the variant incipit *There are, & tedious is their faith
who say* (OVQ 67b).

Levin

All common joys of common days we miss,
As those banned Afric rocks where travellers trace
Continuously the tortured lightning's race,
That feel but storm and wind— nor any kiss
Of dew at secret in their crevices,
With leaf or shooting fibre or the grace
And tinct of verdure creeping o'er the place;
But keep their station where the lightning is,
Exposed and evermore to be assailed.
Thus, O my God, the life about the head
I love— my life! Thy levin hath not failed
To sear, and then hot-breathed to sear again.
So of a face most gentle it is said
That all its record is the brand of pain.

Both *Old Ivories* and *Vale!* were originally part of *The Longer Allegiance* cycle.

T0890   This fine italian sonnet, known from at least five autographs, was written by Michael *Richmond August 20th 1899* (ZJN 96a). The original title was *Abnormal* (OVU 39b). It was also composed as part of the sequence *The Longer Allegiance*, numbered at one point XLV (OVQ 68b), but placed eventually at XXII when published in WILD HONEY, WDH 158. The content of the sonnet however indicates that Michael's thoughts are less with James than with Henry; she, after all, was her aunt's longest allegiance. Michael had written in the Journal 'It is August 20th now— ten years since the Mother One rose up to God— ... Storm after storm has burst over us— fever, & love-fever, disillusion & loss...— we have left Durdans: we are colonists,—...' (ZJN 94b). The actual trigger for the poem, as often, was a chance remark by Ricketts. Henry picks up the tale: 'On Friday 18th night the Artists come to see the Japanese lilies & our satinwood tables. Ricketts perched like a fairy man on our rose-patterned divan-cushion, sitting on it as if it were the top of a toadstool with his small hands round his knees. When we spoke of our troubles he said we reminded him of rocks in West Africa round wh: the lightnings play for ever, so that there is not a trace of vegetation on them' (ZJN 96b). Michael, repeating the tale, decides 'Well, we must get a little moss & a saxifrage' (ZJN 94b). Ricketts's sobriquet was to stick— though he would become more usually known as *Fay* (sa *Balsam*, T0891: and the second note to *An Enchanter*, T0988).

Levin:	Lightning.
we miss:	Michael at first wrote *I miss* (OVU,ZJN).
tinct:	tint, a tinge or slight colouring.
That feel:	The Journal draft has *That feel no winds at all, nor any kiss.*
record:	One autograph reads *That its sole record* (OVU).
brand:	See the final note to *Sanctuary*, T0879.

Leaves

Where are they? I have never missed before
The whole wide kingdom of the cherishing leaves,
Or waft, or drifted into golden heaves
With all their scents, or dead upon the floor!
We left at sundown; but shall see no more
The air a film of multitudinous leaves;
For, lo, a sudden ravishing bereaves
The air that threaded them, the earth that bore!
And now of all their gorgeous, solemn realms
No sign: of unseen arrows came their fall;
They are not. Clematis and ivy curl
Their wavering tissues on the river wall—
Nothing afloat: the river a dark pearl;
The jagged acacia and the misted elms.

T0895   On Sunday 19 November 1899 Michael wrote in the Journal 'Suddenly,
         the beauty has vanished. The air is no longer full of golden leaves. The
         river is a very dark pearl. Never before have I missed the leaves. Even
children miss the flowers; & the harvests we all miss. But the wide, wide populations
of the leaves, so innocent, so fostering, so gay in growing-time, & in their falling
melancholy but without complaint.— I feel the passing of their kingdom as never
before. And the winter days are rather stern here' (ZJN 122b). Some three weeks
later she began work on the new poem. The Journal drafts, all in Michael's hand,
are untitled and run to four pages (ZJN 131a-2b); there are at least three variants
(for example OVU 45b) of the middle six verses v5-10 which experiment with the
italian octave rhyme scheme, and one departure (v.i.). One full draft has the
subscript *Dec 7th 1899* (ZJN 131b) and the next Journal date is the 9th (H ZJN
133a); so the final draft was most probably written within this interval.

A loose Oxford autograph has the title, and a subscript *1900 To C.H.S.* (OYR 2),
which relates to Michael's Journal entry for 05 January 1900: 'On Friday afternoon I
leave 2 Sonnets— "O white, o lovely lilac, o profound" *(ICT: T0894)* for C.R. & 'The
whole, wide Kingdom of the cherishing leaves" for C.H.S. I run fleetly away, leaving
housekeeper Marie with a burning face, as if from the glow of a guest-lunch' (ZJO
3a). Michael had made the Painters a similar gift of a pair of sonnets in 1898
(T0861-2). Other Oxford autographs place the sonnet in *The Longer Allegiance*
sequence, but in WILD HONEY it was transferred to the *Mane et Vespere* section,
WDH 112. Other memorable leaf poems include T0806, T0858 and T1663.

We left: One variant v5-10 (ZJN 131a) draws further on the original prose:

> *It is most natural that we should weep*
> *The summer flowers snatched by the scythe away,*
> *Or linger where the sorrel fell asleep*
> *Hush in her crevice: but the leaves should stay*
> *And very slowly yield their solemn realms.*
> *This year by unseen arrows came their fall*

acacia: 'The servants find the outlook on to the jagged acacia, & the misted elms uncomfortable. "In London" I growl, "all the maids see is the feet of the passers-by"' (M ZJN 123a).

To my Queen   Christmas Day 1899

'Day of humiliation' cries the priest,
Of our quick sins we must be shriven clean.
But thou, amidst thy mourners, sit'st a queen,
Giving God praise. Not fearing in the least
Thy people's stubbornness & pride decreast,
Looking across the darkness that hath been,
By the moving Fire that marshalled thee, serene,
Humble & confident, thou keep'st the feast,
Thy soldiers' children round thee. O most wise,
The glory of the years not yet in sight
Is on thy visage; thou dost feel the swell
And rush of empire under Southern skies,
And dwellest with us, not in fading light,
Strong dawn upon thee, incorruptible.

T0896   Known only from a Journal draft (ZJN 138b) and a fair copy (ZKF 135o), here we have the public face of Michael. It might almost be a Laureate sonnet: Henry called it 'Miltonic' (ZJN 139b). Certainly one for the blue-rinse Conservative chairwoman swathed in a Union Jack and declaiming "Many's the battle been fought under this grand old Flag!" The second Boer war was 10 weeks old. Michael too could be appallingly, mindlessly, jingoistic (see T0907). MacDonald, covering the Ladysmith fighting for the *Argus*, saw the reality: "In Natal war was divested of absolutely everything that once lent it meretricious glamour—..just plain primeval killing, without redemption..." Battles indeed are at the back of the poem. On 10 December, the start of 'Black Week' heralded a series of unmitigated disasters (at Stormberg, Magersfontein and Colenso). And the British losses continued. In the New Year Michael would pen other 'war-sonnets'; *A Lament*, T0898 and *Ladysmith*, T0907 (sa T0899).

the priest: Bums in the air were advocated by, amongst others, a Rear Admiral, C.B.; at least one correspondent however protested against this "whining cry" and "the cowardly, pagan course of fawning on the God of Battles" (letters to *The Times*, 18 and 21 December).
moving Fire: Presumably Victoria seen as Moses, Exodus XIII 21.
confident: On 18 December the 80 year old Queen famously rallied Arthur Balfour "we are not interested in the possibilities of defeat."
Thy soldiers':   Her command that every man receive a tin box of chocolate that Christmas is easily derided; yet the records prove genuine concern.
children: On Boxing Day Victoria would give a tea for the wives and children of the Windsor troops. "Everyone helped to serve them, including my family.. It was a very touching sight, when one thinks of the poor husbands and fathers, .. some of whom may not return."

146

Mood

As God creating did not yet create,
But, quickened in His spirit, moving stood,
And felt the light, and saw that it was good
Before the lesser lights, before the great
Were fashioned, not impatient to relate
The open, clear befalling of His mood,
So dwell I in the Muses' neighbourhood,
And in the infinite soft chaos wait.
More and yet more of sights, of scents that move,
More of that silent joy about the head,
The undisturbed beholding ere the hour,
More of that resting with the dawn outspread,
The assured, the tranquil vagueness of a flower
That Time has never seen the opening of!

T0901   'Henry is on a wave of inspiration such as he has not known since the
          great year of the Trilogy— 96.' So Michael wrote in the Journal on the
          evening of 08 February 1900 (ZJO 21a). The autograph of *Mood*
follows, in her hand, on the next page; it bears an epigraph *Septuagesima Sunday
February 11th* (ZJO 22b). The following entry clearly reveals the background. 'I write
this sonnet, but Henry is busy with the great Flood Scene Act IV of Deirdre (*ICT:
DEIRDRE would be published by Sturge Moore in 1918*). She comes to me & says
that it is finished. Before lunch I take Whym on the towing-path. — There is the
stationary snow on the banks, the river a great, swirling current, a west wind with
knives under its cruel feathers. After lunch I grow ill— .. But we wrap in furs & hot
water bottles & sleep— then I demand the great Flood scene— As she reads, the
great old days return; it is as when the Mother's eyes kindled over the Father's
tragedy (*a reference to Emma Cooper and the play of that name, sa T0219*). Three
years ago, on a Yorkshire moor, I listened to a scene like this— It was in Julia
Domna (*the final play of the Roman trilogy*). There is no longer question of diction,
or passages, or art— but the jangle & dissonance of life. I am doing well to stand
aside, & let the young dramatist swirl on to the end ... After reading the scene Henry
is violently sick: we touch no supper' (ZJO 22-3).

Oxford holds three other autographs, and the poem was eventually published in
WILD HONEY, WDH 94.

creating: Genesis I 1-3.
Muses: See last note to *Long Ago VI*, T0311.

147

Ladysmith

Yea, for a third time toward our leaguered men
Devon's slow-hearted son doth slowly reach,
From day to day forcing the sullen breach:
And guns are flashed, & guns flash back again,
The darkness thunders & is heard. But when
The two great companies of English speech
Clash up in one exultant uproar, then
Who prophesy from venom-lips, who preach
Shall be as impish shadows backward beat
By the widening day home to their smoke of hell. —
So with the fourth fierce onslaught it befell;
Slowly through labyrinthine hills of flame
On, through his dead, avenging them he came:
And the great anthem surges up the street.

T0907   Michael took an active interest in the early stages of the second
Boer war, often including news clippings in the Journal. On 13
February she replied to a letter from Amy Bell. 'Calmly I go on
writing my war-sonnets (*ICT: sa T0896,8-9*)— one on "the two great companies of
English speech (Buller, White & their armies) clashing up together. Neither shall their
failure to fulfil that poetic behest damage the sonnet, because they are doing greater
than popular things. Amy, it is good to feel even the little errand-boys, Yea, even the
grocers'-assistants (after all the cocoa-smelling "assistants" are Englishmen) have a
chance now of living, being wounded in their bodies, not their "susceptibilities",
learning something about dying, & being born again. I rejoice' (ZJO 23-4). On 01
March: 'I am in the street— ..the news "Ladysmith is relieved." Home to Henry, but
already cannon are speaking it— And the parish bells break through the air. We
have not lived through such a great day before: .. London's citizens are singing
together the National Anthem. .. In the afternoon I go forth to get ribbons for the
dogs.' She even sewed a tricolour favour into the Journal (ZJO 33ab).

The garrison town of Ladysmith was besieged for 118 days after the rout of Sir
George White's Natal Field Force on 'Mournful Monday' (30 October 1899).
General Sir Redvers Buller, British Commander-in-Chief, failed in his first attempt at
relief on 15 December, at another disaster (the Colenso offensive). Lord Roberts of
Kandahar was brought in to replace him. Buller suffered an even worse defeat in
January at Spion Kop and 10 days later failed again. He was now known as 'Sir
Reverse Buller'. His fourth attempt (28 February) succeeded. There are two Journal
drafts of Michael's patriotic piece, a ten verse sketch on 09 February (ZJO 21b), and
the completion 23 days later, with title and an epigraph *Begun morning of Friday,
February 9th 1900 Completed morning of Sunday, March 4th 1900* (ZJO 34b).

impish shadows: The original sketch paused *Shall be as impish shadows blown
aside / In their smoke of hell by the pure, widening day.*

Gifts

How huge is passion, & how ill-content!
Four odours in one garland blent—
Keen, cold, a seraph's blossom-rod,
A fresh-torn fruit, a fragrant turf,
A flower as if salt ocean's surf,
Wrested by gales, awhile had pined
On trembling earth beside the seas,
On earth that was a grave: all these
Wild wreaths he left for me, all these—
O Saint, for gifts thou hast no mind:
Thou wilt have nothing but thy God.

T0910   As March turned to April, Henry had a bout of illness. This occasioned
         a gift of flowers from Ricketts. Michael made a Journal entry dated
         31 March: 'Ricketts brings flowers— violets, lilies, fresias &
mignonette— the four great scents— brings them to my sick fellow' (ZJO 43b). The
first draft of the poem, in Michael's hand *but in the voice of Henry*, is dated *April 4
1900* (ZJO 45a). There follows a reworking of the same material in *Henry's* hand
(T0911). Michael copied out the first version (untitled) into an Oxford notebook,
where it appears as the second of a group *In Persian Gardens* (curiously, this has
joined for *pined* in v6, OVX 13b); to add to the fun, she also copied out the second
version (dated *From April 4th to 15th 1900*) in a different book with the same overall
title (OWE 7b). Henry later unambiguously states 'Michael has written.... some
strange, new-moulded little poems— In Persian Gardens' (ZJO 182b). Which would
seem (despite the sense of v9-11) to settle the matter of authorship; but the poem is
a prime example of the pitfalls inherent in dismembering Michael Field.

How huge: Michael's first draft opens more simply—
                        How huge is passion, ill-content!   (ZJO 45a)
Four odours: On a visit the previous October 'Ricketts conversed on <u>Smell</u>, & how
                intense & enjoyable the difference is between the dead leaves at the
                feet of the different trees in spring... Shannon has the English
                suspicion that any smell in a room is a <u>stink</u> & dangerous. Whereas,
                even many strong odours in small quantities are delightful' (H ZJN
                115b). See also *Sirenusa* (T1177).
blent: Henry's version of the middle section of the poem runs:
                        There are four odours: one is as a rind
                        Of fresh-torn fruit; one is a surfy breeze;
                        One pierces as a seraph's blossom-rod;
                            And one is as a sod
                        From Earth that is a grave. ....   (T0911, v2-6)
for me: This must be Henry.
O Saint: Presumably Michael: 'It is all one to me; flowers from him may give
                pleasure not instead of him—' (M ZJO 43b).

Dying

There was a dawn when it befell
My loved one drooped to die;
Parting was by— O strange to tell!—
Parting was close, and there was no farewell.
    But the grey face forlorn
Slowly took on the sober shades of dawn,
    And the slow breath
Heaved solitary from the airless coasts of Death.

T0922   Henry had been alarmingly ill in Dresden in 1891; now in June 1900 her health suddenly and dramatically broke down again. On Monday 25 June Michael confided to the Journal 'After a month's gravest illness Henry is convalescing upstairs... the doctor told me— it was rheumatic fever pure & simple— ... —As for our little home, it is just frame-work for Henry; & in the gold-room & in the sun-room I sit, staring at the hole where the canvas has been cut out.' By midweek, 'I feel parting close; but there is no farewell': the poem draft follows (ZJO 78-9). The Oxford fair copy has a full footnote *July 1st Sunday III after Trinity: the first red lily unfolds* (OVX 20b). Anticipation of Henry's imminent demise, as usual, proved to be premature. The poem appeared in WILD HONEY, WDH 175.

drooped: Both Journal draft and Oxford fair copy read *came*; only at the proof stage (OWL 170), Henry (?) made this magical alteration.

airless coasts: Though the poem is by Michael, it seems likely Henry had a verbal input. In December she wrote: 'My illness was a marvellous time— love was close by me through all agony;... Tremendous pain has a spaciousness of its own— then those gray coasts I beheld were of shadowed magnitude, & I gladly came back...' (H ZJO 182ab).

T0927   This unpublished italian sonnet occurs in three autographs. One, untitled and undated, has a dedication to Ricketts; someone has added the pencil note *Persephone speaks of the Pomegranate seeds she ate and will confine her for the 3 Winter Months* (OYR 12o). The other Oxford autograph has a title *Proserpina*, and the footnote *Forest: summer* (OVX 25b); both are in Michael's hand. The third autograph is also undated, a draft in the 1900 Journal apparently composed over the bank holiday 06 August. This is in the hand of Henry, with two afterthoughts; however she adds the footnote *Michael* (ZJO 102a). All this is specially interesting as the whole Persephone/Demeter sequence of pieces offers a teasing slant on the Henry/Michael fellowship; much uninformed academic mileage could be obtained from viewing this piece as Henry's work, particularly v10-11. However, it is quite certain this is indeed Michael's work, and another promising thesis must be consigned to the trashcan. Michael's Journal entry on the previous page reads: 'I want to write of passion that is remote,— a long, long way off, & yet so hurting, & so alive. Proserpine holds me in her homesickness for the shades' (ZJO 101b). This is even more apparent in *Domina* (T0928), a sonnet

150

Proserpine

Yea, but I grieve not I did pluck & eat
In that bowed orchard nigh to Acheron;
The long six months are slowly drawing on,
More slow to him in hell. Ah, darksome seat,
Lone King, narcissus-crowned:- he did entreat
For Enna's flowers, my flowers; & I am gone!
The ghosts look for their judgment, one by one
Listless he censures. All the fields of wheat
Were soured & whitened when my mother sought—
My mother sleeps beside me comforted,
And yet I am not hers, thanks to these red
Small seeds I feel the graunch of in my teeth:
With each of them a priceless month was bought;
I am his; I hasten to his realm beneath.

that *was* published (WDH 92). Here speaks no clinging aunt— nor rebellious niece
for that matter; it is *Michael* who aches as Persephone. One wonders, considering
the attribution in OYR, whether Ricketts is subconsciously cast as Hades.

Demeter, goddess of crops, swears to Zeus the earth will remain barren until and
unless her daughter is returned to her, and Zeus rules that his brother must release
Persephone— provided that she has not eaten or drunk in the Underworld. All seems
set for her freedom, when Hades's odd-job man Ascalaphus says he has seen her
eat seven seeds of a pomegranate she picked in the King's orchard (the number of
seeds varies from 'a few' to 'a single one' in different accounts). As a result,
Persephone may spend the months of growth and harvest in the upper world, but
must return to the Kingdom of Hades for the rest of the year (germination). By this
delightful story the Greeks accounted for the annual renewal of the seasons.
Demeter turned Ascalaphus into a short-eared owl for his sneaky behaviour.

Proserpine:	Or Proserpina; the Roman equivalent of Persephone. Proserpina occurs fleetingly in Henry's *The God of Silence* (T0969), and her abduction is the starting point of Michael's *Enna's Cave* (T0877). Henry wrote about Demeter in drafts now at Oxford, (T0963,5); sa 'Demetia' in T0333.
Acheron:	See the third note to *Acheron*, T0286.
Lone King:	One Oxford draft reads *Of my dark King, white-garlanded with sweet / Narcissus-flowers, ...* (OVX 25b).
narcissus:	By tradition the last flower gathered by Persephone before her enravishment by Hades. It is sacred to both Hades and Demeter.
Enna:	See the first note to *Enna's Cave*, T0877.
graunch:	Crush and grind, as in 'scrunch'; a word peculiarly Henry's (as in *Delphica*, T0955). For more on the seeds , see *Pomegranates*, T1635.
month:	The original (deleted) word is *boon*. Henry adds a footnote which could be read as a fifteenth verse: *And love, of my lone King.* (ZJO 102a).

151

Amethyst

It was a day most marvellous & fair,
Nor yet one glory of it had he missed,
But all the precious stones caught in the air,
The topaz, beryl, last the amethyst
I found repeated in his countenance,
As in a landscape that is growing dun
Sweet glimpses of the sundown still enhance,
And breeze, & dew, & passing of the sun.
O Nature, not for woman is thy treasure,
Thy moonlight, nor thy pearl-light in the shell;
For woman can but match them in her measure,
Snow to their golden snows assorting well:
But man doth take these fair hues borne along,
Receive, & give them back as in a song.

T0950   Ricketts visited Paragon on 15 December. Michael recorded in the Journal:
'Last night the Fairy man called. He had been walking by the river under a
Basaite* sky. The mother o' pearl lights that had waked him, & all the
precious stones in the air of that marvellous yesterday were repeated in his
countenance. He looked profoundly handsome. He & Henry talked art. I watched,
from my bundle by the fire. Mary° had chosen a good part; it was not taken away
from her' (ZJO 169ab). *(!CT: *probably Basanite, a velvet-black touchstone used for
trying the purity of gold; °Luke X 42)*. The english sonnet, in her hand, follows
immediately, dated *Dec 16th. 3rd Sunday in Advent* (ZJO 169b); there is one other
autograph, also dated and in her hand, in an Oxford autograph (OVX 50b). The
poem was never published until now.

topaz: A fluorine aluminium silicate which is commonly yellow or colourless.
beryl: Beryllium aluminium silicate, occurring in a variety of coloured gemstones
such as aquamarine (pale blue-green), emerald (deep green), heliodor
(golden yellow), and morganite (pink).
amethyst: A manganese-bearing quartz which produces clear purple or violet
gemstones believed to protect the wearer from drunkenness.

Motley

His wit was favoured & of happy clime:
He dreamed & mocked his dreams that with more ease
And flagrance of defying he might please,
Setting youth's chronicle to vulgar rhyme.
Benign & dazzling, of full folly's prime,
He led the mummers, yet, as none of these,
He was of the high places, & a breeze
Set from him of the hill-sides & the thyme.
He loved to lead the choir, &, when he fell,
Still loving music of his ear, he needs
Must cry for music to the church that leads
Its train of ritual o'er the fated world:
We look down to the abysm where he was hurled;
And plant our comfort in the God of Hell.

T0951 As in the parallel cases of the sonnets to Sturge Moore (*The Poet*,
T0986) and to Santayana (*One of the Wise*, T1130), the individual at
the heart of this poem is not immediately obvious. The approximate
date of composition— late December 1900— is however a telling clue, abundantly
elaborated by Journal entries at the beginning of the month: Oscar Wilde, newly
dead in Paris, is the man in motley. Michael was at work on the sonnet over a period
of time, and the many surviving Oxford sketches (as OPO 21ab, OVX 51ab) show
that she experienced her usual problems with the sestet. This Journal fair copy,
perhaps the best, still shows her indecision in that the sestet appears in two versions
(ZJO 170a); probably at least one reason why the poem was never published. The
matter all seems to stem from Henry's prose musings (ZKF 142). Wilde makes
scattered appearances more than once in the run of the Journals. They met him in
July 1890; 'Edith said I looked so "radiantly comfortable" while talking to him, she
refused to interrupt our conversation. He is indeed delightful in converse— not
profound, but touching "profondeurs" with swallow-wings. And he is ironical in a
delicious, persistent way' (M ZCD 53r-4o). Michael Field even visited the Wildes in
the following June (ZJD 54b-5a)— and was snubbed the June after that 'When he
shows himself as a <u>snob</u> he is disgustingly repulsive' (H ZJE 98b). This may in part
have accounted for a later disenchantment (ZJM 18b, ZJT 29ab). Ricketts, as ever,
was a source of anecdote (ZJO 165-8). A handful of letters is extant (sa MFC).

Motley: A Shakespearian clown, or his particoloured garment.
mummers: Masqueraders, actors in a dumb show; it is unlikely that the elegant
             sophisticate Wilde would have found any of these allusions flattering.
thyme: 'In work in life there was, spite of all his degeneracies, a breeziness of
             high places— yes, even a breath of thyme' (H ZJO 163a).
choir: Michael also experimented with a coarser *chorus-noise* (as OSQ 161o).
church: Wilde apparently turned Catholic *in extremis* (newsprint clipping, ZJO
             162b). The *train of ritual* would also prove irresistible to Michael Field.

The God of Silence

Who should be worshipped on these days
That idle February fulfil?
For Flora has no tassels yet,
No daisy roses; she is still
A weanling child that seldom plays:
Adonis, by his death the pet
Of Tyrus, now is fast asleep:
Proserpina doth quite forget
The fields that buried her so deep.

And yet there is a god about,
With spell upon him, young as Love,
Naked and pleasant, of a mien
To brightly whiten clouds above,
And through the gardens in and out
To flush the pulse and lentils green.
Oft in a rain shower, by the side
Of silvering streams, his form is seen
Past the sad fishermen to glide.

Who is the stripling— mitre-crowned
Of Egypt, and his mitre-points
As two rich buds of persea tree
The deep, concealing gum anoints?
The horn he shoulders— why enwound
With persea, sacred persea tree—
A horn full-heaped with all he dreams
The earth will bring forth plenteously,
When leaves start out and April beams?

His wings are Cupid's, but his hand
No torch nor arrow tempts to harm;
His finger on his mouth is laid
As to the centre of his charm:
For 'tis his silence, young and bland,
We feel in every patient glade,
A silence, not the sleep of night,
But silence, store of bounty, planned
By Isis for the world's delight:

And he, her son, we must adore
Before the powers of spring are come—
Harpocrates, his mother's woe,
And ever from his cradle dumb;
The wondrous, little god she bore
To dead Osiris, by the flow
Of wintry Nile— yet pledge to man
She might not, though in grief brought low,
On spring or harvest lay a ban.

He has no altar but our hearts,
As mute as the sown fields are mute;
No greeting but free breath: our eyes
Behold him as a soundless lute,
That by its aphony imparts
Dear promise of gold harmonies.
We love him while Adonis sleeps,
While Flora for a daisy cries,
While Proserpine in darkness keeps.

T0969   We know that this poem was written by Henry sometime in late January
1901; verse 2 must be taken literally. On 30 January Michael wrote in
the Journal 'Henry is looking very young & pretty & has written a handful
of poems— the latest of rare charm about Harpo-crates, the little Egyptian god of
silence' (ZJP 20b). A single undated Oxford autograph in Henry's hand survives
(OWL 51-4). The poem was published in WILD HONEY (WDH 47-9). Though named
as Harpocrates, it is patently clear this is an Egyptian God— in fact it is Horus, the
falcon-headed sungod whose eyes are the sun and moon: it was the Greeks who
knew him as Harpokrates, and pictured him with his finger to his mouth.

Flora: See the third note to T0457,MAS.
Adonis: Another vegetation god, with many of the characteristics of Osiris.
pulse: Leguminous plants such as peas, beans— and indeed, the lentil!
persea: A sacred 'tree of life' in Egypt and Persia, now equated with the avocado.
horn: The cornucopia; yet it was the dead Adonis who was supposed to return to
earth (and the arms of Aphrodite) each springtime.
Osiris: Osiris and his twin sister Isis were an item; their brother Set killed Osiris by
enticing him into a chest which he then threw in the Nile. The chest
washed up in the papyrus swamps, where Isis found it. Set, not to be
outdone, tore the body of Osiris into fourteen pieces, and hid them all
over Egypt. Isis managed to find all the pieces except the tadger, which
had been eaten by fishes. She resuscitated Osiris using enchantments, and
with, in the circumstances, astonishing ingenuity, conceived Horus, who
eventually killed Set. But in the battle his left eye (the moon) was injured,
which accounts for the the lunar cycle. Osiris is the god of resurrection.
aphony: Voicelessness.

Penetration

I love thee; never dream that I am dumb:
By day, by night, my tongue besiegeth thee,
As a bat's voice, set in too fine a key,
Too tender in its circumstance to come
To ears beset by havoc and harsh hum
Of the arraigning world; yet secretly
I may attain: lo, even a dead bee
Dropt sudden from thy open hand by some
Too careless wind is laid among thy flowers,
Dear to thee as the bees that sing and roam:
Thou watchest when the angry moon drops foam;
Thou answerest the faun's soft-footed stare;
No influence, but thou feelest it is there,
And drawest it, profound, into thy hours.

T0982   One of 'Michael's perfect Pan-sonnets' (H ZJP 176ab) written in May
         1901 and included by the 23rd in Fit I of her masque *SILENCE AND
         MUSIC* (ZJP 70ab sa T1012). It appears in two typescripts of the
masque (OWB 12,OWC 15), and there are also two undated autographs, both in
Michael's hand (OVY 8b,OWG 39b). It was eventually published in WILD HONEY,
WDH 13. Michael herself directly compared it with T0333 (q.v.): 'the one is a small
lyric cry— the other something more of the universe— a new star that quietly takes
rank with other stars' (ZJQ 75b). Sturge Moore ensured the masque context was not
lost, when he added the epigraph *(Syrinx to Pan)* to his own reprint (SMF 59).

fine a key: Angela Leighton comments "Pan must have his Syrinx, or rather, Syrinx
               her Pan. ... Even if such poetry does not always speak overtly for the
               cause of woman, it always speaks, 'secretly', in a woman's voice
               which, like Syrinx's, penetrates by its different 'key'" (FAL 241-2).
arraigning: Accusing, calling to account.
dead bee: Syrinx may be addressing Pan, but it seems clear Michael is thinking of
               Ricketts; on Friday May 10 she wrote in the Journal 'Painter gives me a
               dead bumble bee— found frozen at Kew Gardens. "We have kept the
               little chap ever since"' (M ZJP 67b). Michael still remembered this
               strange gift six years later (see the final note to T0001,MAS).
sudden from: Both typescripts read *sudden in*, and *thine hours* at verse 14.
thy flowers: "Ricketts had once placed a dead bee among some flowers he had
               given them" (Delaney, VCR 25).

156

Gabriel's Wand

Mother of Heaven, throw down thy lily-rod!
The stars are thine: to this thou hast no right.
Once it was bowed to thee in all its white,
But Gabriel held it, messenger of God.

It was his pure caduceus, fledged with plumes
Of seraphim; & his great wings were pale
Against them. Queen of Heaven, this white is male,
And of a strength no womanhood assumes.

Young & austere, full-dusted, fiercely still
In pureness, the fresh lilies bow to thee,
Maid-Mother of star-tremulous purity.

They kept the rigour of devoted will,
While thou wert sore afraid beholding them,
And how they swept thy feet with virile stem.

T0990   A *sonnet libre* in Michael's hand— although the underlying premise is
Henry's. There is a single undated autograph (OWl 5b), but both
internal and external evidence indicate a date of composition
somewhere in early June 1901. On June 1st Henry recorded in the Journal:
'Gardener made a hedge of lilies on the rim of our balcony. They are of the Song of
Solomon; we stand among them. The virility of their pureness is such we feel they
are for Gabriel's hand & not Mary's. Their youth & austerity combine with the glister
of heavenly feathers. The line of their long heads is stretched over the stream as it
goes past them' (ZJP 75a). At the end of 1903 there is another entry: 'Maeterlinck
has joined me in the contention that the tall white lily is male. Maeterlinck speaks of
it as "the authentic Prince ...whose nobility dates back to the Gods themselves, the
immemorial lily, who raises his ancient sceptre, august, inviolate, wh: creates around
it a zone of chastity, silence & light"' (H ZJR 196b). Lilies appear again in T0992-3.

Gabriel: Perhaps the paramount archangel: his name translates as *God has
shown Himself mighty*, with the mystical significance that where the
messenger is, there God is fully present (Exodus III 2-4). He is alleged
to have talked with Daniel (Daniel VIII-IX), and also with Zacharias and
his wife's cousin Mary (Luke I 11-38); and, as *Jibril*, to have dictated
the *Qur'ān* to Muhammad.
caduceus: Hermes' staff of office, a garlanded olive branch with two shoots,
carried as symbol of peace; later the shoots became wings, and the
garlands two facing coiled serpents (sa T0455 v2-3; note to T0281).
seraphim: See T1253, note 4.
feet: The first choice (then deleted) was *stool*.

157

A Living Altar

Silence behind the colonnade of pines
Is built a temple hidden by their boles:
Below the unlit, grassy hillside rolls
Its pathway space, and where its slope declines

Sits an old fox, as in Rome's Forum sat
The central wolf. Dim 'mid the solitude,
Its sombre, tutelary image rude,
He concentrates the forest round his plat.

But, as our presence reaches to him, lo,
He trots away with outstretched tail, with spring
Of his spare paws to bramble covering:

While we, blank, superstitious, see him go,
And, our eyes fixed upon the way he clove,
Watch a religion fall, a shrine remove.

T0995 A *sonnet libre*, probably the work of Michael; there are two surviving autographs, one in each hand. Michael's fair copy has the date *July 19th, 1901* with the sestet in both an early draft and the final version (OWI 10ab). Henry had recorded in the Journal on Sunday July 14 'Behind the shafts of the fir-trees silence is built like a temple— on a green space in front sits an old fox— the deity of the loneliness, as the wolf was of Forum & Senate-house. He is motionless as if for ritual, his dignity signalises the sanctuary. ..It is like the fall of a religion to see him perceive us & trot off from his sacred sward with outstretched tail & a leap of spare paws. He was the most necessary thing I had seen in the Forest, for he gave it a rude shrine. I shall never forget him' (ZJP 94-5). And again 'That old solemn fox, the inhabitant of Silence' (ZJP 95a, sa OCH 61b). The following July, a return visit rekindled memories of 'where the old fox sat to be venerated...' (H ZJQ 120b). In the long, probably ultimately futile, arguments on attribution, this sonnet is a good example of what can be at stake. If the thoughts are Henry's, but the metrical rendering Michael's, how indeed can the 'flower' be 'plucked asunder'? The poem was eventually published in WILD HONEY, WDH 64.

wolf: Possibly the famous 6th/7th century BCE Etruscan bronze now in the Capitoline museum; the site of the cave in which the she-wolf purportedly suckled Romulus & Remus, the founders of Rome, is lost.
Dim: The draft has *dun* (OWI 10b).
tutelary: Having a spiritual guardianship, in the sense of a *genius loci*.
plat: A *plot* of ground, here with overtones of territory.
clove: Went, possibly also in the sense of dividing the undergrowth.

Noon

Strength of the world, O Noon, strange things are done
'Neath thy prepollence, when the fir-spines bake
A rare feast for our nostrils, and the snake
With yellow-fleckered body courts the sun,

Till all its reptile's blood is ichor-flame,
And it becomes at once and for the hour
A Prince of Heaven. We receive thy power
As if the hands of some gigantic frame

Beneath our arms lifted us up on high,
Till we breathe sun-rays and our feet are hot,
And space and shadows are remembered not.

There are two moments of Earth's wizardry,
Moonlight and noon: one female, of dread lure;
And one in crisis giant-like, blazing, pure.

T0996   Here we have a situation identical with that of T0995; another *sonnet libre*, and two autographs, one in each hand. But whereas Henry's *A Living Altar* fair copy was part of a shared task for WILD HONEY (OWL 71b), in this case it is an undated manuscript for her own collection DEDICATED (OWQ 47b). Michael's copy has annotations at v8,11 in her niece's hand, and the footnote *Henry: Friday 19th 1901* (OWI 11b). We know Michael could— and did— write a *sonnet libre* (as T0997); but this poem must be Henry's work. The month was July. Henry wrote in the Journal *(ICT: the 18th/?19th)* 'At Noon To feel round one the shadow of the woods! It tempers the heat & yet through it come spaces of open sunlight, where the spines bake a feast for the nostrils & the yellow-fleckered snake lies with his cold reptile-blood in flame' (ZJP 98b). The following summer, returning to the forest, she remembered 'where the snake lay roasting on spines as on embers' (ZJQ 120b). The poem was published in DEDICATED, DDD 95.

prepollence: Predominance, superior power.
reptile's blood: The snake, like other poikilothermic ('cold-blooded') beasts, can only achieve maximum activity by basking. The possibility of an independence from ambient temperatures (homoiothermy, or 'warm-bloodedness'), now thought by some to have occurred first in certain of the dinosaurs, was a crucial evolutionary step.
ichor-flame: Ichor was the name given by the Greeks to the ethereal fluid that flowed in the veins of their gods: nothing so common as blood.
gigantic: Michael's copy reads *Herculean*, amended thus by her niece.
And space: Michael has *And fear;* Henry changed the whole line:
              Severed a space from every shadow-plot.   (OWI 11b)
dread lure: A reference to the malevolent powers of Artemis.

A Kiss

The fury of a creature when it drips
Wet-fanged, and thirsty with the desert dust,
The clench in battle of a sword that must
Ravish the foe, the pang of finger-tips—
Joy of a captain in recovered ships,
Joy, verity of a long-buried lust
Delightsome to the flesh, is in the thrust
Toward Absalom of the king's tarried lips.
And, lo, beneath that awful benison,
A thief's face glittered, sniffing at the gems
Of the bent crown as they were cassia-stems;
While the young ears heard but the rolling on
Of chariots, and a tumult, broke amain
By rumour of an agèd monarch slain.

T1001   This, the first and perhaps best known of a curious group of 'Royal
          Sonnets', drips decadence. It could have come from *The Yellow
          Book*, and certainly demands the illustrative pen of an Aubrey
Beardsley. The epithet 'Royal' refers to the fact that the sonnets centre on events in II
Samuel, and King David. Only *Listening* (T1005) is drawn actually from Kings. *A Kiss*
was published in WILD HONEY, WDH 127, and has been reprinted several times,
most recently in Dilworth's anthology (AID, 1945). On 31 July 1901 Henry recorded
'Michael finishes the splendid David & Absalom sonnet'; the poem draft follows in a
page in Michael's hand, with the further footnote *the Forest* (ZJP 105a-6b).

A Kiss: An Oxford typescript bears the written epigraph *II Samuel XV [ICT:
                 XIV] 33* (OWD 91b); Sturge Moore adds an appropriate one of his
                 own, *David's reconciliation with Absalom* (SMF 105).
lust: Possibly an allusion to Jonathan, and *I Samuel XX 41*, one of those
                 inconvenient verses from "holy" writ *chers pères* prefer not to gloss.
Absalom: The third and favourite son of David. He fled after contriving the
                 murder of David's eldest son, his half-brother Amnon— who had
                 raped Absalom's sister, Tamar (II Samuel XIII). David eventually was
                 persuaded to recall him: this is the moment luridly conjured in the
                 sonnet. Absalom later almost succeeded in seizing the crown, but in
                 the event it was he, not the 'agèd monarch', who was slain (v14).
sniffing: The Journal draft has *snuffing*.
cassia-stems: From the 'Chinese cinnamon', *Cinnamomum cassia*, of the family
                 Lauraceae. The powdered bark has an aroma reminiscent of
                 cinnamon; *cassia* was a metaphor for opulence. In the resplendent
                 words of the Duchess of Malfi (Act IV ii 216-8),
                 *What would it pleasure me to have my throat cut /With diamonds? or
                 to be smothered /With cassia? or to be shot to death with pearls?*
young ears: Sturge Moore's printer exhibits a straying literal, *young years*.

160

Maidenhair

Plato of the clear, dreaming eye and brave
Imaginings, conceived, withdrawn from light,
The hollow of man's heart even as a cave.
With century-slow dropping stalactite
My heart was dripping tedious in despair.
But yesterday, awhile before I slept:
I wake to find it live with maidenhair
And mosses to the spiky pendants crept.
Great prodigies there are— Jehovah's flood
Widening the margin of the Red Sea shore,—
Great marvel when the moon is turned to blood
It is to mortals, yet I marvel more
At the soft rifts, the pushings at my heart,
That lift the great stones of its rock apart.

T1032   One of Michael's more spectacular conjurings, which was written *Dec 20th. 1901* (OWK 42b). The nearest dated Journal entry in Michael's hand, 'It must be about December 19th.— a Thursday', shows that the Painters were contemplating a move back to town. Ricketts 'said he had only known he was happy at Richmond—..' (ZJP 172a). This might well account for Michael's 'despair' (v5). Yet on the following page she writes 'How I wake different in my heart! Yesterday it was a cave with slow dropping stalactytes *(sic)* — to-day it is all soft & luminous with maiden-hair!' (ZJP 173a). The classical attribution has not proved traceable. Plato certainly refers to the heart, as a kind of guard-house accountable to reason (*Timaeus*); there is also his much more famous metaphor in which prisoners in a cave mistake shadows for realities (*Republic*). But one would probably need the detailed knowledge of a Jowett to recognise Michael's allusion. The single previous publication of this poem was in the Sturge Moore selection (SMF 116). He attributes it to WILD HONEY, where the only 'available' blank page (WDH 164) seems to result from a proof-reading error at *Enna's Cave*, T0877 (OWM 160).

The disciples of Luce (being more interested in the 'metaphorical field' than Michael Field) luckily have not so far discovered *Maidenhair*. Where the cave of the Nymphs (T0366, v6-7) becomes "explicitly associated with the female body", a "lesbian space" for their "autoeroticism", it is not too difficult to imagine what the Irigarayan sorority would read into *this* innocent poem. Or *Come with me down to this grot* T0707, for that matter. Yet despite the central rimous image, the fortuitously menstrual overtones of v10-11— and not least the title— neither poem, as their contexts make abundantly plain, is a slyly veiled description of feminine *impudenda*.

Maidenhair: The familiar fern *Adiantum capillus-veneris*, whose fronds divide into small fan-shaped segments on very slender wiry black stipes.
Red Sea: Exodus XIV.
blood: Joel II 31; Revelation VI 12.

Not Lethe

"Of Lethe thou shalt drink no drop for me"
So cried a poet nameless & unknown,
So crieth every creature that makes moan,
"Thou shalt forget me never." Close to thee
Spread the shag, unctuous water-weeds: let be!
The infatuating water that alone
Of waters gives no mirror, round the stone
Of the rock-margin slippeth amorously,
Drink thou no drop of it: the shadowy folk
Tempt & affright thee; crouch thou on the ground,
Thy head between thy knees, & thus invoke
All our rich years of love. Take thou no sound
Of Memory's voice, nor bear her vain debate:
In thy moved heart keep solitude, & wait.

T1056   In isolation this italian sonnet could easily be considered yet another of
         Michael's tributes to her niece (see in particular v12). Yet in context it
         seems the person of the second part is most likely Ricketts. Also, although
the piece unquestionably originated with Michael, Henry had a significant input of
her own (v.i.). The poem is the first of five on Lethe, all of them closely related
(T1056,66-8,103); none was considered good enough for publication. The present
piece, with its overtones of a Blake drawing, is easily the best. A Journal entry for 7
May 1902 (ZJQ 69b) records Michael having read in J.A. Symonds's *Studies of the
Greek poets* "(a) sepulchral epigram... by an unknown writer-   ..."Meanwhile, best
friend of friends, do thou,/ If this the cruel fates allow,/ By death's dark river,/
Among those shadowy people, drink/ No drop for me on Lethe's brink:/ Forget me
never!" ". This quotation is the obvious source of the Lethe poems; the present one
survives in the undated Journal draft in her hand (ZJQ 73a), and two Oxford
autographs, each dated Friday May 9th (OVY 24b,OWK 63b).

Lethe: The underworld river and pool of forgetfulness.
a poet: '—It does not require the bother of a poet to say that— it is the word
            in the eyes of every dying thing' (M ZJQ 69b).
Drink thou: 'Henry gave me the sestet of my sonnet this morning' (M ZJQ 73a);
            both Oxford autographs add *Finished by Henry* (OWK 63b).

— a yellow sheet
Where record of old passions do remain:
    Old passions put away
      Yet live to-day;
Even as of old they buried ears of wheat
    That, planted where the rain
Falls over it, most blithe & sweet
      Will bud again.

T1058   On Thursday 22 May Michael made this entry in the 1902 journal:
              'Tense work at Julia Domna. I propose the London cure for Henry. We
              will go & see Condor's fans: lunch at 12.45. Henry I behold one
instant— beautiful in blue-green hat— his face of springtide. Rain— clothes off—
lunch over at 1.15, & before us infinite afternoon. We route about among old
drawers & cabinets. I came across the memorials of Alfred Gérente. And I write'
*(here follows the poem text in her hand, ZJQ 75b-6; the fans were probably painted,
but not fainting distaffs— the fan-painter most likely Charles Edward Conder).*

This is the perhaps the last time Michael wrote anything about her own glass-painter.
She may have been looking through her old Paris diary ZJA, or the *Quai d'Anjou*
sketch, even leafing the drafts for the 'Duraute' play XNF. But if the abrupt first verse
is to be taken literally, it seems most likely she was reviewing one or more of the
early Gérente-centred poems, such as *'Tis sweet to bring thy buried love to mind:*
T0083 (sa T0058,70,75).

163

Holy, Holy, Holy!

I do not see the saints; yea, but I see,
In the pure spreading of the ether swim,
Their golden crowns distinct upon the rim
Hollow, & voidness of the glassy sea
How bright, how as one golden cirque they be!
How they remove, & make profound the dim
Coast of the rainbow where the cherubim
Let their great pennon plumes drop reverently!
Great joy I have beholding this fair wreath—
The prowess of their love that hath subdued
And drawn a circle on infinitude:
And humble, far, a little way beneath,
Peering as if through Time's o'er mastering sands,
Their outstretched, open, & adoring hands.

T1059   An unknown, mystic and amazing poem in which Michael 'paints a
           picture', unforgettable, of her own private revelation. She appears to
           have been reading Bishop Reginald Heber's famous hymn (#160). Both
drafts are in her hand; the Oxford autograph has the full date *Tuesday May 27th
1902* (OWK 62b). She traces the full genesis of the sonnet in a Journal entry: 'Trinity
Sunday. ...I read to Henry Newman's Paraclete.— of the irresistible Spring— I read
Milman *(ICT: possibly Henry Hart Milman, Dean of St. Paul's and another hymn-
writer)*— "All the Saints adore Thee— casting down their golden crowns before the
glassy sea"— I paint a picture. The saints all round the veiled, pearl sea— its edges
only discerned by the narrow line of the golden crowns on the rim. In the foreground
the prostrate saints. Through the veiled light above & beyond the prostration of the
Cherubim, in the stretch of poised outstretched wing: others brood over the sea: but
my one impression is the clear rim of gold, cast up as a scurf of sea-wrack— on the
edge of the sea. The saints outlines have to be looked for; the worship of their
offering is distinct, so distinct it makes the glassy sea, profound & remote. It is a
joyous circle of crowns' (M ZJQ 76ab).

Holy, Holy: Revelation IV 8 *And the four beasts had each of them six wings about
                him: and they were full of eyes within: and they rest not day and night,
                saying, Holy, holy, holy, Lord God Almighty, which was, and is, and is
                to come.*
crowns: Revelation IV 10-11 *The four and twenty elders fall down before him
                that sat on the throne, and worship him that liveth for ever and ever,
                and cast their crowns before the throne, saying, / Thou art worthy, O
                Lord, to receive glory and honour and power: for thou hast created all
                things, and for thy pleasure they are and were created.*
glassy sea: Revelation IV 6 *And before the throne there was a sea of glass like
                unto crystal:*

164

Spinet-playing

Yea, I would leave thee, yea my life grows cold,
And in my spirit it is void & still;
Belovèd thou shalt listen to my will,
And, when the measure of my days is told,
Find thee some harpsichord or spinet old,
And play to me; the simple tunes will thrill
And keep our souls in unison until
With fuller equipage I may enfold.
Will it not comfort thee the dead should come,
While we are severed, & most shrilly hum
Through their dead instruments as they were lost?
Yea, it will comfort thee & me, Sweetheart,
While I to thy dear body am a ghost,
To watch thee lonesome at thy little art.

T1061   All three autographs are in Michael's hand, that of the Journal
         unequivocally with her comment 'I finish my sonnet' (ZJQ 83a). The
         Oxford MS. has a full footnote *Finished at sunset of Peace Sunday June
1st 1902* (OWK 61b). This first published text is taken from the *Perpetua* notebook
(YFB 13b). Michael would hazard several possible futures, as 'when we are both
buried in Westminster Abbey' (ZJR 30b); in October 1904 another Journal entry
mentions that she had 'seen herself as a burial-mound with Chow's little mound by
her, & Henry faithfully sorting M.S.S. above' (H ZJS 155b). The engaging scenario
conjured by the present poem is however wildly unlikely. As far as is known, Henry
(unlike her sister) had no keyboard talents (OCB 9o); and neither she nor her aunt
appeared to have much of a musical ear (p114). There were encounters with
Dolmetsch and his experiments with authentic instruments. At a concert in February
the previous year, while Henry sat down to 'my lonely dinner... the soft boiled fowl',
Michael confessed 'The sounds as sounds were of scarcely any significance to me,
nor to my ears lovely enough in themselves to make me glad they were born' (ZJP
31-3). If the harpsichord was a banshee in a wire bedstead, and the beastly recorder
was present in any strength, it is very easy to sympathise.

harpsichord: In May, Michael had 'a dream of buying Janet (Dodge)'s spinette for
                  Henry, & of Henry's thrumming little tunes to me' (ZJQ 75a).
Will it not: The Oxford MS. also includes a less engaging variant on the sestet:
                  O patience— we can meet but on one string
                  While I to thy sweet body am a ghost;
                  While we are severed, it will comfort most
                  For that old music in our ears to cling.
                  To haunt thee striving with thy new-found art,
                  Haunt thee, & unperceived to dote on thee, Sweetheart.
thee & me: The original Journal draft revealingly reads *me at least.*
watch: The Journal draft also suggests *haunt.*

After Soufrière

It is not grief or pain;
But like the even dropping of the rain
   That thou art gone.
It is not like a grave
   To weep upon;
But like the rise and falling of a wave
   When the vessel's gone.

It is like the sudden void
When the city is destroyed,
Where the sun shone:
There is neither grief or pain,
But the wide waste come again.

T1062   Mount Soufrière, a volcano on St. Vincent, erupted May 6/7 1902,
destroying half the island (sa *Visitants* T1060). Angel Leighton, quoting
without checking, repeats Sturge Moore's error of assigning the
eruption to Guadeloupe (SMF 31 fn). Here, admittedly, is another volcano, La
Soufrière; but this had erupted last in 1843. In any case vulcanism (*pace* FAL 240) is
only peripheral; "Why have you called it that— it seems irrelevant, after the manner
poets choose their titles": thus Ricketts on being shown the poem (ZJQ 88a). He was
aware that Michael's theme (v3) was more personal (sa Bridge, OZL 62). Maybe on
June 21st (ZJQ 97b) Michael decided 'I must get Souffrière (sic) written down— Fay
has the only fair copy.' There are six known autographs, and Michael's Journal draft
includes a third stanza which, like the first, is unconnected with Mount Soufrière:
   It is like the traveller's plight/ Who must journey on/ With no home in sight
   And the day at wane—/ There is neither grief or pain.   (ZJQ 98a; OVY 30)
The poem *may* have been intended for THE TRAGEDY OF PARDON; Henry declared
it to be 'the Song for Tristan's anguish— instead of the snatch *(ICT: ?T1045)* we had
always felt to be unworthy his sorrow' (ZJQ 100a). It was "completed" on 04 June
(OWD 18b), and revised throughout the month. But its eventual publication in WILD
HONEY (WDH 34), in 1908, was not without further seismic activity; Fisher Unwin
discovered the poem had already appeared in an anthology in 1907 (AWJ; ZJX 13a).

or pain: Obviously this should be *nor* pain, and Sturge Moore so corrects it.
wide waste: One draft dated June 10, in a letter to Amy, has an extra verse:
           And the winds flow on.   (OCJ 81o)

T1063   Ursula Bridge has surmised, probably correctly, that this sonnet was
also written by Michael about her relationship with Ricketts (OZM 96).
It is certainly true that the published poem lies in a run of sonnets on
'the Painter' and Michael's Journal entry immediately before the draft reads: 'At

Armour

Why lack I so in prowess to oppose?
What quality enfeebles my defence?
Spirit I have, courage that courts her foes,
And I am very proud and nice of sense.
Is it, of Love himself I am equipt
For contest, and with Love I must contend,—
In treachery has he some buckle slipt,
The breastplate not set even to defend?
Though to the rush of onset I am fleet,
And guard within my heart most bitter rage,
I know I am predestined to defeat,
My helm, my spears, a ghostly equipage:
All the fair panoply about me spread
Thin as the thin gold armour of the dead.

night a note from Fay... He is teasing me. I tell him the walls of his brain are thick as
the walls of Mycenae' (ZJQ 97b). This seems an obvious allusion to v14. Also all six
extant autographs are in her hand, all but one dated *June 18th.1902* (OWK 69b).
Yet one remains uneasy. A case *might* be made that the loved 'foe' is her niece. In
radical opposition to both these readings is the possibility that Michael is 'working up'
material which is Henry's own; it is not just that v14 seems to originate in one of her
remarks (v.i.)— Berenson had also been visiting Paragon. In February 1904, after an
account of one of Ricketts's visits, Henry would write: 'Fay has noticed that I seem
always to be defending my opinion from a blow. He knows I have not talked enough
in my life— this causes me to be very slow in approaching a good remark & so swift
in uttering it that it is lost— & falls ineffective, unless special attention catches it' (ZJS
31b, see v9-11). She would also admit in November 1907 that pride (v4) was 'the
essential fault of my being' (H ZJX 44a). One may hypothesise but it seems unlikely
one will ever get at the truth of this puzzling poem, with its reminiscences of *Antony
and Cleopatra* IV iv. There may in fact be no actual personalities in it; the poem may
be 'merely' a construct back from that magnificent last line. This is hard to believe
(sa T1137). The original draft (ZJQ 97b), and other autographs, is split at the octave;
the poem was first published in WILD HONEY, WDH 18.

even: The Journal draft also offers *justly*— and *and* for *All* in v13.
heart: Originally *breast*, obviously a too immediate echo of *breastplate* in v8.
armour: Henry had been enjoying William Ridgeway's *The Early Age of Greece*
           (published at Cambridge the year before). 'I love to read of the gold
           leaves thin on the dust of pre-historic heroes, & of the thin gold armour
           made for the dead to wear, as he sat in useless splendour, & the blood
           of victims dripped a moment's warmth on him' (H ZJQ 97a). A
           reference to Schliemann's discovery, in November 1876, of the gold
           portrait masks in the shaft graves at Mycenae, seems inescapable.

The Lament for Cheiron

Through the deer's-milk and the sorrel,
Where the beeches shred,
I lament for Cheiron!
Where the hawk is over head
And the wood-dove is in peril,
I lament for Cheiron.

In the grove of the venomed arrow,
Where his blood was in a pool,
Where I plucked the plantain
With the leaves that heal and cool,
With the vervain and the yarrow,
I lament for Cheiron.

Where afar he reared up heroes
'Mid the rocks of honeycomb,
I lament for Cheiron;
Where the wild goat never clomb,
In a gulley where no flower grows
I lament for Cheiron.

Where in the valley's cover
The sun shoots up and sings
In the soft of sundown;
Where the black moths spread their wings,
And furl them again and hover
I lament for Cheiron.

In the heights above the coppice
Where the desert-land is high
I lament for Cheiron;
Where the crag-tops are moist with sky,
In a crevice of wild poppies
I lament for Cheiron.

T1093   This poem is the last of a group of four that Michael had been writing
about the famous centaur that summer, and perhaps the most successful.
(It is his wife, the naiad Chariclo, who laments him). All this is clear from
Journal entries: by Michael (in a copy of a letter to Ricketts around August 5) 'I have

been writing about Chariclo', and by Henry on August 12 '..She has read me Calichlo (sic)— it has the rustle of wild things in its cadences' (ZJQ 135a, 137b). Michael's autograph reads *Finished the eleventh Sunday after Trinity August 10th 1902* (OWK 90b). The poem was published in WILD HONEY, WDH 4-5 immediately after one on Chariclo herself, the second (T1082) of Michael's four pieces:

> She is safe on his breast,
> This child of Apollo;
> She has no fear; she loves divineness;
> Cheiron is shag;
> A front like a rock; she loves the shock,
> And twines her arms
> Round his neck, in the rock-side hollow.
>
> *(Chariclo)* T1082, s2

Cheiron was the son of Cronus by the nymph Philyra, whom Cronus had (no doubt agreeably) surprised as a horse; like his stepbrother Zeus, Cheiron was therefore an immortal. He became the friend of Apollo, who gave him a skill in archery as well as a wife (see above, though Chariclo's father is sometimes named as Oceanus, or Perses). Cheiron, the kindly and wise tutor of heroes, was king of the centaurs until an accident with one of Heracles's poisoned arrows; there are several versions. This left him in such agony that he voluntarily relinquished his immortality— some say to Prometheus— and became a constellation (sa *The Return to Apollo*, T1084):

> Pierced he looks up, though sunken on his knees,
> To learn who sped the shaft; but when he sees
> The arrow started from loved Heracles
> He gave his immortality to one,
> From such ill-omened sorrow to be gone.
>
> *(The Arrow)* T1078, s3

Henry described Ricketts's reaction to both poems: 'He does not care for "Chariclo" but esteems the "Lament for Cheiron" "very beautiful indeed". He pauses— "a most beautiful poem"' (ZJY 8b). In fact it seemed 'Everyone has loved the "Lament for Cheiron"' (H ZJY 34b). Including Sturge Moore, who wrote in two letters: "Chariclo.. really did delight me.. Chariclo & The Lament for Cheiron have something altogether new and attaching which I have not yet had the time to yeild to" (ZCF 216o, sic 9r).

deer's-milk: The wood spurge *Euphorbia amygdaloides* is a robust, downy plant bleeding a milky latex when damaged; the small yellowish-green flowers are arranged in compound cymes, and have crescent-shaped glands with two horns (which may explain the local name).

sorrel: *Oxalis acetosella*, the shade-loving wood sorrel of beechland.

plantain: *Plantago major* and related mucilaginous species. The bruised ovate leaves are well known to alleviate the pain of a wasp or nettle sting: infusions have been used to treat bronchitis, and diarrhoea.

vervain: *Verbena officinalis*, a wayside herb with pale lilac flowers. Its leaves are astringent, and have been employed in poultices.

yarrow: *Achillea millefolium*, a stoloniferous scented member of the Compositae, also has astringent and antiseptic properties; an infusion of the dried flower corymbs was recommended for bathing wounds.

Where afar: In his cave on Mount Pelion in Thessaly.

heroes: Amongst others, Achilles, Jason, Actaeon (and Asclepius, to whom he taught the arts of surgery and medicine).

Autumn Pansies

Why is it, vexedly I must complain—
Why is it there is something that is small,
Fine, disappearing, & ephemeral,
As things for finest use about thy brain?
I watch the even breakers of the main,
And turn back dully: from the sea-weed haul
A brittle-sanded shell in flush & whorl
Presents thee, thou art live to me again.
Nor in the uplands can I find thy like,
Furrow, tinged farness no incentive yield,
No thought of thee, till riseth from its spike
One minute pansy on the stubble-field;
And thou at once art with me in the power
Of that inscribed & penetrating flower.

T1096   An italian sonnet known only from two autographs, both in Michael's
hand, and dated *Rottingdean- October 1902* (OVY 47b,OWK 100b).
       The Journal is not helpful, but it seems most likely that it is Ricketts
who is brought to mind in the cosmos of small things. In the pagan world the pansy
was said to be the flower of Jove (Zeus), but to the monks it was the flower of Trinity.
The story goes that it once had an irresistible perfume, that caused the peasantry to
trample down cattle forage and their own growing vegetables in an attempt to find
and gather the flowers. The pansy, pious in the way of all simples, prayed to the
Trinity to take away its perfume so that it would no longer incite such rural
mammocking; naturally all Three willingly obliged.

Michael's flower might have been the wild pansy (Heart's ease, one of her favourite
flowers— see note to T1725); but in view of her adjective *minute*, it was possibly the
field pansy *Viola arvensis*. This is also a weed of disturbed ground (almost ideally a
stubble-field), but has much smaller flowers only 8-20mm across.

ephemeral: Lasting but a day.
No thought: In the language of flowers, the pansy (*pensée*) stands for thoughts.

In one Time

Love, do you mark how poignant & how dear
It is to be contemporaneous?
Ver may have broken on the earth more clear
When the earth was young, she did not break on us,
We are alive: & we the wonder are:-
While we awake & ponder in the night,
The branches of the curled japonica
Bud scarlet, flower on flower, for our delight.

We hear the ilex' little pebbly hiss,
And O— we see the willow's long green hairs
But sense of answering sense must feel the bliss.
The sea is for the message that it bears:
And Echo plaineth to the fronting hills—
Then be no longer sick, thy sickness kills.

T1110   There are two autographs, both in Michael's hand, and dated *Feb.
           12th 1903* (OWK 109b). There is no question the author is Michael;
           the sonnet is one of the many she wrote for Ricketts, though it seems
unlikely he ever saw it. The date is also confirmed by her Journal entry: 'February
12th. We are anxious concerning Fay, ill with influenza. The gardener comes early
for the dogs, & I pace the towing-path alone. How I enjoy the little pebbly hiss of the ilex—
& my willows in their long, green hairs. How I love my border trees, my own milky
acacia among them. There is a branch of japonica in flower in one of the gardens I
would fain steal for Fay. By what slender threads our happiness hangs!' (M ZJR 22b).

In one Time: Michael also experimented with *Reverberation* and *Together in Time*,
               but rejected both earlier titles (OVY 50b). This was a favourite theme
               (sa T0209).
Ver: Spring. In 1390 seen as male by Gower, *Whan Ver his Seson hath
               begoune* ; but by 1568 Howell comments *Now Lady Ver in liuely
               greene doth showe her grace in fielde*. Ver is addressed directly in a
               poem with this title (T0835, sa T0975).
we awake: Most memorably in T1055.
japonica: Probably (and paradoxically) the chinese quince *Cydonia speciosa*, a
               large shrub included in the apple subfamily of Rosaceae. Two years
               before Michael had written a whole sonnet on another japonica, *To
               Love: a prayer for punishment* (T0971).
ilex: Holly.
Echo: See the note to T0415.
plaineth: laments (complains).

171

The Beloved

Love only comes to me when thou art gone:
Then he draws to me in his might,
Sundering with his infinite
Power, as a far, wide space,
Till I cannot see thy face;
   And I wonder
If Love so great will not keep us forever asunder.

T1115   There are three known autographs, two in the hand of Michael. The
earliest has a full date *May 14th (Thursday evening- gold room) 1903*
(OVY 53a), but the title appeared only on publication in WILD HONEY,
WDH 69. This early draft has two stanzas, the first being omitted when Michael
transferred the poem to her fair copy book (OWK 113b). The Journal offers no
additional information. Bearing in mind a current preoccupation with Isolde, it seems
just possible the piece was meant for one of the Tristan dramas. The suppressed first
stanza of the draft reads:

> *Love only comes to me when thou art gone,*
> *Love only stands with me to quell,*
> *When thou hast bid farewell.*
>   *The god I deny not*
>   *The god I fly not*
>   *My heart he breaks:*
> *Warm through his feathers, warm & soft are*
>   *The words he speaks.*

The following day Michael wrote another untitled piece (*Buried at sea*) directly into
the fair copy book. The third stanza in particular, with its overtones of separation
(and of Cleopatra) strengthen the argument for an Isolde/Tristan context to both
poems:

> *Buried from me /My Love shall be /As a melted pearl.*
> *And the cup I hurl— /No draught for me /From the goblet of the melted pearl.*
> T1116,s3

In the Prologue to TRISTAN DE LÉONOIS, written perhaps that June, *Amor* will hold
up such a 'goblet, hung with sea-weeds and tarnished':

> *Up from the sea-depths I have brought*
> *This my cup in which was wrought*
> *My spell long years afar—*
> T1123,v1-3

In February 1911 McNabb, on a visit from Leicester, read poems alternately with
Michael; she recorded 'among the selections he likes the Beloved' (ZKB 22b). *The
Beloved* was also one of ten Michael Field pieces that Margaret Sackville included in
her anthology *A Book of Verse by Living Women* (1910).

If Love: This version appears only in Henry's fair copy (OWL 76b); both drafts read
              If the great Lord Love will keep us for ever asunder.

Missed Pleasures

Love, how I crave thee for the common hours,
In Time's interstices, how much is dear,
While we are held apart, how many flowers
Spread on the air, & fade, & disappear.
So I have seen the small convolvulus
Warm in her shell; & the white centaury
I greeted her first morn is dead from us:
The iris from the wood fails presently,
And there is no vibration in the wood.
O sorrow, & more sorrowful, rich sighs
For all that lives between us, lives & dies
And will not live again: too fierce our mood
When once we meet, too terrible the gaze
Of the Lord Love for memory's lingering haze.

T1127   This unpublished quatorzain survives in two Oxford autographs, both in Michael's hand with the footnote *Richmond, end of July 1903* (OWK 124b,OVY 56b). Happily, as on several occasions, the Journal fills in the essential background. '<u>Michael's Letter-Card to Fay</u> It was said of me from the tea-leaves, dear Painter, that I should receive a letter that would give me pleasure. But did it need the necromancer! Any one looking into my face might learn so much of my fortune. ...I am glad you are starting for the sea. Go where there is something beautiful, a blue moth, or the valley-swifts mingling their flight with the sea-gulls. ...Many shells & shell-fish, & Donkeys for your Fellow — Michael' (H ZJR 87ab). It is probably unkind to surmise any playful malice in the postscript. Michael and Henry had themselves been at the seaside earlier in the month (Lulworth), and Ricketts had sent a letter which implied he had similar plans, perhaps setting off on the 19th (sa ZJR 86a). But he seems to have changed his mind. '7th Sunday after Trinity, August* 26th. It was a fable Fay was at the sea— I felt this, & I bade him hither. It is fresh season in his Spirit. How the flowers bloom & fade in the intervals between our meeting. The whole warm life of little, shell convolvulus has opened & shrivelled since we parted. He is intensely brilliant, coruscating— his eyes a demon's in roll & slide. Unaccustomed to the swift current of his brain now in full volume, we sit drowsily alongside & assent' (M ZJR 89a). It would seem reasonable to assume that the poem was written very soon after this entry *(*ICT: A slip of the pen for July)*.

Spread: The draft reads *Spread in the air* (OVY 56b).
centaury: The common centaury of dry grasslands, *Centaurium erythraea*, has, as its name implies, pink flowers; a white variety would be most unusual. Possibly this is *C. tenuiflorum*, the slender centaury of damp grasslands.
O sorrow: The draft continues *more sorrow for the sake*.

She prays, she watches by the river-shore;
What while the sentinel years are changing feet,
Attentive to such signs as in the heat
Of fervid-clashing time she may explore:
The silence fallen from the cannon's roar,
The air so fresh in its voluptuous beat
She can interpret; & with ritual sweet
Give token of the days that are before:
She dwelleth very near the Eternal Love
Soft as its dayspring. She has power to see
How the manna, how the dew fall over me
—The florid winds— But what doth this divine
A joy as of carnation in its clove,
A fragrance of carnation & of pine?

T1150 This untitled italian sonnet is known from two autographs in Michael's
hand, one in an Oxford manuscript (OWK 136a), the other in her book
of fair copies *Perpetua* included in the Fortey cache (YFB 15b). Both are
precisely dated *Jan 3rd. 1904*. What is perhaps curious is its omission from the
other *Perpetua* at Oxford (OW), which jumps in an irregular chronology from T0924
to T1194. The poem affords another fascinating insight into life at Paragon, and the
regular rituals at the turn of the year. On the last night of each old year Henry would
both look back over the accomplishments of the previous twelve months, and make
plans and predictions for the year to come. Both women were convinced of her
"psychic" powers, a gentle barminess apparently of some comfort in the absence of
external emotional release— and part and parcel of Henry's personal *mystique*.

fervid: very hot, as in a molten flux of renewal.
cannon's roar: 'New Year's Day. I look forth at midnight (*ICT: 31 December 1903*)
to grimmest fog, fog that is as a garment to the bitter wind. A moon
in the heavens, bells & cannon on the air. Then a human cheer
across the waters   1904 is with us— for our fashioning More &
more I feel this, we are weavers of the stuff of time' (M ZJS 4b).
interpret: 'I feel we shall remain by our Thames, but I am sure there will be
changes in our service, in our moulding of the riverside life... The
Artists will be troublesome— but there is breath of a carnation time
of delight... late or early I cannot say. We make a new friend— it
comes in surprise that a friendship is begun' (H ZJR 221b-2a).
dew: YFB has *dews*, and *does* for *doth* in the following verse.
carnation: On January 31st Michael made a note in the new Journal. 'I review
the month. We have fought well in it, facing many things. Now we
must face the publisher Our mottoes of Diligence & Passion must
continue. The pine & carnation scent must come as they will— they
will be scents across the battlefield' (ZJS 26ab). sa T0875.

174

Better it were that ball on finest wires
Frail Jenny Wren should perish of the cold
In the thick rime, afar from winter fires,
Far from the crumbs that in my hands I hold,
Far better than the murder I have done,
Letting thee see the verse that I have writ,
Too deft, too delicate the couplets run,
Subtle in fancy, tender but in wit.—
Thou wilt not freeze them, that is not my fear—
Terror will strike them dead against thy breast,
And very wintry thou wilt make their bier,
And the bare ground, instead of woven nest.
O Sorrow that a woman must not speak
Save in pure symbol from the lip, the cheek.

T1153   One of Michael's unpublished poems, known only from the two
         autographs in her hand. The Journal draft (ZJS 18a) has the epigraph
         Friday. Bitter fog; the Oxford fair copy (OWK 138b) an additional date,
January 22nd (ICT: 1904). The first verse affords a picture of *Troglodytes troglodytes*
probably more recognisable to Picasso than to one's average mittened twitcher; but
Michael's real concern is quite different— the fate of a packet of poems she had sent
to Ricketts the previous day: '... I write to Painter. You are painting to-day, — you are
as a bee at her honey. I can speak to you. You can listen to one or two of my songs
about shells— & a sonnet, & another. I have chosen, but who knows how wisely, for
the poet cannot choose, or distinguish one song from another. Comfort yourself with
anything you like in these dateless fragments, & forget the rest' (M ZJS 17b). The
poems she sent (ZJS 18a) were *Camellias (T1104)*, *Onycha II (T1147)*, *Heralds
(T1152)*, *For Ever (T1143)* and *The lonely Shepherd (T1128)*. The extended
metaphor, after its unfortunate start, is one of her loveliest. The final couplet offers a
late resonance of *The New Minnesinger*: in the fair copy the verses are scored
through, an indication that she may have intended to revise them.

It is also possible that she remembered an episode two years before, at the time the
Painters were leaving Richmond for central London; they were making 'their last state
visit'. 'Then Fay gives me a M.S. (typed) of John Gray's. They have been looking
over their papers— It may amuse me to look at it. I need not return it. "Oh," I retort
"that is what you will do with Michael Field's sonnets— come across them when you
are looking over some rubbish, & toss them to a friend for a moment's
amusement"— He makes no defence' (ZJQ 66a). She need have had few qualms:
the poems she sent included some of her finest.

Katharine Harris Bradley (1846-1914)   The Sturgeon portrait, copied several
times, but of no known date or provenance. Carta Sturge vouches for its authenticity
"These two* photographs on the cover° are excellent portraits of the aunt & niece
who together constituted Michael Field. ..her very sprightly aunt, who could be easily
roused to wrath, but somehow wrath of a very fascinating kind. The portrait on the
cover° represents Catharine as I mostly knew her" (YCA: * "The fine medallion of
Ricketts" reproduced on the back cover SZD: ° Mary Sturgeon's Michael Field FMS).

Michael is probably in her late 40's; one might hazard a guess at *circa* 1895; it is
barely possible that the portrait is one of those referred to by Henry in 1898, when
she mentions 'Two other pictures of my Love in her black satin evening dress— a
noble head & ¾ face' (ZJM 15b). Certainly noble enough to be painted by Singer
Sargent. But she was repeatedly told that she was not a 'suitable subject': to the
lasting shame, at least, of Ricketts and of Rothenstein. The present illustration has
been enlarged (x2.5) from the FMS original (Bodleian Library Oxford Walpole e.235).

On beholding a ring set with a star-sapphire

What is it? not the fetter of troth-plight,
What is it? not the signet of a king,
Nor ceremonial, nor prodigious ring,
With alleys for the venoms that requite,
Nor wrought for any separate delight;
It is a dream, a mighty compiling,
A flame through many windows flickering,
A dome of Heaven with one deep star in sight.
It is a shrine, and from the fourfold tier
Of solemn towers that bind its cupola,
From the high windows and the golden doors,
Glimpses there are that fall and disappear:
The passing of trailed spices and the stir
Of a god moving secret 'mid the floors.

T1160   One of two closely related sonnets written probably by Michael, in early 1904; this text was first published in *Letters from Charles Ricketts to 'Michael Field' (1903—1913)*, VCR 14. There are three autographs in her hand, partially dated, but the related T1159 has a full date *Saturday Feb 6th 1904* (OWK 141b). The ring is now in the Fitzwilliam Museum (sa illustration, *Apollo* (JAP CXVI #247, p163). The references below to Sabbatai (another Christ claimant, but one who eventually capitulated) relate to A MESSIAH, the play in hand in 1903.

On 9 December 1903 Ricketts first offered 'to use... (Michael's) star-sapphire for a "Sabbatai Ring"— the star sapphire to be the Mosque of Omar, floating over Jerusalem, & to be supported by a shrine. With joy Michael goes to fetch a ring the right finger-size;' (H ZJR 201a). He later elaborated 'the Star-sapphire ring was that given to Sabbatai to make him change his religion—... "There is Solomon inside"— adds Shannon "reduced to a star"' (H ZJR 212b). On 25 January 1904 Ricketts visited Paragon again. 'Suddenly we learn the Sabbatai Ring is come in its first state— It is brought out, with its doors, & spotted dome, its butresses & its windows, through wh: a loose emerald flashes with ranging green, & the tinkle of it is heard like a God inside. What fancy assails & prompts one in this strange inward life of sound & flash from their prison!' (H ZJS 22b). On 05 February Michael took 'love-apples to the Palace,... The Sabbatai ring is there— the generous ring:- the Shrine, & the presence, & the blue dome-... "This ring will cause much offence" Painter says, & I add "That pleases you" (M ZJS 27b); 'Shannon calls it "Solomon", & the tinkling within "The Song of Solomon." ...Its doors are to be smeared with ambergris, so that it may appeal to all the five senses' (M ZJS 28b, sa OCZ 22o). A copy of the sonnet was sent to Ricketts, who liked it 'immensely' and thought 'the last line very fine indeed' (VCR 14). In its earlier version it had a flatter sestet, and there were many consequent small adjustments; this draft did however pick up on his remark:
> It will work much offence, needs must it be / To the wan world matter of injury / Being of itself profound & generous.   T1159, v12-4

Secret, yet not through veils that can be torn,
Or mystery the heavens must unfrock,
Not as a magic door where men may knock
And greatly enter, or those doors of horn
That shut behind us & the world withdrawn,
Nor petals opening gradual in their flock—
Jewel thou art, & jewel of the rock
For kings to wear, or to be laid forlorn.
Jewel, my sole clear, sovereign ornament
That with the light, the dark, wert wont to mix
How many times, or locked in silver shrine,
Or beddest trembling in the awful pyx
How comes it thou shouldst ever be content,
Long as thou burnest simply to be mine?

T1167   Two autographs of this untitled and unpublished italian sonnet have
survived, both in Michael's hand and dated *June 19th 1904*; that it
is another devotion to her niece is made quite certain by its inclusion
in the little 1902 book *Perpetua to My Soul's Idol* (YFB 16b). The revised version of
the sestet is the one given here (OWK 144a). The central image of the jewel seems
to arise from the circumstance of a visit they made on the 17th to Sturge Moore and
his wife (ZJS 101b). Henry was never far from Michael's thoughts, even when, as
usual that Easter (April 3rd), she indulged ghostly colloquies from which Michael was
excluded. 'Now I commit Henry to Heaven's care in the perilous hour of her
communion with the dead. I should not like to meet her that way, nor do I believe
the attempt would prosper; side by side— the chink of two oboli— & one boat— that
is my prayer for us' (ZJS 60a). Henry that same June was to open a secret most men
(Freud included) have never been able to comprehend— "what a woman wants."
'The men we know all believe that a woman's one need is to love a man— that is
enough, for it is her ideal. They think so. . . But woman's own ideal is to be loved—
she wants herself infinitely surpassed, her power of loving left behind by that in man.
This is why she is religious & Christian— .. why the man who loves is her adoration
& her dream. Father had this talisman— he loved' (ZJS 104b; sa M OYB 40a).

doors of horn: See first footnote to *Long Ago II*, T0306.
Jewel, my sole: The variant (?original) sestet also occurs in both MSS:
         Jewel, that with the elements has blent/ With light, with darkness
         many times to mix,/ Stored in old tombs, or radiant in a shrine,/ Or
         deep-embedded in the awful pyx,/ How does it come that thou
         shouldst be content/ Long as thou burnest simply to be mine?
shrine: Probably the "Sabbatai Ring" (See T1160); on the 18th she wrote 'I
love my Paragon, I love the shrine;...' (ZJS 98b).
pyx: In general a box (as for test coins at the Mint); in hieratic use, the
vessel in which the Eucharist wafers are kept after consecration.

Looking up to the Stars

Not as the sun that presently must drop,
And in damp night no comfort for the eye;
Not as the moon that climbeth by and by,
Too late for my sad eve: as the full crop
Of stars that, clear or trembling, without stop
Amass in myriad feature on the sky,
Is manifest the love that as I die
Fills all my heaven to the archèd top.
What feats of gods are there in permanence,
Conflicts and reconciliations there,
As in a crystal, moving to the sense!
Glad am I, through these draughts of quiet air,
To breathe such visitings, and, in pale stream,
The crossing and recrossing of a dream.

T1173   The return from Rottingdean was on 02 November. 'I loved my Birthday
spent new in the great air. And oh— I love the Painter's letter, laid
topmost of all my letters on the pile. It is, as I write to him, a plaything
to be carried about & laughed over, from the gold-room to the grot, & again to the
high river-room. The rocks of my heart are moist & warm' (M ZJS 171ab). There was
a visit to the Palace: 'Of Friday Nov 4th He is not as a setting sun to me. He is stars.
He covers my eve with an exceeding starriness of light. He illumines every atom of
the Heavens. He is the softness of the Milky Way... We meet in his loneliness, behind
the crystal wall where he dreams the Renaissance. And why remove from behind that
crystal wall even after death? I saw him turn back to his sharp solitude. I am safe in
the munitions of these rocks.' The poem, in her hand and dated *Nov 5th. 1904*,
follows immediately (ZJS 172ab). Three other autographs in her hand survive, but
there was never any doubt about the authorship (or the inspirer) 'Michael has written
a Star-Sonnet— it is gone by post' (H ZJS 176a). The only clue to the new 'starriness'
of Ricketts lies in his letter: "I am going to paint Heliodorus expelled from the Temple
by the Traditional St. Michael on horseback brandishing a flame..." (ZJS 173b).
Michael wished to see the picture— twice— that Friday, and this viewing (let alone St.
Michael) may have been the ultimate starburst. The sonnet was published in WILD
HONEY, WDH 95, and reprinted by H. J. Massingham in *Letters to X*, 1919.

by and by: All the autographs read *by and bye*.
full crop: See also *Stars* T0021; *Stars at dawn* T0738. That August, Henry
                    recorded in the Journal 'Michael has just been out to the stars. She finds
                    "all rustling & the Milky Way"' (ZJS 130a).
the Stars: A discarded title was *Looking up at the Stars* (ZJS 172b, OWK 146b).
Amass: In the Journal this is *Stands forth*; another draft has *Burn out* (OYR 4b).
feats: Michael had already, that May, written a group of three indifferent
                    poems *From the Stars* (T1117-9), treating of actual constellations; still to
                    come was an astonishing unpublished sonnet, *The Open Stars* (T1193).

Sirenusa

Caught unawares the moments that enchant!
"Civet or bergamot, or holy basil?—
But close your eyes!" . . . And while the nostrils pant,
With the kaleidoscopic sweets a-dazzle,
"Oh stay, you strive; draw in a deeper breath:
You cannot fail: do not too quick reply!"
And the great lids before me, not in death,
But vivid as one feels the sea, being by,
Are stretched unsentried. Lovely Gorgon mask,
Kind betwixt me and doom! White siren coast,
And all the sirens whelmèd, in their host
Trembling unseen their perilous harps! Secure,
I leave the chafing senses to their task,
And profit of those brows serene and pure.

T1177   There are three autographs in Michael's hand, all untitled; two of them
are precisely dated 22 November 1904, with a further note *Fay comes
in afternoon* (OWJ 11b,OWK 152b). So it is fairly clear the sonnet
relates to Ricketts, though not *'On Shannon's drawing of C.R.'* as someone (?Sturge
Moore) has pencilled on the loose autograph OYR 9o. On Thursday 27 October
Michael was 58. Henry gave her aunt 'A blue case from Piesse & Lubin containing at
my caprice Holy Basil Bergamotte Civit': later 'We open our scents. Michael is
fugitive from Civet, Birgamotte has the hair & stings of hedge-flowers in its rusticity—
holy Basil has taken Salvia to its nectarous coolness.' After dinner 'we smell scents
blindfold & pay forfeits for ill-success in naming them...' (ZJS 163b,5a). Ricketts's visit
was possibly on Tuesday afternoon 8 November; whether or not he also paid forfeits
is not recorded. The poem was eventually published in WILD HONEY, WDH 116.

Sirenusa: Not to be confused with Henry's poem *Sirenusae* (T0938), directly
concerned with the Sirens— the sea-nymphs, part woman, part bird,
whose wild sweet singing lured sailors to their deaths.

enchant!:   'Only once did he enchant, when he shut his eyes for Michael to put her
scents to his nostrils that he might guess their names. Then all the
coast-lines of his unsentried face lay open to admiration in their
excellence, in their undefended lure— a territory of sirens with the sirens
whelmed under the eyelids— a coast safe & magic' (H ZJS 177ab).

Civet: African and oriental cat-like carnivore of the family *Viverridae*; the oily
secretion of the anal glands is musk-like and used in perfumes.

bergamot: Probably oil from the rind of the Calabrian orange, *Citrus bergamia*

basil: Plants of the (mint) family Labiatae, with fragrant to pungent leaves.

Gorgon: Another sea-nymph (one of three), once beautiful, changed by Athene
into a winged snake-haired monster whose gaze turned men to stone. All
Michael's autographs read *masque* for *mask* (and *Holy Basil* in v2).

unseen: She also tried *Beneath those solemn, covering lids! Secure,* (OWJ 11b).

The Open Stars

What can secure from earth's frail shadiness
Like the completion of a starry night,
And mortal passions current through the stress,
Fixed & for ever in undaunted light?
What lettering of strange loves, what mailèd feet,
What stalk of apparitions on that road,
What flux, what light!— Passion of Juno's teat,
And all the fragrant milk that overflowed,
Those deep incised, those graven heavens we sweep,
And human miseries no more appal;
Stable it is where the great symbols are:
We reck not of Orion on the deep
Tossed so tempestuously: or rise & fall
Of billows chafing round Andromeda.

T1193   Michael had completed an earlier "stars" poem on 05 November (see
T1173) and in this unpublished quatorzain she returned to the theme.
    About mid-November she wrote to Berenson 'I look forth & amuse
myself with the stars' (H ZJS 180a). There are four known autographs, two with the
footnote *Written out (in Sonnet book) the morning of Saturday Nov 12th— the
morning of the 5 reflected stars* (OWK 147/8 b, sa 325o). The text here is the first
OWK version. The third autograph (OWJ 13b) is identical with that of the 1905
Journal, which has Michael's note *finished in the very last hours of 94* (ZJT 5b); this
presumably dates it at 31 December 1904. There are significant departures at v6:
                    What stalk of apparitions among those,
        And how astonied!— Fire of Juno's teat, /And all the fragrant milk that overflows.
        Nothing can now dismay us on our road /Of fear, of agony, of frenzied call;
        Stable it is where the great symbols are: /And, from her even constellation glowed,
        Cassandra triumphs: even rise & fall /The billows chafing round Andromeda.
One approves the innovations of the fire of Juno's teat, and of Cassandra, but
otherwise this version seems undoubtedly inferior.

Open Stars: 'The first sight to me of Ninety-5 is of Stars— Orion— glittering
            through the boughs' (M ZJT 5a; sa H ZJS 206ab). In 1906 Henry
            would declare 'Why should we find the losses of youth so bitter if we
            can be full of stars clothed with their beauty in Age?' (ZJV 196a).
Juno's teat: Fabled origin of the Milky Way. Hera (the Greek Juno) snatched her
            breast from the infant Heracles (another of Zeus's by-blows),
            scattering milk across the sky to form our galaxy. An udderly similar
            expression is credited to the Iranian goddess Yakut Kubai-Khotun,
            whose breasts are "as large as leather sacks" (Middendorf).
Orion: sa second note to T0323.
Andromeda: Daughter of Cepheus, King of Ethiopia. Chained to a rock to be
            devoured by a sea-monster, she was rescued by Perseus.

181

Order

The passion that my heart so wildly took
Most sweetly now is tutored to command;
It was as bells the riving earthquake shook
That now in lovely chimes run through the land
It was— but I forget, so fierce it sped,
Torn & caught up, & spreading with no track
Now on its whispered fulness flowers are fed,
So that its easy banks no beauty lack.
How art thou loved! Chaos no secret has,
It opens noisy fissures to the light;
But Love is that brings happy things to pass
Opening its triumph to the clear daylight
Yet secret— Oh how falsely they surmise
Who hold that candour has no mysteries.

T1199 This english sonnet was never published, but has survived in two Oxford autographs, both in Michael's hand and obviously her work; the final version appears to be that given here (OWK 154b), though the title and full date *May 14 1905* occur only in the other manuscript (OWJ 14b). The relationship with Ricketts (for he is the subject) did not always run smoothly; in fact by this time it was on the wane: by June (v.i.) he had realised "a small pause seemed desirable in a cataract of recent visits, in which I had become as cheap as a relative" (OZB 174). Michael by contrast could not have enough of him, though she also had come to realise that she had to make compromises to retain the friendship. In April she wrote in the Journal 'My relation with "Fay" is spoiled because I must have affairs with him— ..it is when we seek each other we are at peace'. In the previous sentence she proposes to stop 'business relations with God. Never have affairs with God' (ZJT 46b). These reflections seem to be at the back of the current poem.

passion: As for *affairs*, it is important that this word be not misconstrued; the implications are evidently *agitation* and *rage* rather than sexual desire.

noisy: There was plenty of noise to come. Friends watching Wilde's *Salome* 'witnessed some of Herod's wildest moments (and) they all three at once exclaimed Miss Bradley!'. Ricketts when told of this (May 19) 'confesses, with many reservations, that he too traced Michael in Herod's outbreaks.. he has seen quite enough of Herod & of Queen Elizabeth in his visits to Paragon' (H ZJT 62-3). In June Michael wrote to him 'I do not care a straw what you think of Borgia or any other damned play— in comparison with the good of our being "very pleasant to each other"— like David & Jonathan' (ZJT 68a). The strength of her feeling (most likely in defence of her niece) is patent in the cuss-word, perhaps the only one in all the Michael Field papers; it was this "outbreak" that made Ricketts decide on "a small pause."

candour: Frankness, but possibly used in the old sense of *kindliness*.

Eros

"I have no Temple!"— "O young god,
Give me that wide, protecting hand . . .
    No Temple in the land!"
He gave the hand, and foot by foot we trod.

Supine before us lay the Earth,
Held of impregning light and half-enskied,
    Yet adverse— woe betide!—
Uneasy, as the starving in their dearth.

A restless bull clanged on the air;
Bitten young buds, once red, were pressing red
    Up to frost-edges dead:
And on young things fell an unwearied care.

Birds were dark-cradled lutes, and men
And women listened, tho' they knew it not,
    But in a trance forgot,
Till from their flesh lutes echoed back again.

And secret in a green-leaved place,
The Beautiful, the Idalian goddess lay
    Watching a spring-flower's way
Up from the dark, with tremulous breast and face.

T1203   The single autograph in Henry's hand has no date, but the
manuscript context is not incompatible with 1905 (OWQ 53-4).
        The Journal offers tenuous backing evidence. Francis had met up
with them at the end of July, during their return visit to Derbyshire: Henry recorded
'Chatted with the Prof. on childhood & Eros.. walked on the hill among the
fragments of a rain-bow, many clouds at sail, many hill-tops..' (H ZJT 94a). There
might even be a direct reference to this walk at v4-6. There are at least two other
Michael Field pieces on Eros, one with the identical title (T0821, sa T0993). The
present poem was eventually published in DEDICATED, DDD 100.

Temple:	But see note six to *To the Lord Love*, T1155.
Supine:	*Idle, lethargic*; possibly *sloping*. Perhaps even *looking up*.
impregning:	See note four to *Ebbtide at Sundown*, T0873.
enskied:	*In the sky*; which certainly seems to imply a hill-top.
clanged:	*Bellowed*. Henry also mentions 'evening fields of wide landscape,.. the rush of cattle at sun-setting to the river..' (ZJT 93b).
Idalian goddess:	Aphrodite, from her ancient cult centre at Idalium in Cyprus.

September

But why is Nature at such heavy pause,
And the earth slowly ceasing to revolve?
Only the lapping tides abide their laws,
And very softly on the sand dissolve.
The fruit is gathered— not an apple drops:
In little mists above the garden bed
The petals of the last gold dahlia shed;
The spider central 'mid his wreathed dewdrops!
Oh still, oh quiet!— and no issue found;
No laying up to rest of callow things,
Or scale, or sheaf, or tissue of armed wings:
Open the tilth, open the fallow ground!
The fragrance of the air that has no home
Spreads vague and dissolute, nor cares to roam.

T1208   This is the first of two pieces that (presumably) Michael wrote on *Sunday Sept 17th. 1905* (OWJ 15b); two other autographs have survived, another in Michael's hand (OWK 157b), with a fair copy in the hand of Henry (OWL 112). The quatorzain eventually appeared in WILD HONEY as # IX in the *Mane et Vespere* group, WDH 110; it was then not reprinted until the Higonnet anthology of 1996 (AMH).

During the month they had been at work on QUEEN MARIAMNE. On the 30th Michael resumed 'this neglected journal' and on the same page, but dated Oct 5th, Henry repeated these exact words. 'Why so neglected? Well, September has been a mountain of Purgatory: the weather has hugged me indoors to suffocation-point; cold fogs, cold rains, or the warm slackening damps of the grave. We have been afflicted with inhuman melancholia, that does not bear to be remembered. Our isolation in Paragon under these circumstances has been a curse. Day after day we have spoken to no-one, save our ever-soothing dogs. And the sense of great powers of converse lying by in ever-corroding inertness, in seclusion that is not even safe from time, has been despair to us— despair on the dangerous road the end of wh: Wordsworth foretold Gout & Solitude— who can fight such an alliance?' (H ZJT 111b-2a).

sand: The first thought was *sands* (OWJ 15b).
callow: Unfledged, inexperienced; (also applied to alluvial flats).
tilth: Arable (tilled) land.
fallow: Untilled.

184

Disillusion

There is another autumn & more rich,
More sorrowful of its sad mysteries
Than stain of changing colour on the trees,
Or the unravelling vineyards, stitch on stitch.
For love, in season's progress, to its lych
Gate must pass on; & slowly through disease,
Long weeping, & more long aridities
Must re-adjust itself in every niche.
For Love must ease his burthen— no more song.
Love's birds must bear their song to the salt sea
And no sweet odour, when Love walks along,
Nor music of his breath may ever be;
Yet, being a god, Love lingers on the coast
And smiles across the treasure he has lost.

T1209   In this companion italian sonnet, also written that September Sunday
(OWK 158b), Michael contemplates and accepts the inevitable loss of
the Stranger to whom for so long she has been in leash. For one
reason or another (v.i.) the poem was never published, but strangely her words
would soon become reality. The friendship with Ricketts had already begun to
'unravel', and within a month Francis would be engaged; verses 6-7 would also
prove horribly prophetic. Mercifully, she could not know this. Like 'Love's birds' (and
Sappho) she bears her song to the cliff, and 'the salt sea'.

lych-gate: A roofed gate at which the corpse (lich) on its bier would rest before
entering the churchyard.
aridities: See T1409.
niche: Michael was not altogether happy with v8; the other surviving
autograph has a line through it, and the note *rewrite* (OWJ 16ab).
burthen: Burden, or load; with the possible extra sense of *refrain* (of a song).

Her Profile

Nought from the changing seasons can we win:
I have desired that men should learn her spell
As it abides, profound, perpetual,
In contour from the forehead to the chin:
But there is such a tremor in the line,
Such quick beneath the chiselling— what art
The shore of her breath's egress can define?
What lips in all the world part as hers part?
Lo, of a chance, one night, she in her chair
A little from the hearth, a radiance swims
From candles lit beyond that face of hers,
So holden of a dream it never stirs,
While all its tender marge in shadow rims,
Even as a dusky pearl caresses air.

T1215   One of the magical quatorzains (metrically it is not a strict sonnet) that
Michael wrote for Henry. It is dated *Sunday Nov 26th 1905* (YFB 19b)
and four autographs have survived. The moment of inspiration is
detailed in a Journal entry for 24 November. Michael writes: 'Sitting by the nice
log-fire in the sun-room, Henry silhouettes— fine in angle & ridge to the upper lip—
& then a series of curves with margin soft as a bloom misted grape. No lips in the
world part as her lips part. And the line from the lower lip to the chin defines as a
pearl by light caressing the air. When in full-face (the shadow of) her coronet of
plaits gives lovely ripple to the contour of her head' (ZJT 129a). The first draft of the
new piece is on the facing page of the Journal. In September 1924 Carta Sturge
wrote of Henry "It was.. the still side that one generally saw. Her speech was slow
and low and scarce, and had just that suggestion of chant which Mr. Pearsall Smith
exaggeratedly attributes to both. She had, too, a slight lisp which the irreverent were
tempted to mimic a little..." (JWL V16 #35 281).

The poem was first published in WILD HONEY, WDH 178 and reprinted by Edwin
Essex in *Carmina*, when he commented on the "observant love" that "united aunt and
niece." "Miss Bradley's affection was always the more articulate: hers was the
temperament romantic, expansive, glowing" (JCM #8, 1931). The poem was printed
again in *The Catholic Literary Revival* (1935), but surprisingly this is its first
appearance in a modern anthology.

seasons: In the draft, and an Oxford autograph, this word is *features*, and hence
directly related to the main theme (ZJT 129b,OWK 160b); the Fortey
autograph agrees with the published text of WILD HONEY.
So holden: The Journal draft also offers a variant v12:

That is deep in a dream nor ever stirs

(Johannes's Song)

People, rejoice!
Christ is beheld,
Oh, oh, lu, lu!   Light of the East,
Oh, the Wise Men,   Shown to the South;
On camels, mules,   Brought by the Wise
Laden with myrrh,   Down the old road
Chetahs and tusks   Where— on God's Ark
Of elephants wild,   Came from God's Hill,
Journeying on   Came in the days
Where in her hut   Of Menelik, son,
Maryam sits,   Of Nikaula Wise!—
God on her knee!   Down the old road
Oh, the Wise Men,   From Sheba made,
Wise as our Queen,   On which the Queen
Leaving with gifts   Went forth with gifts,
Sheba behind,   With spice and gold,
Leaving the south   With questions hard—
For Soloman!   Down the old road
Oh, oh, lu, lu!   Our Queen trod back
With all she asked
From Soloman.

T*1221*   These two stanzas, here placed together, occur separately as a prelude
(XRB 161) and postlude (XRB 171) to Act III of RAS BYZANCE (sa
T1214). Since the play is in three Acts, the second stanza effectively
ends the drama. Only the first stanza is placed in the mouth of Johannes, 'A lad with
shaved head' who 'twangs a one-stringed instrument and wails a strange, piping
song, as he stands on one leg.' It seems likely that they were both written in late
1905, when work on the play was most active, but at present a closer dating is not
possible. Nor can one say with any certainty who the ultimate author is; but a guess,
and it can be no more than that, would attribute the evocative blank verse to Henry.
Oxford holds an autograph in her hand (OSF 53,79) and two typescripts (OSG,H).

Sheba: An account of the Queen's famous journey is given in I Kings X 1-13.
Soloman: In Ethiopian tradition he *married* the Queen (aka Makeda) and their
son Menelik I founded the royal dynasty.
God's Ark: The ark or chest of the covenant (Exodus XXVI 10, I-II Samuel *passim*).
questions: I Kings X 1. One purpose of her visit seems to have been to 'prove',
through a series of riddles, the fabled wisdom of Solomon.

O little Chow, hast thou no tryst to keep?
   Where is thy pain
  To reach me in the dark,
The flicker of thy paws up to my bed,
        Thy waiting head,
My hand that stirs; & then
   Back to thy couch again,
And for us both wide, shining sleep!

In January 1906 Michael's dog Whym Chow died from an infected cut: the blow was a devastating one. Their lives were to alter irrevocably.

T1232   A short sketch in Michael's hand that exists in working drafts (ZJV 31a) and a fair copy (OWK 165a); both sources are dated *Feb 9th 1906*.
      The piece paints a delightful picture which would be a perfect poem if only Michael had resolved the syntactical ambiguities. The dog had apparently slept in her bedroom. 'Every Dawn speaks of his brave tugging. Our folk at Rottingdean loved him' (H ZJV 27a). Even as late as 14 July Michael was writing that he was 'with us every day... all night long he was with us— & sometimes, he came— in the depth of the night— with soft breath for my hand' (ZJV 125b). In 1907 the theme recurs in another untitled fragment dated October 4, in which Musico the basset hound *(ICT: Music)* makes a guest appearance (sa T1334):

> *That it should be - - -*
> *Down at my knee*
> *The nosing-breath of him should come to me!*
> *I sighed— "How like, but it is Music now,*
> *It must be Music." —And the hound*
> *Far off, asleep is found.*
> *O Touch, O Breath, O little Chow,*
> *And it was thou!*   T1335

Mary Costelloe seems to have discussed the Whym Chow crisis with Ricketts, and his response was unfortunate. Henry recorded 'Michael has a brutal note from Fay "I have heard from the good Mary who reserves her affections for real & wholesome things, people & motors". Henry erupted. '.. The vulgar tirade— all mean pique & jealousy of a glorious Creature & Companion. Well may he be jealous— Michael & I love Chow as we have loved no human being— for central & to us is his Love— our

(Whym Chow XXIX)

O Chow, the Peace of her I love above
All else, O Feeder of her heart forlorn,
Sustainer of her torn,
Conflicted Nature with a seamless love!

Her Silence!— Light her, as with torch of fir,
O little flambeau, that hath never smoked,
Never grown dim, but ever leapt for her
Forth of its Bacchic resin; and evoked
By breath of her alone, would blaze and stir
Through desolation mountain-mists that choked
Dead hollows, till its presence came
Through them triumphant, with unbated flame.

Still love her, little Chow, still love thy Own,
For solely by thy leaping love she keeps
Live now on earth; and, of thy light alone,
By surety of thy brand that never sleeps,
Will she tread out her wandering with no moan,
Nor die! Unless thy ruddy flambeau leaps,
Nothing can assuage her grief,
No mortal nor immortal give relief.

Flame of Love. What are Ice-Countries* or Doctrines° with their Countesses to us
beside a flawless devotion, a complete Response, a Mystic Enhancing of every hour,
a caress— a passion as betwen God & man' (ZJV 25b-6a).

(!CT: *see T1218,MAS; °Berenson.)

tryst: Agreed appointment.
Where is: The Journal copy has verses 2-3 heavily scored through.

T1251   Known from the usual autograph in Michael's hand (OWO 26b), and
        published in WHYM CHOW FLAME OF LOVE, WCF 57. Henry, with a
        panache worthy of her aunt, here sets Michael's words into verse. On
28 February Michael wrote 'O Chow, my peace, my silence, Feeder of my Heart, &
sustainer of my torn conflicted Nature, by the unity of a seamless love, light me with
thy little flambeau that never smoked, or grew dim— that leapt from its Bacchic resin
for me— still love me, little Chow— for by thy leaping love alone I can keep alive
now on earth— Nor mortal, nor immortal can assuage my grief as thou' (ZJV 42-3).

The Goad

Eros, why should one or two small notes
    Of thrilled birds in Spring—
Why should one or two gay motes
Tangled round the beams on wing—
Why should delicate, first flowers,
        Have such powers
That all music sweeps me wild,
That all light of June is piled
In my eyes, and gardens flow
All the colour to me they shall grow?

By thy eloquence, O God of Love,
    We are made alive . . .
Thou with art all arts above
Dost against our slumber drive
Little shudderings of voice,
        Clear and choice;
Stroke of slender rays to wake
Our desire that summer break
On us in meridian heat,
Primroses by roses made effete.

T1259   This poem by Henry, which appears to break the Chow sequence, is difficult to date; a manuscript conflation at Oxford contains the only known autograph (OWQ 66-7). The fair copy occurs in a group of plain white papers, with those of two others— *Dry is the voice of Mystery*, and *In Aznac* (T1275-6), which might be taken to imply they were all three written around the same date; and T1275 can be independently dated to July 1906. Attribution of *The Goad* to March/April in this year is admittedly tenuous, but not improbable.

If this attribution is correct, the break in the Chow sequence is only apparent. There are two significant entries in the Journal for late March. 'I order crimson rose-bushes to put above our Little Fellow's grave..' (H ZJV 58a); 'On Wednesday (March 28th) gardener- made a thick rose-bush bed of the little grave. Since then- our hearts have lightened.- Even the maids say- there is something new to live for' (M ZJV 60b). This may be why 'in Spring' Henry longs for 'light of June', that primroses may be 'by roses made effete'. Or of course these references may be of no significance.

The poem was eventually published in DEDICATED, DDD 109, and not reprinted until the Leighton/Reynolds anthology VICTORIAN WOMEN POETS, in 1995.

Dry is the voice of Mystery

Dry is the voice of Mystery:
O Sphinx, it comes as out of sand,
With shards and grit of worlds upon the air;
It comes in arid murmurs from the land;
It comes across wide deserts everywhere;
Thirsty from thirsty throat it comes to thee.

From fir-woods loosening dust in grains,
That aromatic swim the wind,
Then whistle round thy head-dress in thine ear:
Even from the sea a dry voice is divined,
Deep from its hidden heart where sounds are drear,
A voice that rushes toward thee and attains.

The fields of wheat resound thy speech,
Their eager flood of sand makes hum,
Loosening its yellow syllables as though
It would into thy noon, a-wandering, come,
And, in its shifted circles wandering so,
Announce thy wealth across the Nubian beach.

With voice distinct, barren of tears,
Across thy terrible blue air,
O music-loving mask, my voice I lift,
From memory clean, unmuffled by despair,
And while before thy face the dust-clouds shift,
My song haunts whispering where thy Presence rears!

T1275   One of Henry's characteristic pieces, this is known only from an undated
         Oxford autograph (OWQ 68-9), and its inclusion in Part II of
         DEDICATED, DDD 110. However it seems most probable that the poem
dates from the late summer of 1906, and that the source inspiration is in the third
stanza. They were at Rottingdean (again). In a Journal entry for 28 July Henry writes:
'And I listen & hear the sound of sand, & desert grit in the flow of their sound: I feel
how dry is the voice of mystery, & it seems as if the wheatfield were taking on the
voice of desert-sand round the Sphinx ... The voice of all Mystery is dry. We must
never lament near the Sphinx' (ZJV 133b-4a). It is probably coincidental that later in
the year Ricketts was 'at work again on a thirsty Sphinx' (M ZJV 193a); in 1909 the
outcome of *that* was to be the unremarkable *A Drinking Sphinx*, T1461.

Vain Strife

They had fought a single combat fell,
   In the Court of Listenese,
So the wild histories of Arthur tell.
Sudden, as the wind snaps trees,
Burst Sir Balim's sword asunder;
And it checked the strife with wonder
At that steely crack of thunder . . .
Just one moment of great awe
Turned the quarrel into peace, then broke—
For Sir Balim through an open door
Darted from King Pelam's threatened stroke.

Through the unknown Castle shot
In mad haste Sir Balim, seeking
Sword, that he discovered not,
For revenge he would be wreaking:
As in vain he ran and sought,
Footfall of the King he caught
Following and full of stress
'Mid the Castle's loneliness:
For King Pelam followed fast;
Through each hall and chamber passed,
Fanning like a moth or bird
All the air Sir Balim stirred,
Till a little tempest beat
Round the foemen's tireless feet . . .
Down the Castle-halls and through
All the rooms they fled into . . .
And the terror of that air
Was of woe beyond compare—
Those who sought each other's death
Drew with cruel feet this breath.

Oh, a room! A hope 'mid fear . . .
Sharp on Balim's eyes appear
Spokes of gold from gold-cloth of a bed,
From the clean gold of a table spread
With a spear, a marvellous wrought spear.

Swift, amid the glow from bed and board,
Sir Balim sees the spear-ray leap . . .
Then he faces swift his foe abhorred,
Driving in his flesh the weapon deep.

Swoon upon King Pelam falls;
Terror shakes the Castle-walls—
The walls and ceiling tremble, break and fall,
Down sinks on his face Sir Balim— all
Lie sunken with the Chamber as a pall.

Only Galahad, when seeking far
The san graal, with forehead like a star,
Having found the Vessel of God's Blood,
That within the Castle-chapel stood,
May revive those sleepers from the dead:
For 'mid gold festoonings of that bed
Joseph, out of Aramathy, lay
Balmed and silent, day and night and day;
And the wondrous spear that Balim sped
Fierce against his foe, when Christ hung dead,
Had been by Longius struck with force
In the well-spring of the Holy Corse.

T1278   Henry's poem is the final piece in DEDICATED, DDD 119-21 before
         Michael's moving *envoi*. It is impossible to date; 1906 can only be an
         informed guesstimate (there is no autograph). The plot is taken from
Chapter XL in Part I of Sir Thomas Malory's *The History of Prince Arthur, King of
Britaine* (1634), which details the epic battle of King Pellam and Sir Balin. The
original tale is grand and robust. Balin kills Pellam's brother Garlon (Chapter XXXIX),
which precipitates the quarrel: *Then King Pellam caught in his hand a grim weapon,
and smote eagerly at Balin, but Balin put the sword between his head and the stroke,
and therewith his sword burst in sunder*. Chased into a chapel of the castle, Balin
discovers a wondrous-wrought spear on which he impales the King, and the whole
castle collapses— *And so the most part of the castle that was fallen down through
that dolorous stroke lay upon King Pellam and Balin three days*. The rest is
predictable pious claptrap dreamed up by christian mythographers

Listenese: Listenise in Malory; this cannot be Lyonnesse, the mythical birthplace of
           Tristram, which appears as *Liones* in Part II, Chapter I of *The History*.
Galahad: The pure or 'maiden' knight who alone could sit in the *Siege Perilous*,
           an empty seat at the Table Round reserved for one worthy to succeed in
           the Quest for the San Graal (*The History* Part III, Chapter XXXII).
san graal: Holy Grail, the Cup of the Last Supper: or a vessel purporting to contain
           some of the blood shed at Christ's crucifixion, perhaps from the further
           fantastication *sang real* ('royal blood').   *Notes continue overleaf.*

Without Hope

If we must part, that are so dear,
And of each other's sweetness near,
If we must part, then be it so
That the great sea between us flow.
Secure me an eternal space
For the descrying of thy Face,
    Let but the horizon line
Close me in pitiless confine,
My heart will turn back to her rest
As she were laid in quiet on thy breast

Joseph: Of Arimathea (Mark XV 43); allegedly arrived in Gaul in AD 63, *en route* to Britain. After a quick pop to Glastonbury to found an oratory, he seems to have turned up in Listenise to visit his 'kinsman' Pellam, to whom he obligingly bequeathed both Grail and spear (v.i.).

Longius: Or *Longinus*. He is identified in the Rabulas MS. (AD 586) as the soldier who thrust his spear into the dead Christ (John XIX 34).

T1280   Known only from a single autograph in Michael's hand, dated *Aug 11th. 1906* (ZJV 145b). On Friday the 10th they had travelled to Ireland via Chester for a first visit to the Ryans, who were now living at Grove House 'an eighteenth century house with a little tower' in Milltown, Dublin (ZJV 125b,OCM 158). In the garden of Grove House '...I hear Michael introduced to the Lar— a little Echo who can say all the vowels except ε, & returns one's goodnight through the leaves of the trees in a little familiar voice.' Their apartment was in the tower— 'Michael takes possession & dedicates it to Chow in her lines on the heart-sprung Rose' (H ZJV 148b-50a). That poem was T1279, and on the Sunday Michael wrote another poem linking both the garden echo and the dog, *Echoless* T1281. So one might at first (v4) imagine T1280 is also about Whym Chow, were it not for the inappropriateness of the final verse. Another possibility which overcomes this is that the dedicatee is Amy, with Michael viewing a future in which her married niece seems settled in Ireland. But the one from whom she really feared permanent separation (after death) was Henry, as the Journal makes abundantly clear: 'We take possession of our mountain tower.. . And when parting comes, if we may not go together— here there is for the one who is left a refuge; & here one will learn the beauty of the lonely life' (M ZJV 145a). The dower-house potentialities of the 'mountain tower' were to prove academic (and render the poem title strangely prophetic): Michael could not have foreseen both her nieces would predecease her.

descrying: Revealing: the least unlikely interpretation of a word which is both clearly written and tantalisingly illegible; other possibilities include *denying* and *devizing*, neither making much evident sense.

horizon line: 'I liked the voyage— with that one safe line left in the world— the horizon line— & all life .. drawn from another element' (M ZJV 145a).

It had been well if thou hadst smitten me,
For, at thy cleaving, I had fallen quite,
Full-leaved in all my noisiness of light,
And 'mid the brimming mosses ceased to be!
So had I fallen from thy memory
With quiet touches, & not chid thy sight
A scare-crow in the room of thy delight;—
But thou most cruelly hast withered me
With hacking blows severing my linkèd bark;
Nor sap may rise, nor heavenly dews descend—
Nor with the air's sweet breath my being bend
Rigid above the field, a brand, a mark
Disfiguring! Love, when thou passest by
As from a gallows-tree wilt thou not fly?

T1289   Known only from a Journal draft in Michael's hand, with the epigraph
          This of the old ring-barked ash tree of Eastfield (ZJV 170a). There is no
          date, but the last entry was for Sunday 16 September 1906 (ZJV 169b);
when this was written they had been in the Eildon Hills, a short range in Roxburgh,
just south of Melrose. Michael records: 'We see the hills once behind blinding
sunset— often in dark, solid grey. Once in a bean-field we come across a skeleton
ash, ring-barked. In all its strong life it stretches out thorny patched (ICT: this word is
possibly *parched*) branches to the wind— cruel, & athirst it stands— Its winter
nakedness was that of a man at his bath— This thrust-on bareness is that of a sinner
shuddering before God' (ZJV 168a). The hills themselves appear in the Journal in
two inserted photographs (ZJV 169b,170b), and are the subject of another
unpublished sonnet *Trimontium*, T1288.

sap may rise: The removal of a ring of bark could have no effect on the ascent of
          sap, since the water-conducting tracheids and vessels lie entirely in
          the xylem (wood) of the trunk. It is only the function of the
          food-translocating sieve tubes in the phloem that would be
          disorganised. Bark ringing in apple trees is sometimes done in early
          June to increase yield of blossom and fruit the next year, since this
          conserves foodstuffs which would otherwise pass down through the
          bark to the roots. But in the case of the ash tree *Fraxinus*, it is
          conceivable the bark itself had been harvested that spring. Extracts
          contain a glycoside (fraxin), which is both diuretic and purgative:
          infusions provide a bitter tonic (at one time used as a quinine
          substitute), and decoctions have been incorporated in compresses.

"In an old Music I have found your face—

In an old music I have found your face—
Lover of mine, how you shine on me,
  As the old music dances dizzily,
An old, dance music of a dizzying pace.
       Where one fleeth amain,
Mad-footed, devouring the race;
While the music dreams on, as of twain
That eddy round in a locked embrace.
Lover of mine, in your olden place, how you shine on me
  You are glowing with love, & the pain
    That you are not loved back again.

T1290   This unpublished poem with Francis in mind is undated, but from the
         Journal context (ZJV 170b) was written 14-18 September— for the full
         background see *But if our love be dying let it die*, T1287. It appears
to be Michael's recast final thoughts on the piece she wrote at the end of August:

> In an old music I have found your voice—
>   Not as in a crystal glass
>   Full of sorrows that must pass—
> An old dance-music of a dizzing pace,
>   Singing the doom
> Of the rose that forever must bloom;
> Carrying our love along as in race
> Of the circling stars, & free
> As the moan of their harmony.   T1286

'..Amy plays bits of music that belong, as it were, to her hand... Suddenly the yearning clangor of Chopin's George Sand Valse! It breaks through the past; it tears its way down time. . . Michael is dragged half-conscious with me through the reft it makes till we reach the lovely little parlour at Stoke Green— see, clear, as if we were looking at cameos, the illumed face of the Mother under the head of lovely hair, like a spindle-ful of silver thread— the handsome complaisance of the Father to this music;.. (and Francis) so one with the music its sounds were almost as a satisfaction of desire— a <u>Nunc dimitis</u> of one of the senses at least. Amy & I graceful figures among the others in aesthetic dresses, clinging & <u>unies</u> in colour' (H ZJV 162a).

A late letter from Francis, dated Oct 21/11, shows the withdrawal and formality Henry had remarked on (SZD 112). It opens "Dearest Cousin K.," and ends "..I remain, with best & tenderest love to dear Edith, Always your devoted & affectionate, Francis" (ZKF 216-7). What else could she have expected a married man to write?

amain: At full speed, with great haste.
race: Rapid onward movement (sa T1286, v7-8).
olden place: The last phrase of v9, (the refrain from v2) was an afterthought.

How glad was I that I had got
Of cyclamen a flowery pot!—
So level, lovely did they troop,
And when the hour fell they must stoop,
Their stems, turned round as finger-tip
That from itself a ring lets slip,
Let go the white flowers on the soil,
Then reared themselves in noble coil—
Lifting for sake of those sweet looks
Trophies, & monuments, & crooks.

T1301   On Sunday October 21st Michael had recorded in the Journal the terminal throes of one of her cyclamen plants, *possibly* a present from Ricketts (v.i.). '— I am watching one of our little white cyclamens die— Her stalk in an arch rolls over— & her little white head drops over on to the soil. With such intention she struck upward to the sun— now groping in her white— she seeks the darkness. And it is one rhythm' (ZJV 192b). In November she also copied into the Journal part of a letter she had written to him. 'All I can offer you is these wonderful little crosiers of your cyclamen. "O draw me some!" I have watched them in the window-sill, day by day, as they bent & contorted themselves, &, dropping their little white flowers in the soil, twisted above them, trophies & monuments & signal crooks.' The poem, untitled, but dated *Nov 6th*, follows immediately in her hand (ZJV 203ab). There exists one other autograph at Oxford (OWK 172b).

Though not as fine as *Cyclamens* (T0582), this poem— after an uncertain start— conjures up a memorable image from the lovely trope of v5-6; anyone who has seen this plant in senescence will immediately recognise its aptness. Here we have some of the magic and dying fall of another of Michael's peerless flower poems, *Camellias* (T1105).

It was at the time of Whym Chow's death that Henry finally switched off her brain and took refuge in superstition. Everlasting loss and the futility of all things being too appalling to contemplate, let alone accept, she turned to a source which promised, with a full theatre of mumbo-jumbo, a single certainty. Since she <u>needed</u> it to be true, it <u>had</u> to be true; this, as with all religion, was the fallacy at the heart of the matter. The splendid games of paganism were abandoned for the equally baseless, but deadly serious, entrenchments of dogma. And of course where Henry led, Michael had perforce to follow. In April/May 1907 they became Catholics, consequently meeting Emily Fortey (see T1341,SZD), and probably through her Vincent McNabb, Michael's eventual confessor (MFC 60).

Wild was the honey thou did'st eat;
The rocks and the free bees
Entombed thy honeycomb.
Take thou our gifts, take these:
No more in thy retreat
Do we attend thine ears; no more we roam
Or taste of desert food;
We have beheld thy Vision on the road.

T1329   This untitled stanza appears, precisely dated *July 14th, 1907* as the
             preface to WILD HONEY (WDH pe). Two drafts survive, both in
             Michael's hand, in her ledger of 'Catholic Poems' (YFD 12ab,79o).
The idea of a collection to be called "Wild Honey" dates back to March 1893, when
Henry recorded 'We write poems for the first time on Wild Honey...— We the Knights
of the Modern' (HZJF 24b). The earliest known poem to make the final collection
would be *On a Portrait by Tintoret in the Colonna Gallery* (T0599), written that May.

On 20 April 1907, a review of the American edition of UNDERNEATH THE BOUGH
appeared in *The Academy* (JAC #1824); it was headed *A NEGLECTED POET*, and
signed A.D. (sa ZJW 82ab). It seems this was the stimulus for a hotfoot letter from
the publisher Fisher Unwin, scenting a quick profit, on the 22nd (ZJW 85b). Henry
coolly replied 'I could prepare a volume of short lyrics & sonnets which I should call
"Wild Honey"' (OKE 72-80). The next issue of *The Academy* (JAC #1825) carried a
further surprise. 'The Academy has a poem obviously written to Michael Field by his
Reviewer A.D. To a Silent Poet. It is a charming poem. Who can this seraph be with
his initials of the Year of the Lord?' (H ZJW 98b). Then, while Michael Field was in
Edinburgh, John ('Dorian') Gray — who better informed— let the catamite out of the
bag. 'The sonnet by Anno Domini Father Gray says is by the Seducer of Oscar. "He
was the wicked man!" bursts out the vehement little Priest— but... only laughs like a
school-boy at the thought it is 'Boosy' *(ICT: sic!!)* who has reviewed & be-sonnetted
us' (H ZJW 102a). One imagines Mr. Wilde did not require much "seducing", thank
you very much. Henry and Michael were aghast.

But Douglas had played a crucial *rôle* in the Michael Field story (sa OCP 12r). On
23 April Henry wrote to Amy 'What a book we will give the world this first of our
Catholic Years— Sonnets & Lyrics into the desert— Honey of Neglect has been
distilled into strange sweetness, worthy to dedicate to St John Baptist, who has
brought us out of the desert with the lustral waters' (OCO 141o). In another letter to
Amy, Michael quotes the closing verses to the poem (OCT 86o). Had the book come
out in the early 1890's, the typescript epigraph clearly shows that their wild honey
was originally, and more happily, gathered for Euripides *(The Bacchae)*, Swinburne
and Blake; not a headstrong (and later headless) water-sports Israelite (OVM pe).

Wild..honey: Mark 16.
Vision: sa *God's delight*, T1086.

198

Spello

Spello the name you christened it— a flower
  Grown to my will— so long ago
               That day you came!
  You greet the flower & you repeat the name:
  While I — O Shame
  That age should dim, & age deny me so
What still is shining in your thoughts— Forgive!
      I have recalled the hour;
And it was evening and uncertain rain—
The memory will not fall back again.

T1331   A vivid occasional piece, known only from two autographs in Michael's hand. One, with the partial date *July-19-20th*, occurs in an exercise book of poems all of which seem to relate to Ricketts (OWJ 21b: see the note to *To the Lord Love*, T1155). The poems are almost without exception in chronological order, and T1331 is immediately preceded (20b) by a poem written *January 31 1907*; its immediate successors (22b,3b) are assigned *January 1908* and *Sent to Painter Oct 9th 1907 Wednesday*; at which point the book ends. It seems reasonable therefore to allocate T1331 to 1907.

That Ricketts is indeed the dedicatee appears confirmed by the second autograph, which has neither title nor date; it is on an isolated, very last, sheet— perhaps an enclosure with a letter— in one of the British Library volumes of Ricketts & Shannon Papers, ZCR 184o. There are no further clues as to the identity of the flower, or the occasion on which it received its curious name.

The BL manuscript has a domestic footnote: 'Impossible for Michael to remain a poet. Just called off to dress a burn in cook's hand. Soon there will be matter for confession— if indeed Spello is not a confession.'

to my will: Ricketts may have implied admiration for Michael's skills as horticulturist / mage, the flower having been *spelled* in the sense *conjured*.

He whose lips have touched Christ's lips
Writeth the Apocalypse.

In deep herbage, by a stream,
He beholds the Heavenly Dream.

Lo, he groweth very old,
But his love hath ne'er grown cold!

Only, since his eyes are dim,
Christ hath sent to comfort him

Vision of the very Word
That in Galilee he heard:

And to him whose day declineth
Glory of the Sun that shineth,

Not as when on Earth He trod—
Very God of Very God.

From the sweet mouth of the Lord
There proceedeth now a sword,

Wars of men and angels mingle,
And his ears with trumpets tingle.

Kings are slain and kings arise
In the passing of those skies.

There is left a bloody trail
There is left a rolling wail.

And the day sinks to its brink
And the marshalled spirits sink.

Brown upon the glistened earth,
He perceives another birth.

Very golden is the stream;
And he dreams another dream.

He hath written it all down;
And the sun is going down.

Homeward he must now to sup,
And he rolls the parchment up.

Only, as he ties the bands,
Folding quietly his hands,

To himself, in peace, he saith,
Will it be before my death?

And he prayeth, turning home,
Even so, Lord Jesus, come!

At the door he pondereth,
Will it be before my death?

T1343   An untitled poem which exists in separate drafts in three of the Fortey
               Cache manuscripts, all in Michael's hand. In one instance this only
               amounts to the single stanza s1 (YFD 18b), but luckily a complete
text in another case bears the partial date *Nov 1907* (YFC 18b). The piece was
eventually published in the subgroup *Sword* in MYSTIC TREES, MCT 88-9.

He whose lips: 'The Church seems afraid of the Love St. John learnt from the
               Bosom of Christ. The young eagle with a nest on the Sacred Heart is
               too daring a creation for the Church to speak of ingenuously' (H
               ZJV 227a sa OCN 101r). This hypocrisy of the church down the
               ages is just one of the more detestable aspects of certain of those
               mealy-mouthed men in frocks who preach brimstone while covertly
               eying up their altar boys. Certainly one does not have to be
               gay/queer, only of moderate intelligence, to recognise the special,
               valid, and in no way unusual relationship between the carpenter's
               son and the son of Zebedee. Henry's own specific attempts at
               portraying the "bosom friendship" (T1320-1)— though brave— are
               decidely mawkish.
Writeth: In Patmos (Revelation I 9), probably at the end of the reign of
               Domitian (81-96). Theologians are now less inclined to credit this
               terrifying vision to the 'beloved disciple'.
Apocalypse: Uncovering, or revelation, especially in the eschatological sense.
Dream: A late survival of the Berenson doctrine (see third note, T1132).
sword: Revelation I 16.
trumpets: Revelation VIII 6.
my death?   John XXI 22-4.
Even so: Revelation XXII 20.

Schism

They have nailed Hands & Feet, & to the Storm
That bloweth hard— naked they leave His form.

He looketh up to Heaven, while they dangle
His clothes; &, cutting them in portions wrangle

"Whose shall this be?— Now from your halving cease—
Behold, it is a garment of one piece

Whose shall it be?" The soldiers with one mind
Throw down their dice: the vesture is assigned.

For of God's Majesty that lovely shroud
To mutilate, they are not so allowed.

. . . .

To every one of us in his estate
This shroud is left inviolate.

We may not rend it, we may wear it whole,
As the most lovely garment of the soul.

Drops as of blood— signet of wound & wound:
For us His body in this garment swooned.

Yea, each of us, to each it is complete
Reaching without a flaw from neck to feet.

This— His dear Mother's work— this seamless thing
Shall we to Christ for His division bring?

While we for fragments of His vesture press,
Entire He yields His nakedness.

And rather would we perish of the cold
Than that this single thing be manifold.

T1359   The three autographs of this previously unpublished piece, centred on John
XIX 23-4, are all in the hand of Michael— including this fair copy which
was presumably sent to McNabb (YSL BKF 2.20). Signed *M.F.* and dated
Feb. 21st 1908., its couplets are strongly reminiscent of the mediaeval Mystery plays.

Autograph of *Schism*, T1359
Hand of Katharine Harris Bradley, dated *Feb. 1908*. Notice the three extra stanzas 7,13,14 and the absence of stanza 8.　　　Fortey Cache MS　YFE 14b,5b　(x 0.50).

In Monte Fanno

Sylvester by an open tomb
Beheld Time's vanity and doom—
A lovely body, as a flower,
Left by a ploughman's foot, wet in a shower.

Sylvester meditated, thought
His days to solitude were brought.
Sight of a corpse within its grave! . . .
To be an eremite alone were brave.

Sylvester is a monk: and men
Grow frequent round his holy den:
Thence to a mount he leads them out,
Called *Fannus* . . . through the wood they hear a shout.

Sylvester builds his cloister.— Hush!
Across the doorstep comes a rush,
And all the monks faint with a lure
That those in burgeoning woods lost deep endure.

Sylvester calls into the dark—
There is a breath of those that hark—
"Peace, peace! I am Sylvester! Peace!"
Trespass and echoes and sweet motions cease.

Sylvester in the woods, as still
Even as the grave that bowed his will,
When he became at first a monk,
Rules every power in oak and olive-trunk.

Sylvester conquers by his name:
King Fannus and all Fauns lie tame
Beneath it, and the wild-wood Cross,
That he hath planted deep into the moss.

Sylvester and his monks are clear
From any advent warm and drear
Through any door: but sometimes he
Looks with slant eyes through piles of leafery.

T1383   This narrative poem by Henry is known only from its publication in
           POEMS OF ADORATION, PAD 55-6. It must have been written by 24
           June 1908. In a letter to John Gray about her niece's "chrism",
preserved in Edinburgh and dated *Midsummer Day 1908*, Michael records that
'Henry would like to take the names Michael Sylvester... Sylvester as reprover of the
Fauns she has written a delightful little poem about' (YSH uf). King Fannus is
probably Faunus (often confused with *Silvanus*), the oracular woodland deity who
speaks in the murmurs of the forest, a roman equivalent of Pan. Sylvester may be
the saint who also bound the jaws of a halitotic dragon which poisoned 300 men
every day. Henry's legend has proved untraceable, and though the metre lurches
along in an ungainly fashion, the tale itself is indeed delightful— not least in that
there is obviously still something nasty in the thickets alert to snag a passing cassock.

Baptism

A Babe, still, rosy from the Cherubim,
Set solid by his mother on my knee!
O lovelier the vision that I see,
The oscillating light that sits with him!

O fresh as the first fig-leaf Eden sprung,
Warm as the egg that from the dove we part—
Something thou lackest . . . drops of chrism clung
About thee, and God's charms wrapt round thy heart.

O hidden Sacrament, O second Birth,
O honey-breeding Secret in the hive,
Stealing as Ver by inches through the earth,
Spurring each instinct mightily alive!

Shall they deprive thee of this lovely thing?
O Babe, weep with me for thy christening!

T1408   The only known autograph is in Michael's hand in one of the Fortey
          cache 'Scribble' books. Untitled, it has the footnote *2nd. Sunday in
          Advent* (YFD 50b); from the text and the context the full date of
composition is therefore 06 December 1908. William Rothenstein's son was born on
the 19th of March, and 'Will asks Michael to god-mother the babe' (H JZY 59b).
This request made up for Michael's disappointment when Sturge Moore asked
Ricketts to godfather his own son Daniel (see T1212); her cup ran over when she
heard 'The child is to be William Michael... The H.D. *(ICT: 'Heavenly Dog')* wants his
name & the name of the "noble Michael Field" tied together in the registry & form of
his child's name' (H ZJY 69a). That she took her new duties very seriously is evident:
in August a Jesuit "father" had helpfully told her that an unbaptised baby 'has no
hope of Heaven. It has never been the friend of God' (ZJY 140b). The Journal also
records a consultation with McNabb in mid-December as to 'how Michael can get
him baptised' (ZJY 208ab). The piece was published in the *Sward* section of MYSTIC
TREES (MCT 91), and later reprinted in Will Rothenstein's 1932 memoirs, with what
might have been its original title *To W.M.R.* The child himself reappears (probably) in
T1363, and in T1488 as one of *the souls most innocent that dwell /Hallowed, on the
fringe of hell* (v22-3). Rothenstein commented "Had they lived they would have taken
comfort from the fact that one of my sons became a Roman Catholic; but not he to
whom they dedicated the poem" (FWR 127).

mother: Alice Mary Rothenstein, aka 'Noli'.
honey: The autograph version is subtly but significantly different,
                      O honey, breeding secret in the hive,
Ver: See the second note to *In one Time*, T1110.

206

Gratitude

I love thee in thy perfectness
   As I love the tit
— Love looking at it,
Requiring nothing of song or wit,
Desiring the blue, the gray, the black
   Of its wings and back.
Desiring the black of its head:—
With a joy to bless, to bless
All of its movements, more or less—
And its flight when it has fled.

T1430   This poem has survived as a single manuscript copy on a loose sheet of
paper (OYR 29o). It appears to be in the hand of Emily Fortey; she
appends a date *1909*. A letter she wrote to Thomas Sturge Moore on
12 November 1928 fills out what little background remains. 'Some poems written
after Edith Cooper's death were given to me for the little volume by Michael herself &
I have kept others which have reference to Edith's illness & last days. I am sorry that
the last few poems that I enclose are copies but for the moment I cannot lay my
hand on the original MS. which I have in the house. I can send them later & any
other poems that I may find. There is, I know, one written to "Painter" on his birthday,
but I do not think it could be published for many years to come. What a sting there is
in the last line of Michael's "Gratitude"!' (OYR 15or).

This letter raises several new hares; but the last sentence leaves little doubt that the
poem here is the one referred to in her letter. One would like to believe that this is a
lone survivor of Michael's 'smallest songs possible', written in June 1914; it could
then be read as a latest tribute to her dead niece. But the date on the MS. is an
obstacle which *seems* insurmountable. In all the cases (save one) where Emily added
a date to a poem, that date has been substantiated. The one exception is T1334;
and unfortunately it is only one exception that we need. (We will course one of the
hares. *Old Friendship* (T1706) is virtually certain to be the piece 'written to "Painter"
on his birthday'. This is particularly tantalising, as it implies Emily may have had a
copy of the complete poem. All that survives today is an incomplete draft in one of
the 'Scribble' books. This was written in October 1913; Ricketts was born in Geneva,
02 October 1866.)

thee: If not for Henry, then for whom?   Assuming the piece is late, it is
possible this is another Catholic poem, with an appropriate Dedicatee.

the tit: In November 1911, Michael wrote 'I am giddy with the tits chipping
cocoa-nut at my window— & a wind that has been reading an early
copy of the spring to be issued next year' (ZKB 151b). Then, poignantly,
a year later, of 'the tiny gold room where the tits are no longer fed'
(ZKC 139b). These are rare Journal references to a bird once common
before the Silent Spring. Yet it would be rash to rush to a conclusion on
such precarious evidence.

Suggested by a Picture

It is the brows, the infinite, soft confusing
Of wave on wave and lovely current there;
It is the brows, the marge of the soft hair
In reedy level; or it is the eyes
Where plumes of sea-birds wrangle with the skies;
It is the mouth where bitter shadow lies,
Where in the twilight there are nymphs that mourn
As at the birth of Christ and grow forlorn—
O face, take heed what freedom you are losing!
This cowl is as a cage
For such soft passion's rage;
And, when the temperance of youth is gone,
You will be terrible to look upon.

T1455   Although this poem was printed in the *Sward* subgroup of MYSTIC
TREES (MCT 90), both Journal and a letter to Amy make it clear the
piece was a collaboration— as Henry writes, 'Cut out by me & stitched
by Michael' (ZJZ 134b). The letter includes the text, with its first title *A Portrait*, and
the footnote *Portaferry. Sept. 1909* (OCT 104o). The poem draws on a portrait of
Vincent McNabb 'at about 30.. (he) sits, holding a book delicately.' It was written
Sunday 05 September after a sneaky visit to his birthplace— and his aunt, who
supplied the picture— in Co Down (ZJZ 132-6, sa early drafts ZKF 206o,7o).

The Dominican appears in several 1909 poems, as another MYSTIC TREES piece:
    To see him in his place— / The face and the voice of the face!   T1423,s1
In the unpublished *Vincent*, we have the dispassionate couplet:
    As a bird to God he lifts his throat, / And he cannot sing a note.   T1469,v5-6
Michael is kinder in a 1910 poem *In Retreat*, published in THE WATTLEFOLD:
    To himself I hear him singing low /As a throstle hidden deep in fern. T1568,v3-4
But the 1909 drafts of another piece never stray far from his 'terrible' aspect:
    How he riseth, wrinkled, tall / And majestic to appal   T1468,s4
In the long run McNabb was to prove the sure anchor Michael needed in her last
days. Meanwhile that October (T1460, q.v.) she would conjure him again.

eyes: Earlier in the year Henry referred to his 'eyes tamarisk-coloured.. the
        line of his broken nose, dried skin, lips half of the Egyptian Sphinx, half
        of the Egyptian anchorite; eye-lids carved as in stone..' (ZJZ 82-3).
sea-birds: Michael then wrote another poem about him, and Portaferry itself—
        He was born where the leaves drop into the sea   T1456, v1
mouth: '..the mouth where there is twilight shade in wh the nymphs mourn, as
        at the birth of Christ' (H OCT 100or).
terrible: It was not for nothing that Henry early on described him as 'This elegant
        Wasp of God' (ZJX 20a). On another occasion she remarks 'his lips are
        at their born work when preaching sacramental suffering' (ZJY 67ab).

Before Requiem

Bees from loveliest fields of light,
Make our darksome candles bright!
From the balsam beds ye come
To build glory round the tomb.

Angels from the summer ye,
Angels to our Mystery,
That these golden rods, that stand
Sentry to our dead, have planned!

Pause upon us; stay from hell
Our poor souls with hydromel;
Work us wax so fine, its flame
Be of God's the very name.

Bees, O autumn bees, that fled
Home with tribute for our dead,
Very gentle be your doom,
Dying on the ivy-bloom!

T1463   One of Michael's poems, *probably* written in November 1909; the
              one (undated) autograph YFF 56a lies in a run of 1910 pieces, but
              after a 10 page gap— and follows T1462, known to date from
October 1909. Henry certainly writes in early November 1909 of 'a Requiem Mass—
the dear sticks of golden-wax from the honey-combs' (ZJZ 180a); but also, at Amy's
funeral in January 1910, of 'the dear brown candles the bees make for the dead'
(ZKA 46a). This (see v8,14) makes *absolute* dating to 1909 less sound. The poem
was published in the subgroup *Sword* of MYSTIC TREES, MCT 93.   sa ZJW 222a.

hydromel: A beverage made from honey mixed with water (unfermented mead).

John Ryan, D.Sc., LL.M. (1855-1919)   From a personal greetings card sent at Christmas 1899. Professor of Mechanics and Engineering at University College, Nottingham 1884-5 and then at University College, Bristol 1885-99, in 1899 he was appointed Principal of Woolwich Polytechnic. He married Amy that September. In 1905 they moved to Ireland.   (YCD: Bristol University Library MS. 219).

Amy Cooper Ryan (1863-1910)   A late portrait with no date, possibly 1908, taken from a Catholic memorial card inscribed *Amy Katharine Mary Ryan, who died on January 22nd 1910*.   (ZKF 42o: British Library Add.MS. 46804B, Part I 42r).

Severing

To comfort one who cried to me in need,
Although I knew not how the thing might be
My love stood by me so attentively,
Presumptuous I wrote that I would speed:
When I began to wrestle with the deed
I found she was so fast bound up with me
It was like parting with a mystery;
She stands about my being like a creed.
Then did God gracious set to my mad feet
Clogs & reluctance, & incapable
I stood apart; or, watching as from hell,
Observed her pass: a slow, returning heat
Entered my heart; I lingered, & it grew,
The Itinerarium was said of two—
And round her face spluttered the Irish tide.

T1503   An italian sonnet with an extra final verse, which passed through many
          transformations before its eventual completion by Michael in March
          1910. The earliest sketches are scattered amongst an Oxford conflation
of loose sheets (ORM 21 *passim* 32), and there is an interesting draft in the Fortey
'Porridge Book' (YFF 3ab). The Journal has the first title *Crisis*, and a date *March
11th 1910* (ZKA 52b). When she copied it out in her 'Mystic Trees' notebook, a
second interim title *Parting* was deleted in favour of *Severing*; the, presumably final,
date is *March 12th 1910* (OWN 14b). The poem relates to Amy's fatal illness that
January; a curiosity is that Michael should persist with it two months later. On
Monday 17 January John had sent a telegram *"Bad case— influenza but hopeful"*;
Henry wrote in the Journal 'Michael telegraphs— she will come. ...Michael intends to
leave me at home' but then 'It is revealed.. we must keep together' (ZKA 8b). There
was a daily exchange of telegrams, in which John blew hot and cold on the
proposed crossing (Amy was worried about accomodation); but his telegram at
10.44 on the 19th *"temperature over 102"* (ZKA 11) was too alarming. Michael and
Henry departed for Ireland the next day (ZKA 14). Two days later Amy was dead.

To comfort: The Fortey draft opens with the variant quatrain:
                    How Love has moments of insanity!
                    To comfort one who cried to me in need,
                    I thought of parting from her for the sea;
                    Impulsively I wrote that I would speed.
Itinerarium: A form of prayer at the end of the Roman Breviary for the use of
                monks and clerics who were setting out (as the word implies) on a
                journey. The word occurs again when Amy's body was returned to
                England for burial: 'At home we read the Itinerarium for her who
                crosses the Sea for her burial, & for Johnnie & Emily, who travel with
                her, during the night' (H ZKA 44b).

Answered Prayer

I

But, where her Voice is heard,
　　It is the Voice
Even of the small, grey Bird
　　Of the Greeks' choice,

II

That sang from sorrow's springs,
　　Though open-eyed,
With all the lovely things
　　Of May beside.

III

Lo, God blindfolds my Bird;
　　And, through the scent
Of the dark May, is heard
　　Her song, content.

IV

There are would take my Bird,
　　Would strip her sight,
That, fullest night conferred,
　　She sing the night.

V

But, lo, my prayer is heard;
　　Through full moonlight,
Behold, my small grey Bird
　　Jangles of Love and Night!

T1506　　Henry's grief at her sister's death precipitated a psychosomatic blindness; Michael wrote to John Gray 'pray the dear green eyes may see' (YSG uf).
　　　　　　Other poems (including T1499, T1501 and T1520), apart from the present piece, relate to this distressing episode. On 6 March, Michael wrote in the Journal 'It is "Laetare" Sunday... I have forgiven Vincent *(ICT: see below)*. I offered the Divine Sacrifice in thanksgiving for Henry's restored eyesight, & for Henry's restored wits—' (ZKA 50a). The poem draft follows five pages later, with a footnote

Feast of St. Joseph. March 19th (ZKA 54-5). The earliest sketches survive in one of the Fortey cache notebooks (YFF 5ab); there is also an Oxford fair copy. Michael's first sketch opens:

> There is a small gray bird
> Of the Greeks' choice
> One where the thickets are most dark   (YFF 5b)

On the facing page she tries again:

> God's House withdraweth quite
> And through the stars my Bird
> Jangles of Love & Night—   (YFF 5a)

None of the autographs is titled; the present title appeared only on publication in the subgroup *Sword* of MYSTIC TREES, MCT 139.

where: The Oxford fair copy has *when* (OWN 18-9).

Bird: This is almost certainly Philomela, the nightingale (see T0878); the 'small, gray nightingale' appeared also in *The grave of Schliemann at Colonus*, T0485.
     The draft has *that* small, *gray* Bird (ZKA 54b).

sorrow's: In two autographs this is *Sorrow's*.

blindfolds: 'Miraculously I was borne along of the Blessed One— all through the journey *Amata's illness, & death... Then came the shock of Henry's blindness, & my power got confused by Vincent, & by my blind °priest inferring or suggesting resignation to God's will' (M ZKA 50a. *ICT: *Amy Ryan; °Michael Green, MFC 59*).

There are: Michael's sketch and drafts read   *The priests* would take my Bird;
     It may have been Henry who altered the text (ZKA 55a,OWN 19). But it is quite obvious that she agrees with her aunt. One year later, she wrote in the Journal: 'He *(ICT: McNabb)* had desired I should be blind, & the Son of David had mercy & I am not blind. Now he desires I should suffer...   I am really frightened & revolted by this Dominican, who has been so close to me before' (ZKB 61a).

moonlight: 'Jesus, Son of David, have mercy on me— give Henry his sight was my cry. I said "I want Henry to see the moon." Many holy souls prayed for Henry— In answer to profound prayer Henry is seeing, tho' the Lord has not yet finished his work of healing' (M ZKA 50a).

Jangles: The draft reads *Jangling*, and as before the bird is *gray* (ZKA 55a).

When Henry could see again, she began to sport *lorgnettes*— 'my dear eyes on a stalk' (ZKA 54a). Even Michael did not escape unscathed. 'I am writing this with rimless glasses & the round sources of healthful light & devotion, Michael's eyes, are to be put into glass for reading— we feel a new age has begun, that needs fortitude' (H ZKA 56a).

Fortitude would indeed be required. In February 1911 Henry learned that she had bowel cancer (T1595,SZD); by April she would be in 'atrocious pain.' Then in May 1913 Michael found breast cancer. She endured in her turn; Henry never knew.

Desolation

Who comes? . . .
O Beautiful!
Low thunder thrums,
As if a chorus struck its shawms and drums.
The sun runs forth
To stare at Him, who journeys north
From Edom, from the lonely sands, arrayed
In vesture sanguine as at Bosra made.
O beautiful and whole,
In that red stole!

Behold,
O clustered grapes,
His garment rolled,
And wrung about His waist in fold on fold!
See, there is blood
Now on His garment, vest and hood;
For He hath leapt upon a loaded vat,
And round His motion splashes the wine-fat,
Though there is none to play
The Vintage-lay.

The Word
Of God, His name . . .
But nothing heard
Save beat of His lone feet forever stirred
To tread the press—
None with Him in His loneliness;
No treader with Him in the spume, no man.
His flesh shows dusk with wine: since He began
He hath not stayed, that forth may pour
The Vineyard's store.

He treads
The angry grapes . . .
Their anger spreads,
And all its brangling passion sheds
In blood. O God,
Thy wrath, Thy wine-press He hath trod—

The fume, the carnage, and the murderous heat!
Yet all is changed by patience of the feet:
The blood sinks down; the vine
Is issued wine.

O task
Of sacrifice,
That we may bask
In clemency and keep an undreamt Pasch!
O Treader lone,
How pitiful Thy shadow thrown
Athwart the lake of wine that Thou hast made!
O Thou, most desolate, with limbs that wade
Among the berries, dark and wet,
Thee we forget!

T1543   Henry, with unerring dramatic sense, chose this arresting piece to open
         her collection POEMS OF ADORATION (PAD 1-2). The unmistakable
         source text is Isaiah LXIII 1: *Who is this that cometh from Edom, with
dyed garments from Bozrah?* That the original idea was hers seems borne out by an
entry in the Journal for July 1910: 'It is now the Month of the Precious Blood & I
have written of the Word of God treading the wine-press' (H ZKA 114a); *but* in one
of *Michael's* scribble books there are (the only) surviving sketches, *in her hand*, for
the last two stanzas. This makes active collaboration a near certainty (YFF 57-8).
Mary Sturgeon wrote " Here the conception of Christ the wine-treader is treated with
magnificent audacity of image and metaphor, while underneath runs a stream of
thought which, though it makes great leaps now and then, pouring its strong current
into cataract as it goes, yet bears its craft safely up and on" (FMS 97).

shawm: An oboe-like instrument with globular mouthpiece and a double reed.
Edom: The 'red region' in southwest Jordan between the Dead Sea and the
            gulf of Aqaba, presumably for its red iron-rich rock and soil; inhabited
            by tribes traditionally described as the descendants of Esau (unfortunate
            elder twin brother of the weaselly Jacob, Genesis XXV 25,30).
Bosra: Edomite impregnable fortress city some 20 miles southeast of the Dead
            Sea, and some 35 miles north of Petra— the 'rose-red' city itself.
red stole!: *Wherefore art thou red in thine apparel, and thy garments like him
            that treadeth in the winefat?* Isaiah LXIII 2
blood: .. *he washed his garments in wine, and his clothes in the blood of
            grapes:* Genesis XLIX 11; *I have trodden the winepress alone; and of
            the people there was none with me: for I will tread them in my anger,
            and trample them in my fury; and their blood shall be sprinkled upon
            my garments, and I will stain all my raiment.* Isaiah LXIII 3. One is
            struck afresh by the charm of the unspeakable *YHWH*, and that of his
            chosen people (sa the lip-licking death-to-Edom relish of Obadiah).
Vintage-lay: ..*in the vineyards there shall be no singing..* Isaiah XVI 10
brangling: (wrangling): noisily argumentative.
Pasch: Passover, with overtones of the lamb killed and eaten on that occasion;
            by hieratic extension, Easter.

215

Offence

To see how all the world is growing new
To thee, O Loved, now thou art doomed to die!
Each flower looks on thee with a softer eye;
The alpine flowers, studding the grot at Kew,
Sprinkle and spot and fringe of things half blue
And glints from mountain-sides Himalaya-high
Arrest thee, soothe thee. And I know not why
It should be thus. For what have these to do—
Anemones from Alp and Caucasus—
With thee so close, so piteously near?
O exile, standing by me hand in hand
And yet contracted, drawn as on thy bier,
Take comfort of these strangers where they stand
And then more simply bend thine eyes on us.

T1596   Michael wrote this poem apparently after they had been on a visit to the
         alpine plantings in Kew Gardens. The occasion was probably the 19th of
         April. Henry recorded in the Journal 'This day.. is the Feast Day of my
reception into the Fold four years ago.. we go on a drive to Kew, & wander the Grot,
& dote on Soldanella & welcome the new cineraria of Cardinal Red' (ZKB 72b). The
first fragmentary draft (YFE 47-8) has no date, but we know from the only other
autograph that Michael was writing the poem on *Low Sunday*— ended *April 23rd
1911* (OWN 88b). This is in agreement with Emily Fortey's footnote, *April 23, 1911*
to the published text. She included it in the posthumous collection THE WATTLEFOLD,
within the group *The Fall of the Leaf* (TWF 187).

half blue: Bearing in mind Henry's remark, this might be a reference to the Alpine
              Snowbell *Soldanella alpina*. The violet or bluish flowers open in April.
Himalaya: The accent is on the second syllable.
contracted: 'Holy Week has been a time of atrocious pain to me— The effect of
              Lent Abstinence & the marvellous long services I have had the joy of
              assisting at in their entirety this year. One must pay tribute for all true
              joy & my tribute of suffering has been heavy' (H ZKB 68a).
comfort: In THE WATTLEFOLD this verse is indented; here, the presumed
              typographical error has been corrected. It is to be hoped Henry did
              take some comfort— all her life she had loved blossom (see especially
              T1618). Only that March, Michael had commented in a letter to Mary
              that 'Field (was).... at her old vice of arranging flowers' (ZKB 55a).

T1618   The autograph that Emily used has not survived, although there are
         fragmentary early drafts in one of Michael's scribble books (YFE 70ab).
         The only full text is that printed in THE WATTLEFOLD, in the section *A
Rank of Osiers* (TWF 91); the footnote *Hawkesyard, July-Aug., 1911* is in accord

Golden lilies— gold as gold may be,
Gold in globe and anther glint the trees,
Covetous, thou lookest down on these
From the pool's fair bank. What part to thee
Loved, in this vital, rich simplicity,
This hum of scent from clustered water-bees?
Death is pulling on thee with disease,
Thou art where the ghosts and shadows be.
But I drew a sigh so deep in strife
For thy birthright to this bliss denied,
Heaven that laid the lamb by Abraham's knife
      Doth to my extremity provide
That an angel, presently shall swim
Secret for the flowers. God favour him!

with the Journal record. It was probably through the intervention of McNabb that on 10 July they came to stay at Park View Cottage, near St. Thomas's Dominican Priory, Hawkesyard (at Armitage in Staffordshire). 'A Cottage has been found ... at the very gate of the Novice House of St. Domenic' (H ZKB 91a). They were very taken with the novices, who seemed equally intrigued. 'The nice young Sacristan tells us to go wherever we like in the Park. so our old Protestant takes us.. past the lake, where I see a gold fret-work of water-lilies & desire wakes in me to gather.' Unfortunately 'All the water-lilies are on the far side— save two buds..' The temptation proved irresistible; the following morning '..we come to the pond— I plant my foot on a root, & amazed Michael snatches my dress as I ply my umbrella to hook the lilies. A lunge— & I have secured one— & am holding it out as a Red Indian his fresh scalp..' They are caught redhanded. 'The white brethren.. pace but they look. In pride I still hold out the scalp-water-lily, that the theft may be open' (H ZKB 101b-2b).

Golden lilies: They were probably *Nuphar lutea*, stout-stalked members of the Nymphaeaceae, whose bowl-shaped flowers project out of the water. Their common name 'Brandy-bottle' may refer to the bottle-shaped fruit capsule; however the lilies exhale a faint but undeniable aroma of wine lees. All very cloistral.

Covetous: 'I am sore with longing after those two yellow water-lilies' (ZKB 102b).

knife: It seems doubtful the lamb would have seen this point of view.

an angel: This was Brother Bertrand, one of the hunkier novices. 'On Sunday July 23.. Bro. Bertrand receives warmest thanks for the glorious armful of yellow waterlilies he swam over the Lake to gather for me, one day of the week, leaving them, because he had no permission to enter the house at the door...' (H ZKB 113b). It is possible her hero repeated his Leander act; Henry's copy of a thank-you letter to him from Malvern Wells, dated August 2nd and signed 'Your grateful humble Sister in St Domenic', yet exists (ZKF 214or).

217

Descent from the Cross

Come down from the Cross, my soul, and save thyself—
    come down!
Thou wilt be free as wind. None meeting thee will know
How thou wert hanging stark, my soul, outside the town.
    Thou wilt fare to and fro;
Thy feet in grass will smell of faithful thyme; thy head . . .
Think of the thorns, my soul— how thou wilt cast them off,
With shudder at the bleeding clench they hold!
But on their wounds thou wilt a balsam spread,
And over that a verdurous circle rolled
With gathered violets, sweet bright violets, sweet
As incense of the thyme on thy free feet;
A wreath thou wilt not give away, nor wilt thou doff.

Come down from the Cross, my soul, and save thyself; yea, move
As scudding swans pass lithely on a seaward stream!
Thou wilt have everything thou wert made great to love;
    Thou wilt have ease for every dream;
No nails with fang will hold thy purpose to one aim;
There will be arbours round about thee, not one trunk
Against thy shoulders pressed and burning them with hate,
Yea, burning with intolerable flame.
O lips, such noxious vinegar have drunk,
There are through valley-woods and mountain-glades
Rivers where thirst in naked prowess wades;
And there are wells in solitude whose chill no hour abates!

Come down from the Cross, my soul, and save thyself! A sign
Thou wilt become to many, as a shooting star.
They will believe thou art æthereal, divine,
    When thou art where they are;
They will believe in thee and give thee feasts and praise.
They will believe thy power when thou hast loosed thy nails;
For power to them is fetterless and grand:
For destiny to them, along their ways,
Is one whose Earthly Kingdom never fails.
Thou wilt be as a prophet or a king
In thy tremendous term of flourishing—
And thy hot royalty with acclamations fanned.

Come down from the Cross, my soul, and save thyself!
   . . . Beware!
Art thou not crucified with God, who is thy breath?
Wilt thou not hang as He while mockers laugh and stare?
   Wilt thou not die His death?
Wilt thou not stay as He with nails and thorns and thirst?
Wilt thou not choose to conquer faith in His lone style?
Wilt thou not be with Him and hold thee still?
Voices have cried to Him, *Come down!* Accursed
And vain those voices, striving to beguile!
How heedless, solemn-gray in powerful mass,
Christ droops among the echoes as they pass!
O soul, remain with Him, with Him thy doom fulfil!

T1623   No autograph for this poem, one of Henry's grandest strophic pieces, seems to have survived. Dating is problematic; but given the ever-present thread of stoicism under appalling pain, sometime in the second half of 1911 seems probable. The poem was published in POEMS OF ADORATION, PAD 96-8. Sturge Moore — who found it "magnificent"— also reprinted it in his own selection (SMF 13,127-8). An anonymous note (possibly written by Edwin Essex) in the editorial of *The Hawkesyard Review*, looking back on Henry's work after her death, described the poem as "one of rare beauty, (which)... probably ranks as the author's finest". This note rightly acknowledged "...amidst all her sufferings of body the spirit remained indomitable... She was a true mystic as well as a true poet— perhaps the terms are synonymous..." (JHR March 1914, 142-3). Essex certainly admired the poem (JCM 1931, 239). Its most recent appearance has been in Ann Stanford's *The Women Poets in English* (AAS 1972, 151-2).

free as wind: Leighton discovers in these lines "a celebration of the old natural pleasures"; but she surely overstates her case in saying "Faith did not re-energise their poetry" (FAL 223). Some of it (as here) is powerful stuff indeed, sustained by Henry's dramatic enthusiasms.

violets: This reference to the crown of thorns as a wreath of violets occurs again as the argument of Henry's *A Gift of Sweetness* (T1581), a poem known to date from March 1911:

> *I thought to lay my hands about Thy Crown,*
> *And gather, bleeding, its sharp spines:*
>
> ......
>
> *...... never will a mould-born violet-bed*
> *Smell like the violets from the Sacred Head.*   vs 1-2;16-7

swans: The *seaward stream* could be the Thames at Paragon; sa T1713.

burning: On Ash Wednesday in 1911 (March 01) Henry recorded 'I do not need to be marked with ashes who have been marked with cancer'; and further on April 11 'It may be that in mercy I have had special purgatory for my sinning this week of the Cross...' (ZKB 49b,68a).

Come down!:   Mark XV 30 *Save thyself, and come down from the cross*.

doom fulfil!:   Leighton contrasts this final verse with the last verse of Wilde's *Humanidad*, written in 1881:

> 'Loosen the nails— we shall come down I know'   (FAL 223)

Pomegranates

Proserpine, Proserpine,
Give us of lovely stems,
Give us your fruit—
We with pomegranates will crown our bowers,
So feel the flowers,
So fails desire—
So your fruit is ruddy as a fire.

Winter again, how quick,
Comes! and my loved is sick:
'Proserpine'.
Shuddering she pleads 'I do not want
The pomegranate'—
Desire in tears
Claims an eternity of love and years.

O Love, thy voice! . . . My breath
Warm on thee startles Death.
Mythology
Shrivels as a ghost, beholding me
My lips, O Sweet,
To thine the heat,
Stir of coals, immortal cherishing!

T1635   This poem, otherwise unknown, is taken from the subgroup *The Fall of
the Leaf* in THE WATTLEFOLD, TWF 188. Emily Fortey appends the
footnote *Nov. 8th 1911*, which agrees in some extent with the opening
of the second stanza. One wonders if the poem has any basis in an actual event; its
special interest lies in the new slant on an old legend often treated by Michael Field.

Pomegranates are the fruit of a bush-like tree of the family *Punicaceae*, indigenous
in Iran and widespread throughout Asia. *P. granatum* has long orange-red flowers,
and fruits the size of an orange. The smooth leathery rind conceals numerous
elongated seeds, each enclosed in an edible fleshy aril which releases a bright red
juicy pulp. It is no doubt the appearance of these seeds that make the pomegranate
a symbol of fertility in many cultures from Uzbekistan to Greece and China; in
Turkey a bride may dash a ripe fruit to the floor to count in the spilled seeds the
number of her future children. The fruit has been suggested as that which caused all
the trouble in Eden, and the Greeks believed it grew in the garden of Hades; it may
be for this reason it is also seen as a symbol of wealth. Muhammad says that eating
pomegranates purges the system of envy and hatred.

A Picture

Love, you were dying and one came and drew
The story of your sickness and your pain—
Forlorn you stooped; lover nor loved you knew,
Sucking the salt of sorrow, grain on grain.
You saw my grief for you, thus quite undone
How as at day of judgement you appealed
And sent for an old picture by the sun
As he saw you years ago in a green field—
A vision of your beauty very clear
Of open lip, yet something flashed between
That held and awed and made the face appear
As a shell under water, secret, keen.
O Catholic, sweet face, O gift, O truth
And revelation of thy Spirit's youth.

Proserpine: The first verse is taken (perhaps) from the title of another poem on the subject, written in ?1901 by Henry herself (T0963).

not want: In Michael's poems *Proserpine* (T0927), and *Domina* (T0928), written in August 1900, Proserpina is positively homesick for the Underworld.
> ... *I grieve not I did pluck and eat* (T0927, v1)
> *Dear realm that is my home!* (T0928, v9)
The new reality was too shockingly pressing for the luxury of myth.

T1699 The poem almost certainly refers back to a Journal entry Henry made during their visit to Ireland in late July 1908. 'A little English Lady, sensitive & with a gift for making photography oracular— ..— gets me as a Dryad in the shadowy gleam of the old acacia-tree. I look rather as I did in youth— something yet to be in the burthened but unfulfilled picture. It is an intimate photograph &, alas, it tells nothing of my Catholicity— except in relation to the elements & to imaginings' (ZJY 145ab). The photograph seems to have disappeared. A full draft of the poem, dated *July 29th 1913* but untitled, survives in Michael's final scribble book (YFG 11b); Emily included it in *The Fall of the Leaf*, the final section of THE WATTLEFOLD, TWF 194. She quotes the same date. The title may be her own.

were dying: The draft has *are dying*; that October another poignant poem recalls
> *Lo, my loved is dying, and the call/ Is come that I must die,* ....
> *And the great reconciliation of this pain/ Lies in the full soft rain.*
> (T1710)

one came: William Rothenstein. These pencil sketches, executed 03 June 1913, are also lost (YVH, FWR 279-81). On 12 April 1914, Michael would write 'It is Easter Day. .. I build up in imitation of Henry, a little altar to the dead with her drawing by Rothenstein in the midst..' (ZKE 28b).

the face: The draft reads first *thy*, then *your*.

Remember of me, Loved, but this,
Nothing that I have done,
Nor fame that I have won,
Nor any beauty flashed across my days
    When I lie in my green rest,
One of the happy ones, remember me,
One of the innumerable blest,
Signed with the sign of the Holy Trinity.

T1709   The drafts for this poem occur in Michael's last scribble book (YFG 27a).
              No date is given, but the single fair copy— also unmistakably in her
              hand— has the footnote *M.F. Oct. 1913*. Emily Fortey included this
date when she published the poem as the final piece in the subgroup *The Fall of the
Leaf* in THE WATTLEFOLD, TWF 206. She thus used it as a fitting *envoi* for the
book, and for the published works of Michael Field as a whole. She adds a further
footnote *This poem was written for Father Vincent McNabb*, which may indeed be
so; it is certainly true that the fair copy which has survived is the one that was sent to
him. The attribution may however be secondary. The preceding draft in the scribble
book is for *Esther* (T1708), and this is followed immediately by the isolated couplet:
          Who whilst she lived was signed / with the sign of the Holy Trinity.
Though in the event these verses were not used in *Esther*, they are the obvious
source of the final verse in the present poem. It is of further interest that, after her
first sketch, Michael also briefly considered a less direct opening:
              I would remember of my days but this
As for Vincent McNabb, a note in his handwriting on the reverse of the fair copy
reads "This was written by Katherine Bradley in the days of loneliness (1913-1914)
when she was waiting for death to unite her to her fellow-poet Edith Cooper. She
gave it to me bidding me keep it in my bible. R.I.P." He signed and dated it *22 Dec
1925* (YSN BKF 4-15r). For a photo-reproduction of this fair copy, see MFC 125.

Loved: As in the fair copy, and both drafts; Emily uses lower case.
Nor fame: The first draft reads *And no fame won*.
across: Originally *through*.
Trinity: Michael had a special regard for the Trinity, indeed in 1902 she had
           asked Ricketts to 'fashion.. an ornament that shall express my worship'
           (ZJQ 20b). A month later she approaches him again 'If I am "dead nuts"
           on the Trinity— I say I am— a beautiful sparkling jewel, entirely in gems
           might be produced' (ZJQ 28a). But he seems to have done little about it.
           Michael's poems to the "sacred number" specific to strict christian
           mythology include notably T0748, 1121, 1371 and 1438. See also
           Henry's Whym Chow *Trinity* (T1247).

To Love

I had detached myself, I had grown free—
A creature must not hold me on the rack,
I broke from her, I left her on her track
Of doom and bore to God. Love smiled on me
Fecund from His infinity,
And caught my chains and bade me hurry back
To that lone figure, that she might not lack
One minute's daily assiduity.
O Love, O Majesty— and is it thus—
I may pour nard upon her head and weep?
That I may cover her with tears as rain?
Die for me that the grave I may not keep,
As if we were one breathing cherish us
Give us the loving of our lips again!

T1715   This poem is known only on the authority of Emily Fortey. She included it
in *The Fall of the Leaf*, the final section of THE WATTLEFOLD, TWF 200.
She is most exact about the date of composition: her footnote reads
Feast of Santa Lucia, Dec. 13th, 1913. These separate citations are indeed in
agreement, but what is of prime interest is that this is the actual day of Henry's
death. This further implies that Michael must have written the piece within hours of
the event.

(Lucia was the patron saint of Syracuse, but had no eyes for any of The Boys From
that fair city— possibly because, with a masochistic relish seemingly mandatory to
virgin-martyrs of the christian persuasion, she prefers to carry them around in a dish.
It is therefore no oversight that she is also the patron saint of optometrists).

223

Not in that vesture brave
O Victor King, Thou wearest from the grave
Come to me now I sit beside my Dead—
   A little cold Thou still dost shed
   As if Thou wert a Spirit, and I dare
Scarce speak to Thee, Thou art so fair.
I take Thee from Thy Mother's arms instead—
Warm art Thou in my arms, how warm a thing!
My very tears Thou warmest as they spring
To feel one's God so warm and so alive,
And yet so tender; if He is to thrive
With me for nurse I must learn cradle-songs;
O Birth of the Lord Jesus that belongs
To mourners chief among the mysteries,
I turn from Death, that power of strictest term
And definition that doth so displease,
O babbling Child, O Sacrament in germ,
O passing of the moments, Babe, to Thee—
And, Mary kneeling by me to adore,
I know there is no dying any more.

T1716   One of the poems collected by Emily Fortey, for which no autograph
is known; she included it in the final section *The Fall of the Leaf* in
THE WATTLEFOLD, TWF 201. Her footnote date *1913* is entirely in
accordance with the death of Henry on 13 December, and the text itself corroborates
that the season is Christmas.

Victor King: See the first note to *The Homage of Death*, T1576.
cradle-songs: She may have done nothing about this till the following March, when
she indeed wrote *A Cradle Song*, T1720. But this was not for
Emmanuel, but for Henry, seen most mystically 'in a wood alone.'

          A song of one string,
          Our sharp, keen love!
          ....
      My Love, I have sung thee asleepen, the praise,
      The breath of the years, the breath of the days,
      I have sung thee fast asleep.

I am thy charge, thy care!
Thou art praying for me, and about my bed,
About my ways; but there are things one misses—
    It is the little cup
    That I drank up,
The cup full of thee, offered every day—
I come for it, as birds draw to a brook—
It is the reflex of thee, in thy nook,
Caught sideways in a mirror as I pray—
    My precious Heap,
My jewel, in the casket of thy sleep.
Beloved, it is the little wreath of kisses,
I wove about thy head, thy withering hair.

T1718   This is another piece which Emily Fortey published with a full date
(*January 28th, 1914*) when she included it in *The Fall of the Leaf*, the
final section of THE WATTLEFOLD, TWF 202. It is the date Michael
applied to her drafts in the last 'Scribble Book' (YFG 31-2), so this seems to be
Emily's source. Michael also made a fair copy into the Journal (ZKE 8b). The poem
was republished for the first time in 1997 (AED).

drank: Emily (or her printer) has *drink*, and the draft is admittedly ambiguous.
But the fair copy is clearly and heavily corrected to *drank*. Michael's
Journal entry on the previous page, as well as the sense, support this
reading: 'Hennie, Hennie, Hennie, but it is just the little cup-full of you
I want, just the little draught I drank of you every day. Be with me
exceedingly, my Beloved— Make me sweet & very meek' (ZKE 7b).

cup full: Both autographs favour *cupful*.

Heap: There is no capital in the first drafts.

hair: This most moving image echoes Henry's own words the previous
October 27th: 'It is the early morning of my own Love's birthday. How
dear she is to me— how the sweetness & clench of love grow pain &
joy as I look at her, touch her, & receive her little wreath of kisses in my
withered hair' (ZKD 94a).

Michael rejoined her Fellow early on the morning of September the 26th.

Μνάσασθαί τινά φαμι καί ὗστερον ἄμμεων

O free me, for I take the leap,
Apollo, from thy snowy steep!
Song did'st thou give me, and there fell
O'er Hellas an enchanter's spell;
I heard young lovers catch the strain:
For me there is the hoary main;
I would not hear my words again.

Ah, lord of speech, well dost thou know
The incommunicable woe
Finds not in lyric cry release,
Finds but in Hades' bosom peace;
And therefore on thy temple-ground
Thou pointest lovers to the mound
Set high above the billows' sound.

Though in unfathomed seas I sink,
Men will remember me, I think,
Remember me, my King, as thine;
And must I take a shape divine
As thine immortal, let me be
A dumb sea-bird with breast love-free,
And feel the waves fall over me.

Note on the freestanding poems

T0259   (Page 37) The only autograph, in Henry's hand, is in her notebook 'Songs of sundry natures'; it carries neither date nor title, but has the note *Written for a drama on the subject of Justinia & Cyprian* (OVI 3b). Michael sheds further light in a Journal entry dated 7 March 1897. "Henry reads to me a choice collection of passages from a disused, old drama— of some 13 years ago— (Ignorance: the story of S. Justina & Cyprian) & shows me how so many of them have secretly been hewn to be carried noiselessly to our modern work— <u>Race of Leaves</u>— <u>Carloman</u>— <u>The Loves of Alexander & the Moon</u>. What a rich young poet I was!' (ZJL 17b). This places the 'passage' approximately in 1884, and it was probably that August that she wrote to J.A. Symonds from Alum Bay with the request 'Can you give me any help in my St. Justinia and Cyprian.' Cyprian apparently 'was a heathen magician.. Justinia receives from Cyprian a love-potion which gives her evil thoughts, but, repressing these, she resolves to exalt him to the highest spiritual passion' (OZO 135or). A meller hardly likely to roll them in the aisles. Henry later refers to the autograph in a letter written to Michael (then at Sidmouth) in April 1885: 'Every song has a beautiful red ink heading' (OCB 66r-7o). Did *Henry* write this specific 'passage', rather than Michael? The extract was certainly in existence by August 1886, as its receipt was acknowledged by J.M. Gray on the 28th (ZCC 2-3). It appeared in *The Academy* (#760) that November, as *An* Invocation. The present title appears first in UNDERNEATH THE BOUGH, where the piece serves as a prelude (UTB pe) delightful in itself— mercifully divorced from spiritual passions.

T0341   (Page 227) There are the usual two autographs in Edith's hand, OVF 46-7 and OVG 103, with the usual ambiguities of date and author; but the poem must have been completed by April 1887 (ZCL 91o). The epigraph, also alluded to in v16, is Sapphic fragment #32: *Men I think will remember us even hereafter* (VSW 82). Not something alas, till now, that can honestly be said of Michael Field. The piece was published, fittingly, as an *envoi* in the last pages of LONG AGO (LAG 128)— which may be one reason why an undistinguished and distracting fourth stanza was omitted. It was probably also at this time that the draft *whelming* seas became *unfathomed*.

The story of Sappho's leap is reported by Strabo (for Wharton's excellent account of the legend and its ramifications, see especially the 1895 edition, VSW 15-22). The Leucadian (white) promontory, now part of Santa Maura, was a high place sacred to Apollo; those who threw themselves off its cliff top into the sea were assured of a certain cure for the torments of love, and most probably also the human condition that fostered them. Sappho's apparent metamorphosis into a bird is probably a later accretion; Addison's suggestion of a swan seems an over-egging of the pudding. Wharton further cautions "The story of Sappho's love for Phaon, and her leap from the Leucadian rock in consequence of his disdaining her, though it has been so long implicitly believed, does not seem to rest on any firm historical basis. Indeed, more than one epigrammatist in the Greek Anthology expressly states that she was buried in an Aeolic grave" (VSW 15). Amongst modern writers, Angela Leighton as usual has something intelligent and interesting to say; especially delightful is her Stevie Smith comment "Wrung out of sexual betrayal and impending death, Sappho's last songs are also, as it were, a last fling of passion, a waving and drowning together, in which the woman's body is alluringly and unattainably displayed in a spasm of hopeless desire" (FAL 35-6). Alluringly is of course a matter of opinion.

Index of poems in respect to prior publication

Ninety four of the poems have appeared before in print:

The remaining fifty six are here printed for the first time:

Index of titles and incipits

232

233

Significant addenda 1908-2002, to the bibliographies of **The Michael Field Catalogue**

AAF 10   ABP 30   AMH 19   AMT 34   APV 20   ATT 21   FAV 27   FBL 26
FED 23   FJK 14   FNM 13   FOS 32   FRV 17   FSR 15   FSZ 08   FTP 16
FWC 31   JBD 05   JCF 09   JHS 24   JSS 06   JTW 12   JVP 33   JVS 28
JWH 18   MAS 29   MFC 22   SZD 25   VJE 07   VWK 11   YSI 01   YVJ 02
YVK 03   YVM 04

01 YSI   EDN 9864 f48 Letter nd reported in Shorter and Bulloch papers (Not seen)
02 YVJ   (UNIVERSITY OF TEXAS at AUSTIN, Humanities Research Center Archives)
         NUC# MS 71-1902: Richard Garnett papers includes letter(s). (Not seen)
03 YVK   (UNIVERSITY OF HARVARD at CAMBRIDGE, MA; Houghton Library)
         NUC# MS 82-665: Houghton bMS Eng 1148 (486,1728). Sir William
         Rothenstein papers. 103 letters fr MF, 1897-1914 & nd.   (Not seen)
04 YVM   (HARVARD UNIVERSITY CENTER FOR ITALIAN RENAISSANCE STUDIES)
         Biblioteca Berenson, Villa I Tatti, Florence. Cache of largely undated letters
         from (mainly) KHB and EEC to the Berensons, occasional reply from Mary.
05 JBD   (BOOK REVIEW DIGEST) 1908 Ann. p117 Review of WDH.
06 JSS   (THE SATURDAY REVIEW OF LITERATURE) 1923 V2 p274 Review of SMF.
07 VJE   THINE ELDER THAT I AM   (Michael Field)   For voice and piano
         John Edmunds (1913-)   Inscribed *for Edward Ballantine*. The New York
         Public Library for the Performing Arts.   MS, end-date *Mar 42*
08 FSZ   CATHOLIC SYMBOL AND RITUAL IN MINOR BRITISH POETRY OF THE
         LATER NINETEENTH CENTURY M. Lynn Seitz Unpublished PhD Diss.
         Michael Field 131-85 Arizona State University 1974.   (Not seen)
09 JCF   (CONFLUENTS) Université Lyon 2 Centre d'Études et de Recherches
         Anglaises et Nord-Americaines Etudes Victoriennes Henri Locard (sa FHL)
         1976 #1   Le Journal d'Edmond et Jules de Goncourt & WORKS AND
                   DAYS de "Michael Field"   (pp53-77)
         1977 #1   Michael Field & Music   (pp69-77)
         1979 #2   The Dionysiac Dance & the "Dance Macabre" in the poetry of
                   Michael Field   (pp109-126)
         1983   Bernhard Berenson & 'Michael Field'   (pp31-53)
10 AAF   MARY QUEEN OF SCOTS an anthology of poetry chosen and introduced
         by Antonia Fraser Eyre Methuen 1981. Includes the single piece T0346.
11 VWK   DOUBLE TALK   The erotics of male literary collaboration   Wayne
         Koestenbaum Routledge New York 1989   Michael Field 53,144,73-5.
12 JTW   (TULSA STUDIES IN WOMEN'S LITERATURE) V13 #2, Fall 1994 University
         of Tulsa Screaming Divas: Collaboration as Feminist Practice. Article by
         Susan Leonardi and Rebecca Page, 259-70. Michael Field 262.
13 FNM   LYRIC TRANSVESTISM: Gender and Voice in Modernist Literature
         Norman Madden PhD Thesis University of Texas at Austin 1994 (Not seen)
14 FJK   CONVENTION AND COUNTERPOINT: 19th-Century Women's Poetic
         Language J.M. Knittel PhD Thesis University of Oregon 1995 (Not seen)
15 FSR   VOLCANOES AND PEARL DIVERS: Essays in LesbianFeminist Studies Edited
         Suzanne Raitt Onlywomen Press Ltd London 1995 Pages 74-102.
         **The One Woman (in virgin haunts of poesie) Michael Field's Sapphic
         symbolism by Chris White.   Engrossing study of LAG,MCT; rose imagery.
16 FTP   VICTORIAN WOMEN POETS: A Critical Reader Edited Angela Leighton
         p148-61"The Tiresian poet: Michael Field" by Chris White; p235-44 'Elegy
         and the Woman Poet' Susan Conley's analysis of T0755; pp 295-304

'Sappho's Last Song' Margaret Reynolds LAG & T0884.   Blackwell 1996

17 FRV **SAPPHO AND THE VIRGIN MARY: Same-Sex Love and the English
   Literary Imagination   Ruth Vanita   Columbia University Press NY 1996.
   Michael Field especially 118-35, 228-31 (misallocates WCF to KHB).

18 JWH (WOMEN'S HISTORY REVIEW) 1996 V 5 # 2 239-57 'Michael Field, the
   Two-headed Nightingale': lesbian text as palimpsest. Article, Virginia Blain.

19 AMH BRITISH WOMEN POETS OF THE 19TH CENTURY   Edited Margaret R
   Higonnet Meridian NY 1996 The 27 pieces T0217,336-7,53,89;506,25,
   31,8,637-8,62,755,60,98,805-6,37,78,925,1014,32,57,62,1208, 83,92

20 APV THE PENGUIN BOOK OF VICTORIAN VERSE Edited Daniel Karlin 1997
   The 4 pieces T0455,538,40,82. And T0430 (first stanza only).

21 ATT POETRY OF THE 1890'S Edited R K R Thornton and Marion Thain
   Penguin Books 1997 The 9 pieces T0217,50,347,400,12,53,95,506,64.

22 MFC The MICHAEL FIELD Catalogue: a book of lists De Blackland Press 1998
   Researched and assembled by Ivor C Treby

23 FED *****WE ARE MICHAEL FIELD Absolute Press 1998 Emma Donoghue
   Includes the 10 pieces T0217,44,318,525,62,789,98,817,1315,650.
   [Splendid biographical sketch: the ladies are for once recognisable.]

24 JHS (HENRY STREET) 1998 Fall Vol 7.2 89-93 Review of MFC Suzy Waldman

25 SZD A SHORTER SHĪRAZĀD 101 poems of Michael Field De Blackland Press
   1999 Chosen, annotated, but *not* edited by Ivor C Treby

26 FBL WRITING DOUBLE: Women's Literary Partnerships Bette London Cornell
   University Press Ithaca and London 1999 Michael Field 63-74, 99-103.

27 FAV WOMEN'S POETRY, LATE ROMANTIC TO LATE VICTORIAN: GENDER
   AND GENRE, 1830-1900 Essays edited Isobel Armstrong and Virginia
   Blain. St. Martin's Press, Inc. New York; Macmillan Press Ltd, Basingstoke
   1999. Michael Field 138-9, **Chap 8, Narrative Discoherence in Michael
   Field's *Underneath the Bough* (Robert P. Fletcher) 164-82.

28 JVS (VICTORIAN STUDIES) 1999/2000 Winter V42 #2 312-4 Review FED,
   MFC K.L. Thomas [On MFC, Ms Thomas is *exasperated* (well that's nice)
   that Michael Field is referred to as 'him'. She in her turn is referred to the
   present preface, and the ultimate and only relevant authority. She also
   discovers *significant errors* (which almost certainly there are), though is
   too coy to be specific— save on the 'mislocation' of the Michael Field
   grave. Perhaps she would care to enlighten the rest of us (with an *exact*
   citation please) on the "correct" location? We are all ears, Ms T.]

29 MAS MUSIC AND SILENCE The gamut of Michael Field De Blackland Press
   2000 Chosen, annotated, but *not* edited by Ivor C Treby

30 ABP THE BROADVIEW ANTHOLOGY OF VICTORIAN POETRY AND POETIC
   THEORY Concise edition ed Thomas Collins & Vivienne Rundle Broadview
   Press Ltd 2000 The 9 pieces T0198,212,45,60,354,409,53,57,538.

31 FWC **WOMEN COAUTHORS   Holly A Laird   University of Illinois Press
   Urbana and Chicago 2000 *Especially Chapter 3: Contradictory Legacies:
   Michael Field and Feminist Restoration (p81-96; 282-4); also 22-7;274-5.

32 FOS **MICHAEL FIELD BBC Radio 4 10 part serial written by Moya O'Shea
   with Geraldine James as Michael, Sophie Thompson as Henry. Broadcast
   wkdays 6-17 Nov 2000 during *Woman's Hour* at 10.00am, rpt 7.45pm
   in *Chapters and Verses: Treasures of the British Library*.   (Not heard)

33 JVP (VICTORIAN POETRY) 2001 Winter V39 #4 621-6 Review MFC,SZD,MAS
   Dorothy Mermin. Includes the single piece T0695.

34 AMT VICTORIAN LITERATURE 1830-1900 Edited Dorothy Mermin and Herbert
   F Tucker Harcourt College Publishers Fort Worth 2002. Michael Field
   p1006-14 includes the 25 pieces T0198,209,17,92,336,8-9,47,90,498,
   506,12,25,38,62,82,637,78,98,724,55,98,800,73,8.

Sydney reading, July 1992

IVOR C TREBY researched and assembled
The MICHAEL FIELD Catalogue: a book of lists
(De Blackland Press ISBN 0 907404 03 0)

He chose and annotated
A Shorter Shīrazād,
101 poems of Michael Field
(De Blackland Press ISBN 0 907404 05 7)

together with
Music and Silence,
The gamut of Michael Field
(De Blackland Press ISBN 0 907404 07 3)

He is also the author of five collections of poetry
including
Awareness of the Sea,
Selected Poems 1970-1995
(De Blackland Press ISBN 0 907404 06 5)